THE ILLUSTRATED
ENCYCLOPEDIA OF
DIVINATION

THE ILLUSTRATED ENCYCLOPEDIA OF DIVINATION

A Practical Guide to the Systems that Can Reveal Your Destiny

STEPHEN KARCHER

ELEMENT

Shaftesbury, Dorset • Rockport, Massachusetts • Brisbane, Queensland

© Element Books Limited 1997
Text © Stephen Karcher 1997

First published in Great Britain 1997 by
ELEMENT BOOKS LIMITED
Shaftesbury, Dorset, SP7 8BP

Published in the USA in 1997 by
ELEMENT BOOKS INC.
PO Box 830, Rockport, MA 01966

Published in Australia in 1997 by
ELEMENT BOOKS LIMITED
for JACARANDA WILEY LIMITED
33 Park Road, Milton, Brisbane 4064

Designed and created with The Bridgewater Book Company

ELEMENT BOOKS LIMITED
Editorial Director: Julia McCutchen
Managing Editor: Caro Ness
Production Director: Roger Lane
Production: Sarah Golden

THE BRIDGEWATER BOOK COMPANY
Art Director: Kevin Knight
Designer: Jane Lanaway
Page layout/make-up: Chris Lanaway
Managing Editor: Anne Townley
Editor: Viv Croot
Picture Research: Vanessa Fletcher
Three-dimensional models: Mark Jamieson
Studio photography: Guy Ryecart
Illustrators: Pauline Allen, Ivan Hissey, Katty McMurray

Printed by
New Interlitho, Italy

British Library Cataloguing in Publication
data available.

Library of Congress Cataloging in Publication
data available.

ISBN 1-85230-876-1

Contents

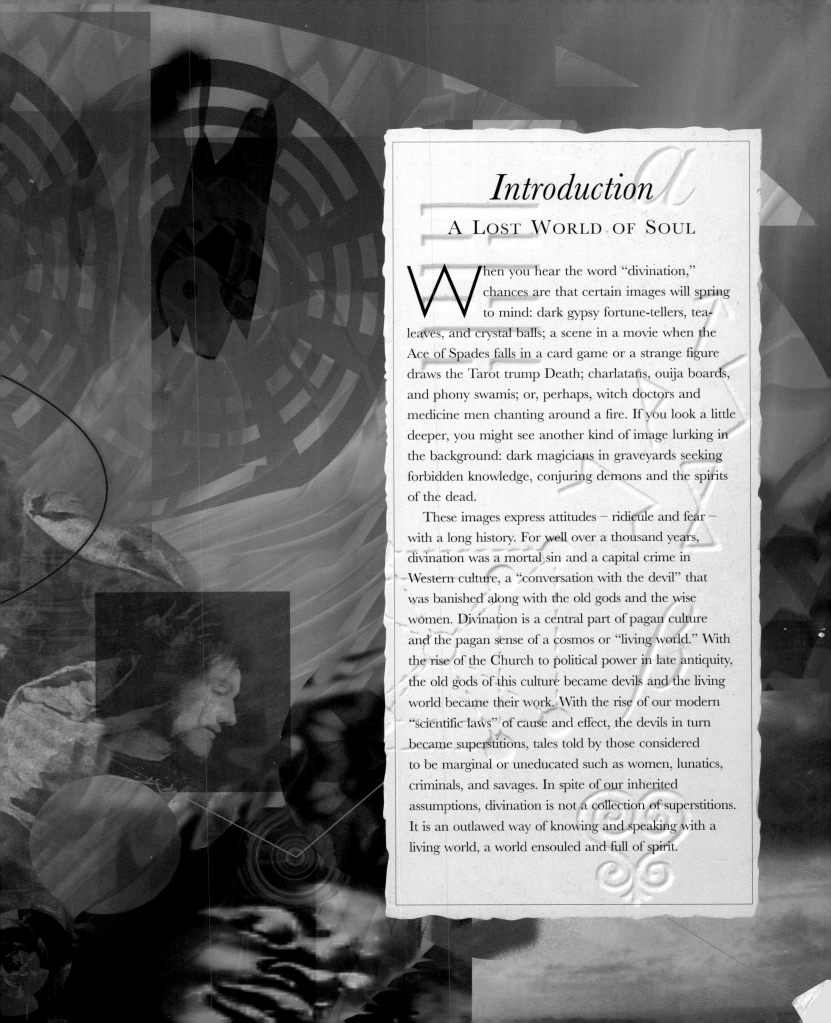

Introduction
A LOST WORLD OF SOUL

When you hear the word "divination," chances are that certain images will spring to mind: dark gypsy fortune-tellers, tea-leaves, and crystal balls; a scene in a movie when the Ace of Spades falls in a card game or a strange figure draws the Tarot trump Death; charlatans, ouija boards, and phony swamis; or, perhaps, witch doctors and medicine men chanting around a fire. If you look a little deeper, you might see another kind of image lurking in the background: dark magicians in graveyards seeking forbidden knowledge, conjuring demons and the spirits of the dead.

These images express attitudes – ridicule and fear – with a long history. For well over a thousand years, divination was a mortal sin and a capital crime in Western culture, a "conversation with the devil" that was banished along with the old gods and the wise women. Divination is a central part of pagan culture and the pagan sense of a cosmos or "living world." With the rise of the Church to political power in late antiquity, the old gods of this culture became devils and the living world became their work. With the rise of our modern "scientific laws" of cause and effect, the devils in turn became superstitions, tales told by those considered to be marginal or uneducated such as women, lunatics, criminals, and savages. In spite of our inherited assumptions, divination is not a collection of superstitions. It is an outlawed way of knowing and speaking with a living world, a world ensouled and full of spirit.

Bringing the World Back to Life

or at least three thousand years, people have used divination to find ways to imagine themselves and their situations. They seek advice, help, and knowledge of their fate to help them connect with the transformative potential of the spirit. In many parts of the world today, people visit shamans, healers, and soul-doctors, consult oracles, check propitious and unpropitious dates in almanacs, read star charts, use sticks, stones, dice, and cards to give them symbols of the spirit-forces surrounding them. They do this because they seek to act in harmony with those forces, with what the Chinese call the *tao*, the "on-going process of the real." When faced with a difficult decision or problem, when they need to find a strategy, when they feel the weight of the spirit pressing on them or are searching for their own way,

these people go to a diviner or use an oracle system. Why? What happens when the oracle speaks or the seer sees, when your cards are read, when you consult the *I Ching*, look at your dreams for messages, or empower things as signs and omens?

The first thing that happens is that the world comes to life. You enter a world of powers, potentialities, and presences in which your destiny and your actions matter. Things and events acquire the capacity to speak with you. The act and language of divination revive a lost world of soul, a world full of spirits, magical helpers, and significant landscapes. We acquire a sense of destiny, the means to negotiate with that destiny, and a guide or helping spirit in the process. The "living world" begins to play an active role in our lives.

ABOVE: The Sun (top) is a potent symbol of life and features in many beliefs and divination systems. Runes (above) carved on stone or wood were the northern European keys to the unseen universe.

LEFT: Tarot cards, probably the most familiar modern oracle system to western European followers of the divinatory arts.

OPPOSITE: Dice (top) can be used for gaming or divining. An "immortal" (right) communes with the *Tao* paradise with the help of a magic mushroom, seen in his pocket.

This mixture of fortunetelling, practical guidance, and spiritual advice may seem strange to us at first, with our culture's concern with great transcendental truths. It cuts across the usual boundaries between what is important and what is unimportant, for anything can become a place where the spirit world enters your life, and thus a matter for divining. The world you meet through divination is full of imaginative forces with attributes, powers, desires, and needs that are creating what we experience. Our souls ask us to recognize the events and emotions that sweep through our lives – our loves and hates, crises, confrontations, problems, and challenges – as gifts of these forces, with lessons to teach and tolls to pay. Recognizing this, giving attention to these forces, is one of the great healing acts that divination has to offer us.

MIRROR OF TRUTH

Divining is one of the oldest and most persistent human acts. There is virtually no human culture that has not used divination as a "mirror that speaks truth" to open a dialogue with the invisible world that surrounds it. The dictionary tells us that divination is both an act and an art that uses images, patterns, and symbols to reveal what is hidden. It interprets, intuits, predicts, and constructs possibilities through what we now call nonrational means: intuition, imaginative induction, inspiration, trance, reflections on dreams, and symbols. The word divination shares a root with "divine." This root connects divination with shining or making things clear; deities, decisions, and riches; light, luminosity, the sky, and the moon; gods, demons, and the course of the day; journeys, journals, and the keepers of fate.

The Purposes of Divination

Another one of our presuppositions is that divination is supposed to reveal the "future." This is not quite accurate. Divination was considered a lumen or light added to our normal intelligence. It was and is first of all a way to see what is there, what spiritual forces are active in your present situation and how you can successfully interact with them. It is used to give you insight into what is behind a given problem or difficulty and what strategies you can use to deal with it, or to tell you if the "way," the basic flow of energy, is open or closed. It can give you information about the way your fate or inner spirit is moving, locate you in a process of transformation, or give you "signs of the time" that connect events in your soul with events in the world. The aim of divination is not to reveal an implacable future, but to place you in the process of that future, to connect you with the flow of life through its signs, symbols, and spirits.

These symbols propose themselves as a crossroad or meeting place with a world of creative energy, the dynamic forces underlying events. They are a way of contacting the hidden – called soul, spirit, *tao*, gods – in and through the events of your daily life. These symbols act as a link, an interchange or interface with the forces involved. The divination system that uses them acts as a kind of inner navigator, a "machine" for creating awareness of spirit.

LEFT: A ritual from a Dionysiac mystery cult from ancient Greece, where regular contact with the gods was part of everyday life.

OPPOSITE TOP: Joseph of Arimathea's vision of the Holy Grail, Christ's cup at the Last Supper; it is revered as an object that was both human and divine, an interface between the physical and the spiritual world.

OPPOSITE BOTTOM: In traditional cultures, images of gods and spirits embody forces beyond human control.

The symbols have two aspects. One aspect acts as a signpost, indicating what is favorable and what is not favorable given the quality of the time. It points out possible traps, hidden dangers, and special opportunities. The idea of "good fortune" connected with these signposts involves the experience of meaning and connection as well as gain and happiness. The idea of "misfortune" involves being cut off from the flow of the spirit. These signposts are there to protect you. The other, more symbolic, part has several layers of possible meaning. It invites you to interact with it, exploring possibilities and letting your awareness of your situation be moved and changed. The divinatory way creates a *temenos*, a protected and creative place, that allows this symbolic interaction to take place.

Divination and Fate

Any divinatory method implies a living world and posits itself as an active participant or double of the creative process. This process mirrors the continual creation of what we call fate or destiny. It is a way of questioning and trying out the possible versions of fate.

The signs and symbols produced by this questioning do not control our actions. They suggest the field in which our lives are being played out and offer a description of potentials. This does not take away your freedom to act. It offers you the chance to interact creatively with these possibilities and help shape your experience rather than being its victim. Your awareness and choice are the seeds of things to come.

Who Is Happening to Me?

People in a traditional culture live surrounded by images of gods and spirits that help them understand the events of their lives. These spirits are recognitions that there are forces beyond our immediate control, things and feelings that "happen" to us. Divination lets you question these forces and experience their friendship and benevolence. By knowing which god was at work, you would know what to do, what to offer, and what the likely directions were in which energy and passion would flow.

When people are troubled or sick, when they want to begin a journey or start an enterprise, when they need to know what is going on "behind the scenes" in their lives, when they approach a fateful moment or encounter, they ask for an oracle, a "talking symbol." Behind each request for knowledge of "what will happen to me?" is a more basic question: "who is happening to me? which god or spirit is presenting me with this situation?" Each of the gods is a way of seeing, acting, and feeling, a shape or sign of the times. So in knowing who it was who was affecting your life, you would know what to do, how to act "in the spirit."

Divination and Culture

nother of our suppositions about divination is that it is "primitive." Yet human culture has expressed itself in some amazingly profound and sophisticated ways through the methods of divining that we will look at in this book. These divinatory ways describe the connection between a world that displays itself in signs, images, and symbols, and the power in the individual to read them. They open a potent imaginative space where individuals interact with the basic images of their culture, and where the myths and deep psychic images are in turn shaped and changed by the individuals they encounter.

We can see this very strikingly in two traditional divination systems: Yoruba *Ifa* divination carries the entire oral culture of its people grouped around 16 main signs and 240 minor ones. The

Chinese *Classic of Change* or *I Ching*, with its 64 "hexagrams" and their short divinatory texts, carried and developed the core of traditional Chinese culture for 2,500 years. The deep images are both carried and continually modified through the opening of "sacred space" in the individual imagination that the act of divination provides.

The dynamic works both ways. If divination has created and carried culture, it has also helped people to free themselves from the hold of a restrictive public morality by establishing an individual connection with its creative spirit. Historically, the divination process moves toward a recognition of the creative relation of the individual to the creative matrix of life and culture. It has helped many to thread their way through times of great social breakdown, upheaval, or repression. This is probably the most important element in traditional divination – the individual encounter with the helping spirit.

Each of the divinatory "ways" we will look at in this book proposes an imaginative world, has a rich history, and offers a way to interact with the "spirits" who inhabit its imaginative world. The symbols in these systems show us the richness of the soul and give us a background in depth to what we are experiencing. They are the ways people have "divined themselves," the ways they use to connect their daily life with the healing gift of the gods.

ABOVE: The Egyptian oasis town of Suwa, famous for its desert oracle.

LEFT: A healing ceremony in Saudi Arabia.

OPPOSITE: The Persian Sultan Iskander and his courtiers visit a cave-dwelling hermit for enlightenment.

The Function of an Oracle

In its most basic form, an oracle is anything that "speaks" to you, revealing what spiritual forces are active in your life and what you might do about them. The ancient world had hundreds of oracles – shrines, altars, incubation sites, temples, grottoes – that used a wide range of divinatory "symbolizing." These sites encouraged a special kind of perception, a way to see through the surface of things and hear what is at work behind them. What the ancient world called "oracles" are fundamentally symbols, places, words, and signs with a special function – they put something together that has come apart. This reflects a quality highly valued in traditional cultures: the capacity to see, hear, and feel spirit moving, which was fostered by innumerable sites of close encounter.

If you asked someone in a traditional culture what divination and oracles do, you would probably get a variation on the idea that they give you access to a "divine mind," a "knower of fates," or a "world soul," and to spirit-figures that relay messages about the way this living whole is moving. When the sense of the existence of such a divine mind, world soul, maker of fates, or world of patterns has vanished, divination falls into the disreputable shadow of rational thought. It becomes superstition, spooky correspondences, and charlatanism. But there has always been something eerie about divining and the "other than ordinary means" it uses to gather information about the invisible world. Much of this "strange" quality is reflected in the figure of the diviner and his involvement with what depth psychologists have called the shadow – not just what is hidden from view, but what we as individuals and as a culture would rather not look at.

There are many images of this figure from traditional cultures. Most of them emphasize the diviner's "wounded" nature as the source of his or her strange power. Like the shaman, the diviner is often chosen and pursued by the spirits. Many attempt, unsuccessfully, to flee their calling. The diviner may cross sexual boundaries as a transvestite, transsexual, or hermaphrodite; be an outcast, wanderer, or hermit; or become a technician of the sacred, full of recondite lore and hard-earned knowledge. Legendary shaman-kings and culture founders, beings full of daimonic power, were quintessential diviners. The Old Wise Woman, the Shaman who travels in spirit, the Medium of the Spirits, or the wandering "Man of God" all suggest that the source of this way of knowing comes from crossing boundaries, from entering into liminal or borderline states of mind sometimes paid for in suffering or dislocation.

These figures give us an intimation of the power latent in our innate intuitive capacity. Divining – which involves seeing patterns that interconnect time, spirit, and soul – cultivates and trains this innate capacity to see outside the way we usually put things together.

Reading the Signs

he most common way of divining involves a reading. An inquirer puts a question to an oracle through a diviner, consultant, or reader, thus establishing an inner field of dialogue with its symbols. The reading is a model for our interaction with an oracle or divinatory system.

A reading is an exploration in which the inquirer becomes the center of cosmic attention, on whom the power and energy of the archetypal images are focused. The symbols invoked yield specific information – "try this," "don't go there," "danger," "opportunity" – and act as catalysts that open the gates to a process of bringing deep patterns to awareness. The process induces a light trance state in which associations become fluid and available. Inner myths are projected into the divinatory symbols. What happens is a kind of "myth therapy," the opening of a space and time where these inner processes can be displayed and opened to creative intervention.

The reader or diviner moves into another kind of altered consciousness, sometimes called a "flow" state. Attention, activity, and involvement are intensely focused without regard for a particular objective. This self-forgetfulness concentrates skill, knowledge, and subliminal awareness at the service of the patterns that emerge in answer to the inquirer's question. What results is a highly creative state that dissociates from the normal personalities involved to weave new patterns and stories through a

heightened awareness. It is a game, played with symbols that have a more than personal power. The results of this game include a feeling of connection and spiritual renewal as well as astoundingly accurate predictions. It develops your ability to see yourself as part of a great interconnected whole, an awareness of spirit moving in and through the events of your daily life.

ABOVE: Inside a Chinese temple. The priest holds a container full of divinatory bamboo stalks while a supplicant seeks an answer or direction.

OPPOSITE TOP: "Chaotic Attractors," a computer graphics representation of a form of fractal geometry. An aspect of the chaos theory introduced by new physics, this image shows the inherent form and beauty that underlies apparent chaos as patterns connect and collide.

OPPOSITE BOTTOM: A Greek *krater*, or cup, showing ritual animal sacrifice during a Dionysiac festival. Bowls, cups, and containers all have special meaning in the symbolic vocabulary of divination.

The World of Symbols

Where do these symbols come from? On a literal level, the origin of the world's divination systems remains a mystery. No one knows who "invented" any of these ways of questioning fate. There are, however, many myths that describe the "world of signs" the symbols come from, the place we go during a divination. Taoist myth sees it as a fertile originating chaos. Ifa diviners invoke a noble trickster, a border-crossing spirit that breaks down and re-forms shapes and circumstances. Greeks saw it as the Garden of Zeus where Eros was born, full of the shapes of possible things, or the girdle of Aphrodite, with all the images of desire.

These myths all point at a paradisical and chaotic place, charged with energy, where shapes change easily and the normal categories of time and space do not apply. Other symbols of this fertile place are the great mixing bowl, or *krater*, where all that lives takes shape; the Divining Bowl that is an image of the alchemical process; the Holy Grail, or Cornucopia pouring out its blessings; the "creative unconscious" of depth psychology; and the unnamed and mysterious fertility of the tao or way. In this mythical place everything is simultaneously present, infolded, yet ready to "unfold" itself into existence.

A striking place where these old myths and magical psychologies cross over into modern thought is in the metaphors for the deep structure of reality that come from new developments in theoretical physics – quantum theory, chaos theory – and theories of the brain at work.

In the last 60 years, high-energy physics – the study of submicroscopic waves and particles – has described a reality underlying what we normally perceive where matter and energy are interchangeable. Normal rules of time and space do not apply in this submicroscopic world. Things can move in any direction, temporally and spatially. The nature of any phenomenon is intimately connected with who or what is observing it and what they expect it to be.

The world described by the new physics, with its protean appearances, disappearances, and reversals of time and space, and by chaos theory, which shows how minute variations at critical moments can affect global systems, is strikingly like the world described by shamans, magicians, seers, and deep diviners. It is a fertile, surging pandemonium in which effects occur simultaneously in widely separated places or move backward and forward in time. Each small piece of this world infolds all information about every other piece. We perceive it as creative patterns, information about unfolding events as they connect, collide, and deflect one another. We can symbolically interact with and influence this world through entering its patterns. The way we perceive and organize knowledge partakes of the same chaotic yet orderly movement of creative patterns.

The process of divination, the interaction with its potent symbols, duplicates this return to chaos, a fertile chaos that underlies the reality we experience.

The Way and the Ways of Divining

Divination has been described as the most aboriginal and persistent of human acts, fundamental to religion, magic, myth, and the soul. It reflects the very deep need we feel for creative contact with spirit and our fate, something that cuts across cultural boundaries.

Analytical thinkers have tended to break divination into two categories, ecstatic and inductive, or inner vision and outer thinking. Each is then further subdivided according to the medium used and the place it comes from. Both of these qualities, however, are present in any divinatory act. Rather than separate them, this book presents divination in terms of its "ways" or traditions: reading signs and omens; traveling in the spirit and "seeing"; the lots and the great oracle systems; reading star signs and patterns; and divining through dreams. It assembles a wide range of examples from very diverse sources with no attempt to analyze their relative importance. These "ways" cut across cultures to point at deep human needs and perceptions, imaginative solutions to our search for contact with the living world. Some are closed to us – the information is lost, the technique has become impossible, the particular culture is untranslatable. Others are still open and, even more, in a current state of transformation and rebirth. The current reimagining of divinatory ways and systems is one of the most fertile and exciting events of our postmodern culture. All are presented as ways of seeing and knowing that have run through virtually all human cultures, old and new, simple and sophisticated. The emphasis is, whenever possible, on experience: how they were used and how you can use them.

These traditions, the ways in which we have "divined ourselves," constitute some of the most profound and bizarre perceptions people have had about what we are and how we might connect with the reality around us. Opening this dialogue is a healing act, for it re-places us in a living, speaking world.

DIVINING THE WORLD

There are various ways in which the oracle is approached, from simple palmistry to high-tech computer readouts. Some examples are given below.

LEFT: Parrots are the divinatory birds of choice in Bangladesh, used like chickens as domestic bird oracles. The birds sit on their perch then flutter to pick up grain scattered on questions written on pieces of paper. The diviner interprets the answers for his clients.

RIGHT: Worlds collide in Khabarovsk, where a computerized fortuneteller offers his services in a fish store.

LEFT: A palm reader concentrates on her client's hand among the bustle on Seragoon Street, in the part of Singapore known as Little India.

OPPOSITE: In the Judeo-Christian tradition, God is seen as the ultimate Divine Being who measures and guides human life. Divinatory practice in this tradition includes prayer, meditation, trancing, speaking in tongues, visions, and miracles.

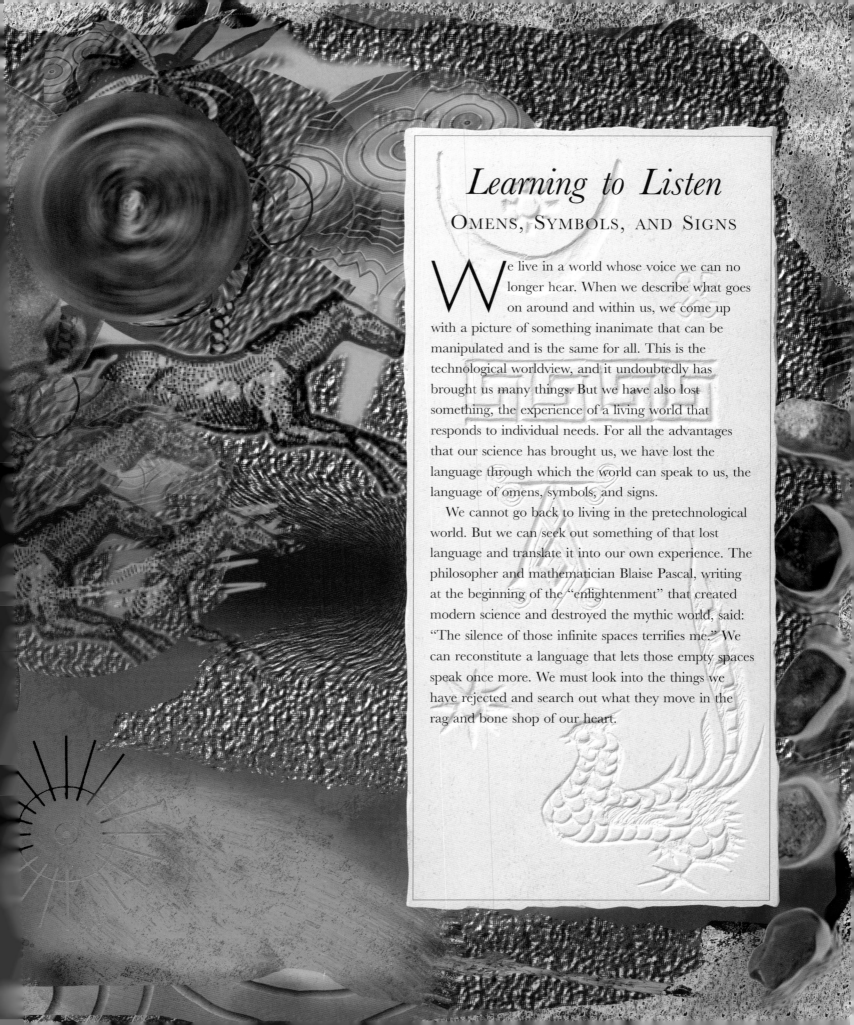

Learning to Listen
OMENS, SYMBOLS, AND SIGNS

We live in a world whose voice we can no longer hear. When we describe what goes on around and within us, we come up with a picture of something inanimate that can be manipulated and is the same for all. This is the technological worldview, and it undoubtedly has brought us many things. But we have also lost something, the experience of a living world that responds to individual needs. For all the advantages that our science has brought us, we have lost the language through which the world can speak to us, the language of omens, symbols, and signs.

We cannot go back to living in the pretechnological world. But we can seek out something of that lost language and translate it into our own experience. The philosopher and mathematician Blaise Pascal, writing at the beginning of the "enlightenment" that created modern science and destroyed the mythic world, said: "The silence of those infinite spaces terrifies me." We can reconstitute a language that lets those empty spaces speak once more. We must look into the things we have rejected and search out what they move in the rag and bone shop of our heart.

Signs, Spirits, and Synchronicity

In the most traditional terms, omens imply the existence of spirits, forces outside our direct conscious control that can, and do, enter into and influence things. Humans are vulnerable to these forces and must learn to deal with them. The world of the spirits, which is also a model of our souls, is mysterious, dangerous, and magically fertile. These spirits have been described as gods, demons, or the souls of the dead. They are a mysterious semidivine force that the Greeks called *daimon* or the Chinese *shen*. In modern terms, they are complexes, autonomous parts of our soul that directly influence interior and exterior events. What we now see as chance, coincidence, or random selection is the instrument of these spirits. They enter into things or human beings and influence the way they act. The result of this entrance is an omen, a word or phrase in the language that they use to communicate with humans.

Another traditional perspective sees omens, symbols, and signs as the self-display of the ongoing processes of nature. Perceiving and recognizing a significant pattern in one part through an omen lets you read how this pattern is affecting any other part, for each part reflects the organization of the whole. In this view, a single pattern connects spirit, nature, society, and the individual, and it is the duty of the individual to conform to the pattern. Things that break "normal" patterns indicate something that calls for redress. Omens indicate whether or not this is being done.

For many modern people, omens and signs are "superstition." Because a sign is not logically or causally connected to the thing it pretends to describe, it is meaningless. The same is often said of dreams and fantasies: they are mere coincidence, only chance, or just your imagination. The language of signs and omens describes something outside this perspective, a kind of meaning that has been called "synchronicity." This is a modern equivalent of traditional views that hold that omens reveal spirits and hidden processes.

CELEBRITY DIVINATION

The use of various divinatory practices is being revived in the realms of worldly celebrities. In the West, astrology is increasingly used by royalty, media stars, politicians, and financial institutions. In the East, feng shui permeates everyday life, and business depends on the harmonious flow of the life force. Some examples of celebrity divination are given below.

LEFT: Nancy Reagan (a Cancerian), former First Lady to President Ronald Reagan (an Aquarian), who consulted an astrologer and used the advice given to organize her husband's day-to-day program.

RIGHT: The Hong Kong Bank, designed by the Western architect Sir Norman Foster to conform with the guidelines laid down by local feng shui practitioners.

LEFT: Indira Gandhi (1917–1984), Prime Minister of India from 1966 to 1977 and 1980 until her death by assassination, also used astrology to help her in her decisions and scheduling.

Synchronicity describes a particular charged quality of time through which an event in the outer world coincides meaningfully with an event in the inner world without a logical or causal connection to explain it. It indicates that a basic structure of our imagination has been activated. When this happens, it violates the "normal" laws of cause and effect and, in doing so, creates new meaning. The synchronistic occurrence is grounded in a psychological conflict, a concern that cannot be dealt with in normal ways. A symbolic event occurs that gives voice to the problem. It is a "little miracle" that offers a suggestion for action and a deepening of your understanding. It introduces a "nonordinary" world hidden behind the screen of "normal" appearances.

Seen from this perspective, omens open the gate to a kind of language that we also see in dreams and fantasies, a language that puts things together in "impossible" ways. They come from a place you can influence but cannot control, something that behaves as if it were alive and aware. They reveal a hidden connection between the psyche and the space-time continuum, a connection we become aware of in certain emotionally charged situations. Perceiving the connections leads you into a deepened creative thought that traditional cultures saw as the source of gods, spirits, and ghosts, the spontaneous "self-display" of a living world.

ABOVE AND BELOW: The dream landscape of Joseph, renowned for his ability to interpret the dreams of the pharaoh. In most cultures dreaming is regarded as a divinatory state.

Opening the Gates to the Omens

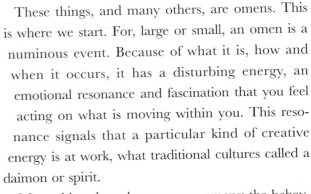

omething happens, something extraordinary. A general rides into the city and an eagle swoops down to seize his hat. A soldier on the march suddenly sees a whirlwind dance behind the troops, scattering debris. Crossing the threshold at the beginning of a journey, you hear a crow call, then fly away to the left. A strange tingling occurs in your thumbs. Walking down the street, thinking of a plan, you hear someone suddenly scream from the crowd, "No, no, the other way, stupid!" You are struck by a stranger's face, a name, or word that keeps recurring. A white horse haunts your dreams. As you say something, the walls groan, there is a loud clap, bells ring, or someone sneezes. Stuck in a dilemma, you suddenly say, "Oh, let's just flip a coin." Thinking of how you will assert your rights in a quarrel, you suddenly turn the corner and see two dogs fighting in the middle of the street.

These things, and many others, are omens. This is where we start. For, large or small, an omen is a numinous event. Because of what it is, how and when it occurs, it has a disturbing energy, an emotional resonance and fascination that you feel acting on what is moving within you. This resonance signals that a particular kind of creative energy is at work, what traditional cultures called a daimon or spirit.

Many things have been seen as omens: the behavior of birds, animals, and insects; random words and surprising events; body intuitions, irritations, and feelings; clouds, wind, and thunder; letters, numbers, and dates; faces, badges, and social types; stars and planets; surprising noises, creaks, and groans; suggestive patterns, particularly when connected with elemental things such as fire, wood, or water. Anything that intersects our thoughts and feelings in an unusual way at an important moment, activating that part of our imagination that sees behind the apparent, is an omen. Omens can be spontaneous – bird flight, a sudden word, event, or feeling, a dream image – or they can be induced. The dream can be incubated, we can search for a vision, draw lots, or ask something beyond our control to choose from a set of symbols. As we work with an omen, when we let it "work on" us, it becomes a symbol, a gate to a hidden world, and a sign, a guidepost to help direct our actions. It opens the gate to a dialogue with imaginative and spiritual processes that lie behind its appearance. The root of the English word omen shows this process, meaning both "to announce" and "to take or hold as meaningful."

Acknowledged or unacknowledged, the concern with omens, symbols, and signs is a universal human preoccupation. Medicine, religion, psychology, all forms of predictive methods from market research to fortunetelling begin in the omen: how do I explain this strange event, what lies behind it, and where is it going, what does it mean to me? Currently, our culture tends to deal with omens as it deals with individuals, through statistical averages and reductive analysis. In traditional cultures, however, it is different. Omens warn, encourage, explain, and direct. They reveal personal destiny and the will of the gods. A tribal group lives in a continually evolving network of these signs, a "dream-world" equivalent of modern science we call superstition. These omens, many of which we now recognize as signs of organic, meteorological, and psychological processes, give information on everything from weather patterns and animal movements to the approach of malevolent spirits and hostile desires. They also act as a kind of initiation, whereby everyday events reveal a mysterious significance. The description of a Melanesian "man of knowledge" (page 24) gives us the flavor of such an awareness.

OPPOSITE TOP RIGHT: The random patterns and overheard conversations of crowds can be used as divinatory tools.

OPPOSITE BOTTOM: Chinese children playing a traditional game in the school playground. The spontaneous collective decision to play a certain game, or sing a certain rhyme, was regarded as an omen by some Chinese diviners.

RIGHT: Flickering lights, unexplained noises, strange apparitions all have a part to play in the unlocking of the gates between the worlds.

Omens open a "hidden language," a way of looking at things that sees behind events to their imaginative significance. Chinese diviners call them "dragon-holes," places where creative energy enters and manifests itself. For many African, Asian, and American diviners, signs are themselves animals that move in a powerful invisible reality parallel to this one. Their appearance signifies a crossover point. Ancient Greeks would mark off anything that intensified meaning and stirred the soul in this "synchronistic" way with fluttering white pieces of cloth to indicate that a link in the invisible net that binds heaven and earth together had momentarily surfaced.

An omen is anything that strikes you and activates your innate desire to "symbolize," to empower events as connections to the invisible world. The appearance of an omen often indicates a critical moment, when psychic energy is moving and pushing toward awareness. Omens really make sense at critical moments when we become aware of the tightening net of circumstances and feel the necessity to act.

ABOVE: A guardian of a dragon-hole, the space where creative energy interacts with earthly existence.

RIGHT: This ramshackle house once belonged to an Hawaiian *kahuna*, a man of knowledge. It is built in the graveyard, so that the *kahuna* has access to influences on both sides of the gate of the world. Melanesian "men of knowledge" live in the same manner.

THE MAN OF KNOWLEDGE

The life of a "man of knowledge" is filled with a subtle but continuous interaction with the realm of the unseen powers. The plants in his garden provide the necessary ingredients for magical potions, like the insect tied up by one leg over the fire, the dried bird's wing, the lizard's skin in the thatch of the roof. The songs he sings to himself when he goes to bed are ritual invocations of the spirits of fathers and grandfathers. The cries of birds, the chirps of insects, the sudden appearance of a bat or firefly are communications from the other world, imbuing his waking consciousness with constant awareness of other realities. This morning he heard the bird *ifi* calling in a bush from the near end of the village: someone in his clan will soon die. In the evening a cicada shrills or a bat swoops low overhead: they are messengers. A sudden sneeze, a ringing in his ears, veins throbbing in his arm, all are meaningful to the "man of knowledge." Each plant or tree is the transformed body substance of a myth-person. The enormous black butterfly with trailing, frilled wings that floats past is the beautiful widow clad in black, and the swarm of bright-colored smaller ones following her are her suitors. They can be used in a love charm. Everything has a secret significance. Awareness of this hidden world gives him conscious knowledge of what will eventually happen in bodily reality. It is his responsibility to know this.

Divination and the God of Knots

People use divination because they want to know what to do, how to act, what to feel about particular situations. Over time, working with the omens and signs of a divinatory way constellates a spirit-guide deep within you and lets you speak with it through the language of symbols. It connects you consciously with the great processes of living and transformation.

The connection between an omen and a critical moment brings up one of the most fundamental and mysterious images the human imagination has ever produced to explain its situation in the world: the net, loom, or labyrinth, the moving fabric of life and the inescapable and fatal interconnection of things. The omen, archaic and powerful, is a part of this net, a knot, noose, or snare. It is a place where the web of fate is drawn tighter, and evokes the mysteries of binding and loosening, fate and freewill, suffering and transformation.

This image of a knot where fate is bound into each person's life lurks behind each divinatory sign. By tying together what is inside us and what is outside us, it opens a mysterious gate and points at a dark mythic figure: the weaver of fate, god and goddess of patterns, tricksters, magicians, illuminations, and traps. Compulsions, problems, symptoms, sicknesses, and desires are the raw material of an

encounter with this figure of fate. The omen points out the crossing-place. It is a nick in time, the entrance to an imaginal world.

ABOVE: The Pillar of the Silver Net is the imagined boundary that marks the beginning of the Otherworld in the Celtic tradition. The net is a striking metaphor for the concept of interlocking fate and the connectedness of all things. It also has echoes in modern physics, which is exploring the lattice theory of the relationship between subatomic particles.

LEFT: Knots are at once useful in the real world and imbued with magic. Sailors believed that certain knots could tie up the wind in their sails or bind sea demons. A bowline (left, above) and a sheet bend (left) are shown here.

26

Cracks in Time

Normal time presents us with a linear flow of minutes, hours, days, and years that move from the past into the future, independent of what is going on inside us. The sign or omen, combined with the attention of the observer, is a gap in this flow that offers the opportunity for another kind of seeing. It is a "window of opportunity" that opens a crack in time.

Seeing the hidden significance of things involves all your faculties, thought, feeling, imagination, memory, but it is particularly associated with the space of the heart, or the heart-mind. This is where we perceive symbolic significance, something that is not quite the same as thinking.

OPENING THE HEART SPACE

Here is a meditation exercise to open this space. You can use it before any divinatory procedure.

Sit relaxed and straight, feet on the floor, and close your eyes. Breathe deeply and naturally, take the stream of the in-flowing breath all the way down into the bowl of your pelvis and release it gently. Let yourself relax. Let thoughts, worries, and tensions slide away. Let the breath open a place inside you, on the level of your heart, where you can feel and see what usually is hidden. Keep breathing, easily and deeply, letting energy flow into this place. Sense the connection between this place in yourself and everything around you. This is your circle. You can call on anything that appears here to help you.

Now imagine there is an open door in front of you, an old stone door marked with cryptic signs. As you cross the threshold you find yourself on a stairway leading down, into a shadow world that has, in many ways, been taboo in the West since late antiquity. Here we find symbols, floating and changing, mysterious images like those in dreams that speak to us by calling up nets of associations, memories, and feelings. We catch glimpses of strange masked faces, at once timeless and threateningly intimate. We see the glimmer of phosphorescent lights and feel sudden dim illuminations. Underneath and around us we sense the great flow of the stream of life as it mysteriously nourishes and gives meaning to all things.

Here in this space imagine you see a vessel, lying on its side, unused. Take the vessel, stand it upright in the center of the space. Feel it expand to include the entire space. It marks off a sacred space where you can interact with the symbols: Whatever is of concern to you, the knots and difficulties in your life, whatever you want to "see into," can be put into the vessel to be "cooked." The watching eyes of the spirits appear at the edge of our awareness, standing all around us. By putting something into the vessel, valuing it as a symbol, you empower the imagination. It is this creative attention, acting out, playing with, imitating the symbols – turning and rolling them in your heart – that lets the spirits play a constructive part in your life.

Now return again. Say farewell to the circle of spirits. They will be there whenever you want to return. Go back through the door onto the stairs. Though the door closes behind you, it will open again whenever you approach it. Climb the stairs and return to the place where you are sitting. See and greet the things around you.

Birds of Omen

A look at what traditional cultures value as signs and omens gives us another clue as to how the divinatory language works. In many cultures, birds are the creatures of omen par excellence. In fact, signs and birds are interchangeable: "Happy is he who can distinguish the birds, and avoid the evils," an old poet said. Birds are messengers of change, fate, illumination, death, and transformation, spirit-guides and vehicles for travel in other realities.

Soul-birds and bird-masked dancers haunt the 15,000-year-old cave-paintings at Lascaux. They descend into the shaman's body to carry him on the heavenly journey. The "feathered guest" and ecstatic journey of the Chinese shaman would draw the spirits to incarnate in human bodies. Raven and crow, crane and diver bring the shape-changing gifts of culture. Owl and vulture announce the opening of the gates of death and wisdom, the dove heralds a visit from the Goddess of Desire or the Holy Spirit, the "calling crane" points at an immortal affinity of souls. The bird sign signals an influx of spirit, a reminder of an old celestial paradise. It gives people the assurance that they are not alone in a world full of demons and hostile forces.

Migratory birds have an uncanny ability to follow electromagnetic currents and predict weather patterns, while trackers know that birds will tell them of everything that is moving in a forest. Birds' movement parallels the gifts of thought; their sudden appearance is the visible sign of what we call intuition. Learning to speak the "language of the birds" is a sign for the clairvoyant ability to perceive hidden patterns. Bird flight was seen as the origin of writing, bird song as the beginning of music. Transformation into a bird is the happiest of fates and sign of the ecstatic journey.

Birds, said Plutarch, a Greek philosopher and oracle-priest of c. 46–120 C.E., because of their speed, intelligence, and the justice of their movements, through which they show themselves aware of everything that strikes the imagination, put themselves, like true instruments, at the service of the divine. It permeates their movements and pulls their songs and calls from them. Sometimes they hold back, sometimes they launch themselves with the impetuous force of the wind to interrupt violently certain of our acts and intentions or to aid their realization. That is why we call them "messengers of the gods."

Birds are the sign for the intervention of spirit in human life. Drawing lots, the random fall of a card or dice, the sudden appearance of a figure in dreams, a sudden body sign, an unexpected voice, event, or vision all have the numinous and mythic quality associated with the bird as spirit-messenger. All these signs were seen as "birds," and further associated with the *daimones*, spirits of the air who hold the world of the gods and the human world together. This is the background to the long effort of medieval Christian literature to turn birds into the helpers of the saints.

Though any bird could be an omen when it appeared in a "charged moment," certain birds were singled out as particular carriers of meaning. In Homeric Greece, as in many Indo-European cultures, the bird of omen was the lone eagle or hawk, the *oinos*, associated with kings, destiny, blood, and sacrifice.

Like many Mediterranean cultures, archaic Greece recognized three kinds of divining and diviners: the *hieros*, who read signs in animal sacrifices; the *onieropolos*, the reader of omens in dreams; and the *mantis*, who read bird signs and "saw" through a kind of imaginative induction that was induced by a sign. This ability was a gift – or curse – that ran in certain families.

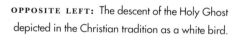

OPPOSITE LEFT: The descent of the Holy Ghost depicted in the Christian tradition as a white bird.

OPPOSITE TOP: The seemingly random freewheeling patterns birds make in flight are seen as instructive omens in many traditions.

LEFT: Zuni and Hopi Indians dress as these spirit birds – this one is known as Koyona – to ward off evil and to contact sacred spirits.

ABOVE: Birds were considered to be associates and messengers of the gods. This is Artemis, fierce goddess of the hunt, seen with her emblematic bow and arrow and her bird.

THEOKLYMENOS AND THE HAWK

Theoklymenos, rescued by Odysseus' son Telemachos in the *Odyssey*, is an example. He was descended from the race of Melampos, who had been given the ability to understand the speech of birds, animals, and snakes. Taken on board Telemachos' ship as it returned to Ithaka, he saw a hawk fly up on the right clutching a dove, at the same time the despairing Telemachos was wishing a dark fate on the men who were oppressing him. Theoklymenos instantly "saw" the connection between the bird-sign and the pressing question haunting everyone, the return of Odysseus. "Telemachos," he said, "this bird did not fly to our right without a god behind it. I knew when I saw it overhead that it was a bird of omen. Do not be afraid. There is no house stronger than yours on Ithaka." In the same way, he later "sees" the net of fate tightening around the men eating and drinking in Telemachos' house. He is suddenly struck by a vision of their heads, faces, and knees shrouded in darkness, the walls covered with blood, and the room peopled by phantoms. He has seen the underworld open and a fateful mist rush to cover the sun (xx, 351–57).

Wretched men! What evil is this you suffer? Your heads
and faces are shrouded in night, and your knees beneath.
Wailing blazes up, and your cheeks are covered with tears.
The walls and the lovely pedestals are sprinkled with blood.
The porch is full of phantoms, the courtyard is also full
of those eager for Erebos under the dusk. The sun
has perished out of heaven, and an evil mist rushes in.

HOMER, *THE ODYSSEY*, XX, 351–57

As the Crow Flies

The crow or raven omen occurs in many cultures, and if you have ever observed how these remarkable birds interact with humans, you will have a sense of their "ominous," unsettling presence. The crow was a sun-bird and a trickster, eater of corpses, and shape-changer in cultures as diverse as those in China, Greece, and North America. No Greek would continue a journey or an activity if a crow flew on or toward his left. In traditional Tibet, the crow or raven was the divinatory bird par excellence. Crows were never killed, for they were regarded as messengers of the Mahakala, the great protectors. People watched their movements and learned to understand their strange, piercing calls and cries. As in Greece, Etruria, and Babylon, there were specific texts dealing with interpreting these bird-signs that combined the direction of flight and the time of day to produce a series of specific omens ranging from the appearance of a guest, enemy, or malevolent demon to where to search for something lost. But this is just a background. Most often the meaning lies in the immediacy of the sign.

A WARNING IGNORED

A Tibetan religious leader who escaped from Tibet at the time of the Chinese takeover told of a crow omen. His party was on its way over a mountain pass, having been assured the road ahead was clear, when a flock of crows appeared from an unfavorable direction and flew directly at them, trying to make them turn back. One was so insistent that it landed on the head of the man's horse and pulled at the bridle. Ignoring the omen, they arrived at the top of the pass a few moments later and found themselves facing a hostile group of Chinese soldiers hunting for potential escapees.

Celtic peoples recognized both the raven and the wren as divinatory birds. Here, too, we see an association of bird-signs, "seeing," dreams, and other divining methods. Later Celtic diviners attempted to locate the appearance of the sign in a divinatory cosmos based on the direction of the birds' calls. Their efforts are noted in medieval manuscripts.

CALLING BIRDS

In a medieval Irish manuscript we find that if a raven calls above your bed, distinguished guests are on the way, the type depending on whether the bird calls *bacah*, *gredh gredh*, *gracc gracc*, or *grob grob*. If a wren flies or calls between you and the sun, someone dear to you will die; if it calls at your left ear, you will unite with a young man from far away or sleep with a young woman; if it calls from behind and above, someone is attempting to seduce your wife; while if it appears on the ground behind you she will be taken away by force. If it calls from the east, you should rejoice – poets and glad tidings are on their way.

ABOVE: A Celtic druid notes the position of a raven before consulting his book and deciding an action.

OPPOSITE TOP LEFT: A flight of crows, recognized as birds of great divinatory importance.

LEFT: Taliesin, the Celtic diviner and bard, accompanied by his eagle.

Other universal birds of omen were the owl and the vulture, who announced the opening of the gates of the dead. Fewer and fewer of us know the larger birds today, living as we do in an urban, postindustrial world that has destroyed them in great numbers. We lack the frightening experience of the sudden appearance of the owl's round white face in the darkness or its strange unsettling cry. But birds in general may assume this function. Jung once told about the wife of a patient of his who had seen a flock of birds gather at her window at the death of both her mother and grandmother. Her husband was on his way home from a medical checkup – ironically he had been given a clean bill of health – when he collapsed in the street, dying. At the moment of his collapse, the birds gathered once more at her window.

Another kind of omen from late Mediterranean antiquity brings together many of the things associated with bird divining. Though very strange to us, it is a model in small of the systems of omen interpretation developed in ancient cultures, combining the symbolic and magical nature of the bird with a network of human meanings. This kind of divination was greatly valued by philosophers and played a role in many magic rituals.

For the Greeks, like many other peoples, the rooster was a bird of omen and a sign of divine courage and strength. Beloved of soldiers, it was thought to have a natural divinatory ability that made it aware of all atmospheric disturbances, literal and metaphorical. The rooster's cry on a marriage day predicted a stormy relation, while the sacrifice of a rooster protected the vines and turned away hail. This bird played a very important part in magical and theurgical ceremonies in Greece and throughout Africa. Through alectryomancy, or divination through roosters, it was given a voice. The diviner drew a circle on the earth and

AVIAN PORTENTS

Eagle

Raven

Duck

Vulture

Birds of all kinds are omens. Ravens and crows, for instance, bring the gift of shape-changing.

Owl

Crane

Dove

Owls are traditionally seen as opening the gates of death, whereas cranes are considered auspicious.

placed the letters of the alphabet around it. On each sign he placed a grain of wheat or barley, which he would constantly renew. He would pose a question, consecrate the bird, and place it in the circle. The bird would eat the grain, thus indicating the letters of the divine response to the inquirer's question.

For most peoples, seeing or hearing an auspicious bird – crane, duck, goose, swan, or pheasant – as a journey or activity begins is an assurance of blessing. Certain African diviners make wooden images of birds and suspend them in a sacred grove, where the slightest air current will move them. By watching these movements, the diviner can answer the questions posed to him.

TALKING WITH BIRDS

Try simply becoming aware of the movements of the birds around you. At the same time, watch your thoughts and feelings. Pay attention to any movement that occurs when you are thinking of something that affects you deeply. Pay particular attention to the crows and how their movements and cries intersect with your thoughts. As you pay attention to the birds, they will become aware of you and begin to interact with you in a kind of extended dialogue. Do not hesitate to let their movement call up personal associations. There have been many interpretative systems developed to give bird-signs a context, but the most basic and functional is the old Greek system of right and left, high and low, forward and backward. Flight on or toward the left indicates closure and caution, a time to retreat, retire, or abandon your plan. Flight on or toward the right indicates opening, expansion, and favor. The bird passing directly overhead indicates insistence, while calling from a stationary position indicates something activated in your psyche. Some people count the number of birds or the number of calls. Pay attention to the way the bird acts toward you.

Most of us no longer live in the sort of environment peopled by the great birds of omen, nor are our imaginations open to their movements. But some of these divinatory messengers can still interact with us.

Here is an example. I live in an urban area inhabited by a large flock of crows and I have learned to watch

their movements on my daily walks. On several occasions when I was contemplating a specific action or feeling, a crow would fly directly overhead, land, and begin to call vehemently at me. The feeling of being spoken to was quite unmistakable. Once, when I was considering one of two alternatives to a deeply felt emotional dilemma, I was surprised by a crow suddenly flying directly overhead, calling, then landing behind and to my left – clearly a very negative omen. I then entertained the other alternative, visualizing and feeling it through. The crow called vehemently, flew overhead, forward and toward the right, again landing and calling to make sure I had seen him – a very favorable omen. From our modern point of view, taking this bird's activity seriously is extremely superstitious thinking. But, as things turned out, it clearly pointed the way to the best solution to my problem.

ABOVE: A Kwakiutl shaman dressed in bird costume performs a ritual dance. Shamans believe that they can enter into the spirits of birds and other animals and travel with them in their search for enlightenment.

Animals and Auguries

nimals as signs take us into the body and the underworld. All the old gods not only had animals as emblematic companions, they *were* animals. The sudden appearance of any animal crossing your path in waking or sleeping life indicated a god was at work. Totem animals describe the mysterious yet powerful identity between humans and animals. Bestiaries full of symbolic meanings show how they epitomize our basic qualities, reflected in the worldwide use of animal masks and dances to take on specific powers. Animals are capable of anticipating changes in the natural environment, so watching their behavior allows you to predict weather changes and sudden disasters such as flood or earthquake.

Aside from direct observation and sudden epiphany, animals become omens in three different ways. One is as a helping spirit that lets you travel in other realities and connects you with the various landscapes of the imagination. All animals are and have been pyschopomps, a paradisical alter ego connected with the "time before time began." Most hunter-gatherer cultures had specific ceremonies to take on an animal helper or guide to solve problems, seek advice, or explore the future. Another way that animals became omens was through sacrifice. The death and the

blood of the animal opened a gate between the worlds. All aspects of it were watched with care – how the smoke rose, the behavior of the victim, and, most important, the animal's internal organs, the liver and the intestines. Extiscipy – analyzing the entrails of sacrificed animals – was one of the ancient world's most widespread divinatory methods, a practice that could include humans. Certain Celtic and Germanic tribes practiced a kind of divination using prisoners of war. White-robed old women would cut the throat of a prisoner above a caldron and predict the outcome of a battle according to which way the blood fell. The body would then be opened and the entrails examined.

LEFT: A Native North American totem pole from Canada. Totems are the animal spirits that guide and help each tribe or nation.

OPPOSITE CENTER: A Babylonian sculpted head, carved to resemble the intestines. It would be used to interpret signs from the entrails of a sacrificial animal.

OPPOSITE BOTTOM LEFT: Cow's entrails are used to divine the future by the Mursi Tribe of Ethiopia.

Examining the Entrails

The liver was the primary focus of this examination. It was considered the seat of the soul and mirror of dreams, over which the "rays of the gods" play continually. The intestines reproduced the complex patterns of celestial movements, which could be read by counting the number of twists, odd or even. Modern theorists think that environmental factors directly affect these organs, so a reading of the sacrificed animal is like an evaluation of the health of the environment. Traditional thinkers say that the gods imprint the shape of the time on the inner organs of the animal at the moment of sacrifice.

THE COSMOS OF THE LIVER

The original pattern for analyzing the "cosmos of the liver" comes from Babylonian omen collections. Babylonians used a sacred grid to divide the liver into 55 zones. Marks found in each of these areas portended specific things. An enormous commentary literature developed, such as:

If there is a cross on the "strong-point," an important one will kill his lord.

If there are two "roads," the traveler will reach his goal.

If there are two "fingers" on the right, the omen is "who is king? who is not king?" – rivals for power.

The intestines, laid flat, formed a spiral labyrinth that reflected planetary movements. The spirals were examined and counted as key to the favor of planetary gods. Even was good, odd was bad.

This developed into a complete universe, shown in the bronze divinatory model of a sheep's liver found at Plaisance. The liver is divided in two, with the concave face divided into a series of houses, each with a god's name. The two lobes of the convex face bear the names of sun and moon, and are divided by a north-south line. The houses that surround the liver are the 16 cardinal divisions of the sky with their god-names. Thus each part of the liver belonged to a god, favorable or hostile, and the whole was a model of the heavens erected on earth, a *templum*.

ABOVE: A clay model of the liver inscribed with magic formulas as a guide for diviners when reading a real liver.

The third way animals became omens was through allowing them to be the agent of random selection. Germanic tribes practiced a sacred horse divination, described by the Roman historian Tacitus. White horses were kept in sacred groves. When the tribe needed to know the will of the gods, the horses would be yoked to a chariot and allowed to run. This evoked an important sacred image, the empty wagon or riderless horse as vehicle of the gods. Priests, servants of this Unseen God, would observe the behavior and cries of the horses, who were in the god's confidence. In another version, nine spears were laid across the horse's path and the priests noticed which of them his hooves touched and which foot he put forward to step over them.

African tribal cultures have many animal oracles that operate in similar ways, joining the mythic power of an animal to a divinatory pattern or grid through "chance."

BELOW: Early Germanic tribes believed that wild horses, particularly white ones, possessed oracular powers.

LEFT: A model horse from Bronze Age Denmark pulls a chariot containing the Sun or Moon.

OPPOSITE CENTER: Termites are one of the divinatory animals of the Azande people. Wood from two different kinds of trees is needed to activate the termite oracle.

The Termite Oracle

The Azande use two animal oracles. The termite oracle is available to all. It involves taking branches of two different types of trees, opening holes in the side of a large termite mound, inserting the branches and leaving them overnight. The consultant associates one side of a question with each branch, then addresses the termites: "O termites, if this business will succeed, eat the dakpa-tree. If this business will not succeed, eat the kpoyo-tree." In the morning, if one or the other branch is eaten, the answer is clear. If both are completely eaten, or both left untouched, the question has been refused. When they are unequally eaten, the answer is a qualified yes or no.

If the question has to do with adultery, death, marriage, sickness, sorcery, a new home site, war, disloyalty, or important appointments, it must be corroborated by the benge or "poison" oracle. Benge is a specially collected and ritually prepared substance. When it is given to a guinea fowl, a common domestic bird, it produces a reaction, it is felt, that can uncover the hidden forces at work in a situation. The usual time for such a consultation is morning. A private space is marked off at the edge between cultivated land and the bush, and a group of senior men gathers to put the questions. The benge is prepared and, at the last minute, mixed with water and forced into the throat of the bird. As it goes through its ordeal, the question is posed in great detail, ending with the injunction: "If so-and-so is the case, benge kill this fowl. If so-and-so is not the case, benge spare this fowl." To be fully established, the same question must be posed in reverse, i.e., if it is true, the bird will be spared, if false, killed.

THE PAWS OF THE PALE FOX

One example of random selection by animals is the kind of divination practiced by the Dogon, a North African tribe. Dogon diviners will lay out a grid in the earth at the edge of a village, based on a very complex set of signs. The grid represents the fields of human endeavor and is "sown" with over 60 possible questions. The divinatory animal is the "pale fox," a trickster animal who "speaks with his paws." He is surrounded by myths of disorder, incest, death, and loss of speech that reflect the hidden part of the human situation. The signs representing questions are sown with peanuts that attract the fox and left overnight. At dawn the signs of his paws and tail give the gods' answers to the questions that have been posed.

ABOVE: A Dogon diviner pores over the grid he has drawn in the earth, set out to attract the divinatory visit of the elusive "pale fox."

Several tribes in the Cameroon divine through the ngam spider, a large, hairy, black earth-dwelling spider that is an aggressive night-hunter. Old laws made it a capital crime to kill such a spider, for it was the messenger of a mysterious supreme power. Its night-sight permits it to see what humans cannot. It has direct contact with the realm of the dead and the ancestors who, bright and happy, live at a continual feast.

When a spider is discovered, a large pot, open top and bottom, is placed over the entrance to its burrow. The spider is fed often, and the feeding is associated with a call. The divination system relies on a deck of up to 300 cards made from the leaves of a particular plum tree. They are dried, flattened, and inscribed with a set of symbols and triangular signs indicating a good or bad augury. Sets of these cards can be up to a hundred years old. They represent a wide range of myths and symbols and are treated with care. Though the cards can be used alone, important questions are put to the spider, who is the mythic sponsor of the system.

A consultation begins with a conversation gently probing the background, the personality, and situation of the inquirer. The diviner will then go to the spider's shrine, whisper the question, and put the cards and insects the spider feeds on in the opening to the spider's burrow. He then covers the pot and calls the spider. After several hours, he returns and examines the cards that the spider has moved. These give the answer to the question posed and form the basis of a further dialogue with the inquirer.

ABOVE: Plum tree leaves are used to make the "cards" left for the ngam spider to select in a Cameroon divinatory system.

ABOVE LEFT: In the Cameroon, certain species of spiders are considered to have a direct line of contact with the nonhuman world.

LEFT: A juju man accompanied by village elders enters a village in the hills of southwest Cameroon.

CONSULTING THE NGAM SPIDER

This is an example of spider divination. Here are the symbolic answers given to a man seeking the cause of the dissension and conflict in his family.

• Bed without "favorable" sign: your sleep is troubled.

• Roof and door of a hut: trouble in your home.

• Assembly without "favorable" sign: family feast is incomplete; you are holding something back.

• Assembly and wife sign, not favorable: improve on the gift to your wife!

• In-law sign plus female breasts, unfavorable: a horror, your mother-in-law is angry with you!

• Two curved lines, sleeping together, unfavorable: illegal sexual intercourse.

• Curved lines back to back, not sleeping together: marital discord.

• Hoe or shovel used to tend fields, unfavorable: your hoe is against you.

• Shed on a farm, site of illegal love affairs, unfavorable.

• Woman, hoe, unfavorable: recall a certain "hoe-meeting" with a woman? Your past catches up with you!

• Knife used to tap palmwine, unfavorable: the palm you tap will not yield wine.

• Prosperity, woman, unfavorable: prosperity does not reward her work.

• Cup used in ceremonial cleansing, favorable: publicly state loyalty and devotion.

• The talk behind one's back, unfavorable: evil plans are being made.

• Trail and two holes, a man trap: danger!

• Crossroads (misfortune and perplexity), woman: women are bringing you misfortune, a crisis.

• Owl-eyes, girl, unfavorable: witchcraft is being practiced by women in your family.

• Brooding, worrying, woman: a woman is brooding over wrongs done to her.

• Oath, swearing, favorable: speak the truth!

• Assembly of men at a crossroads, favorable: men sit in judgment, favorable verdict.

• Hidden thoughts, secret talk, bundle of sacred grass, purification: you are in need of purification.

• Rites to renew ancestor cult objects, favorable: participate in renewing cult objects and values.

Weaving these symbols together, the diviner brought out the story of an angry wife, the harmful effects of a hidden sexual encounter, the potential of "witchcraft" or projection of negative feelings, and the need for purification and renewal of ancestral values if family harmony was to be preserved. The result of this, the oracle states, would be positive.

Body Talk

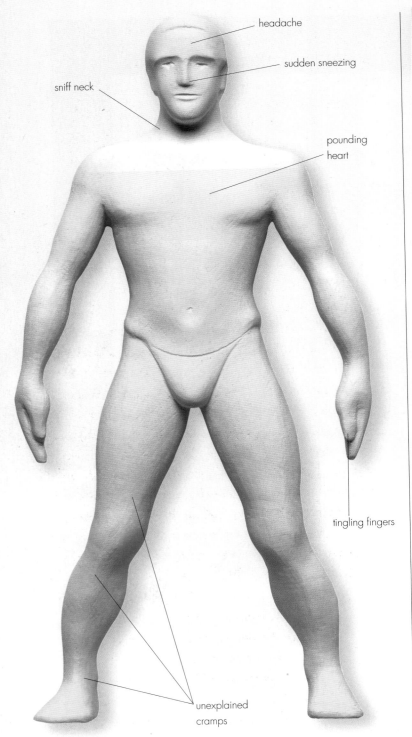

headache

sudden sneezing

sniff neck

pounding
heart

tingling fingers

unexplained
cramps

ur bodies are what we share with the animals. They are the source of a deep intuitive awareness and divinatory response. Head, hands, ears, feet, genitals, guts all have an emblematic quality that constantly sends signals. The Greek god Pan, half human, half goat, with his big ears and careful gaze, is a symbol of this kind of attention to the little spurts and waves of body feeling and their wisdom. Our actions, too, become signs: embrace the idea, find your feet, stiff-necked, itchy fingered. Like the shaman's animal guardians, "helping spirits" live in our bodies, sending signals to inform us about the world.

We can learn to hear their voice through involuntary actions. Sneezing is a widely recognized body sign in old cultures. The conjunction of a sneeze and a statement indicates that what was being talked of would happen. The idea of connection or conjunction is more subtle. An entire divinatory chapter of the *I Ching* is built on showing what happens when an influx of energy connects with the toes, calves, thighs, the border between upper and lower body, the spine, neck, and shoulders, or the mouth and tongue. Another sign shows what happens when each of these body areas is subject to limit and constriction.

Our bodies are both a continual source of signs and metaphors and a very sensitive instrument. The more we are aware of our body and its language, the more we can feel the connection with the world around us.

LEFT: The body picks up and gives out signals seemingly undirected by the conscious mind. You may often find that your body is giving you information about the world via involuntary and intuitive physical signs – shivers down the spine, goose bumps, a suddenly pounding heart.

OPPOSITE BOTTOM: The six body chakras, or energy centers, where the ebb and flow of the life force is measured in the human body. The seventh chakra is considered to be just above the crown of the head.

OPPOSITE TOP: A phrenologist's head, with the zones and lobes carefully marked off. Phrenology was a divining phenomenon of the 19th century.

European astrologers created a "cosmic man" or "astro-man" with each body region controlled by a particular astrological sign, and physical feelings linked to astral images. Chinese diagnosticians see the body as a series of interconnected processes, "orbs" of organs and energy meridians similar to those that run through the earth. These can be "read" through careful attention to the six pulses, which indicate the relative strength, weakness, or balance of energies in the various systems.

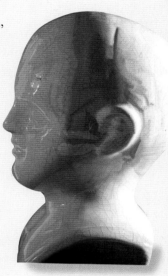

Just as a feeling, a "tingling," can show where and how spirit is influencing the body, so a symptom can begin a dialogue with a spirit or unacknowledged "complex." Old medicine attributed many disorders to gods or spirits that wished to reach or contact a person. The symptom is the sign. These could be treated with "sympathetic substances," things that partake of the god's nature. More often the sufferer must enter into a dialogue with the spirit through ritual, sacrifice, imagination, or art.

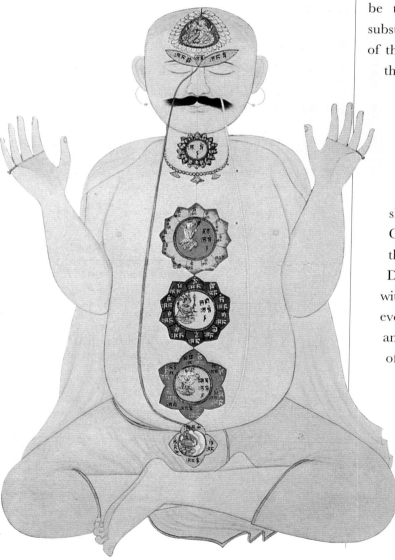

Physiognomy and phrenology are another sort of body talk. The shape of the face and head was felt by many peoples to reveal character. In fact, "head" has often been used to indicate inner spirit, destiny, or daimon. There are old lists of head shapes, facial characteristics and their meanings in Greek, Sanskrit, and Chinese. In 19th-century Europe, this was elaborated as the "science" of physiognomy. Different head shapes and features were associated with long lists of qualities, and an analytical system was evolved through assigning numerical values to virtues and characteristics. Similarly, phrenology, the "science of the head," divided the head into 35 zones or "organs," each associated with a quality. The investigator examines these organs, assigning a value to the development of each, in order to arrive at an assessment of a person's character. Reichian psychology, which reads the presence of various negative emotions held in the body through patterns of chronic muscular tension called "armoring," is a more contemporary form of body divination.

Palmistry and Dowsing

Palmistry, an old divinatory art spread throughout Europe, Africa, and the East, sees the hand as a microcosm on which a life is figured forth. Each part of the hand is associated with a planetary spirit – the "mounds" of Jupiter, Saturn, the Sun, Venus, the fields of Mars, while the general shape of the palm and its relation to the fingers show a person's temperament. The lines on the palm weave the story of an individual life unfolding: life line, heart line, head line, fate line, line of the Sun, girdle of Venus; while smaller patterns like chains, crosses, branches, and islands connect or modify their flow. Reading the interactions gives clues to the potential, problems, and direction of a person's life.

FATE IN YOUR HAND

The palms of the hands are crisscrossed with signs. The left hand (in right-handed people) shows the potential of a person; the right hand shows the actuality. Fingers and thumbs are also significant as is the overall shape and texture of the hand. The wrist wrinkles ("bracelets of life") trace the pattern of overall health.

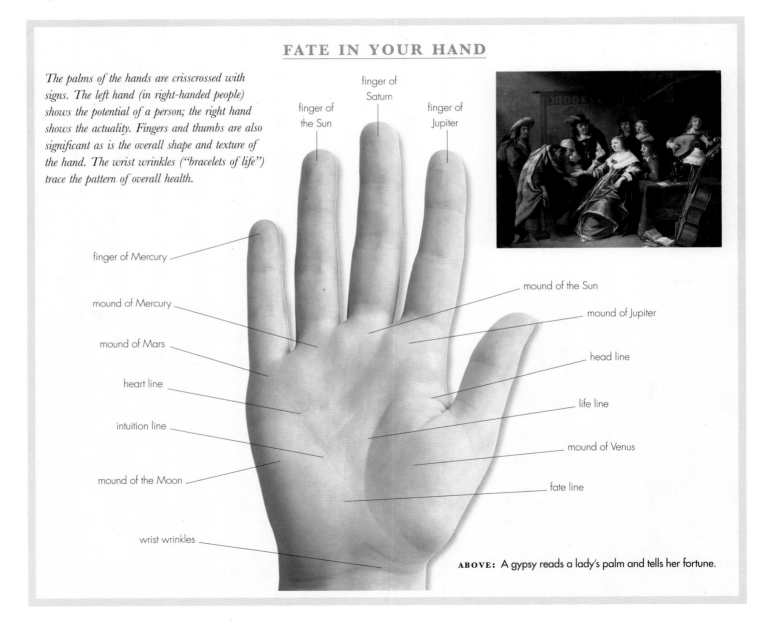

finger of the Sun

finger of Saturn

finger of Jupiter

finger of Mercury

mound of Mercury

mound of Mars

heart line

intuition line

mound of the Moon

wrist wrinkles

mound of the Sun

mound of Jupiter

head line

life line

mound of Venus

fate line

ABOVE: A gypsy reads a lady's palm and tells her fortune.

The art of dowsing relies on a mysterious interaction between the body and concealed forces in the environment, an interaction focused through the diviner's rod. Different-shaped rods are used for different purposes: a traditional Y-shaped rod of wood to locate water; a "bobber" shaped like a fishing pole to locate oil; metal L-rods that swing out in the hands to explore "earth energies" associated with sacred sites; a pendulum bob suspended from the fingers to answer personal questions. In use, the rod is held in both hands, tip pointing up, while the diviner searches. When he is over the target, the tip swings down or out.

PENDULUM DOWSING

The pendulum, which is used to answer more personal questions, is suspended from a finger. The diviner establishes beforehand the sort of movement that will signify yes and no. Professionals may also use the pendulum to explore a region by map before attempting on-site activity. You can use a pendulum very easily to explore personal choices. Make one with a supple chain or cord and a balanced weight. Hold the end of the cord between your fingers. Decide what movements will define the answers, pose a question, and watch the resulting movement.

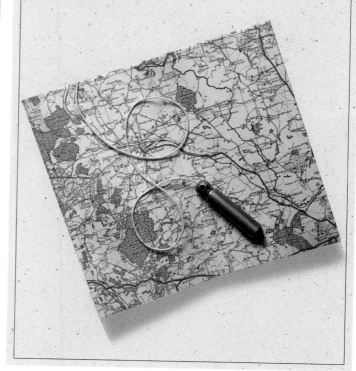

LEFT: Dowsing for water is traditionally done with hazel twigs, but any wooden or metal stick will do; it is simply the focus for the dowser's concentration, not an essential tool.

Talking Bones

nother kind of omen is associated with bones, a sign of what dies endures in death. The dead are a very important part of all traditional cultures; bones are a sign of the concrete presence of death and the souls of the dead. Shamans visualize themselves as skeletons to exit normal consciousness. Skulls and thigh bones, in particular, were often used as ritual objects. Bones actualize spirit realities. Divining with bones relies on this "charged" quality to produce abnormal events.

For many traditional cultures there is a continuity between the living and the dead. Ancestors who die travel to a realm of the dead, where they become spirit-presences capable of influencing the living. At the same time they wish to reenter the world through the rebirth of their name. One form of bone divination is used to find the name of the ancestor present at a child's birth. The priest, shaman, or father holds the bones, makes an invocation, and recites the possible names of those who might be waiting to join with the child's new life. As the correct name is pronounced, the bones suddenly change weight in his hands. The ancestors have spoken through the bones.

The skulls of dead shamans were often set in a wooden figure and questioned about all important events, answering through a similar change in weight. The Germanic god Odin divined with the head of Mimir. The severed head of the Greek shaman-priest Orpheus prophesied after his dismemberment. Mummified heads, bone images, skulls, or teraphim were used in the early Jewish tradition of speaking with the dead. In Melanesia, the "man of

BONES AND SHELLS

When a Melanesian "man of sorrow" consults a bone oracle, he uses bone, cowrie shells, and a stick. After repeating the necessary incantations, he poses the question, then blows on the shell and stick. He places the curved shell on the floor, holds the bone vertically, sets it on the shell and removes his hand. If the answer to the question is positive, the bone will remain standing, held in an "impossible" position by the ancestors. If negative, it will fall. Observers state that the answers are extremely accurate and that it truly seems as if something extraordinary holds up the bone. The diviner experiences the movement as controlled by some force other than conscious will.

RIGHT: Bones loom large in the divinatory traditions of many cultures.

sorrow" or healer-sorcerer uses a piece of his ancestor's upper arm bone and a cowrie shell in divining. Such mementoes of the dead are considered quite "hot" and spiritually dangerous, so it requires ritual preparation to use them.

Bones are also associated with the ordeal and the impartial judgment of the angry ancestors. A person accused of a crime in a Masai or Nandi tribe, for example, will put a skull at his accuser's door, charging it with the spell: "If I have done this thing, head, eat me. If I have not, head, eat

him!" One or the other would soon die. Certain highland tribes in Melanesia practice a sorcery divination to decide whether or not a given group has been inflicting death through magical practices. The exhumed corpse of one of the suspected victims is raised and empowered, invoking vengeful ancestral spirits to act through it and inflict death on the guilty parties. The judgment occurs through counting the number of abnormal deaths that occur in the next few months after the exhumation.

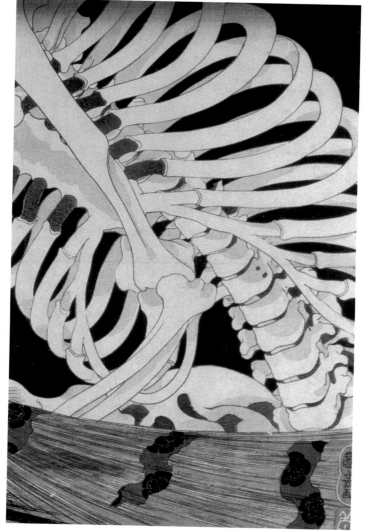

Scapulomancy

The most widespread bone-oracle, however, is scapulomancy, a form of fire-divination that uses the shoulder bone from an ox, sheep, deer or, in later China, the undershell of a turtle. It was used throughout Asia, India, Europe, and North America and is mentioned in medieval Latin texts as one of the Devil's instruments. An example of the most direct form is that of the Naskapi, a Labrador hunting tribe who practice a religion of divination.

When game cannot be found, the Naskapi use scapulomancy to create a new map of the territory. First, someone must dream of the animals they are hunting, an incubated dream induced by sweat baths and drumming. When the dream-animal appears, it must then be located. To do this, a caribou shoulder-blade is cleaned, boiled, and dried, fitted with a small wooden handle and put into the fire. When it emerges, it is held in a predetermined relation to the hunting territory. The burnt spots and cracks form a new map, fixing the location of the dream animals.

Tibetan monks took this method over from shamans and made it into an integral part of Buddhist divination practices. They employ the right shoulder blade of a sacrificed sheep. The general characteristics of the bone describe the inquirer: a light, large bone indicates a rich, intelligent person; a thin, hard bone shows a liar; a thick bone, a miser. The bone is washed, fumigated, and reflected in a mirror. Mantras are recited as it is put into the fire. The surface of the bone is divided into areas called protector, enemy, kindred, king, lord, self, and servant. The cracks and bubbles the fire produces in each area point to events and the specific rituals and purifications needed to deal with them. Overall, white cracks are good; black, bad. Many cracks over the whole bone indicate a lost path. A vertical crack through the whole blade shows sickness; a horizontal crack would indicate robbery and delayed accomplishment.

The greatest users of scapulomancy, however, were the old Chinese. Shang dynasty diviner-kings (2000–1100 B.C.E.) raised it to a sophisticated art used almost daily to insure that the noble ancestors who had become powerful spirit-forces approved of their actions and sacrifices. In this form, which used both ox scapulae and tortoise undershells, the bone was laboriously prepared. A series of pairs of shallow holes was scooped out on the reverse of the shell. The altar ritual was also quite elaborate. The question, which involved the actions of the king and a handful of select nobles, was posed in positive and negative form: "If the king makes war on X, he will take many heads. If the king makes war on X, he will, perhaps, not take many heads." A heated bronze rod was applied to the depressions on the reverse side of the bone. The heat produced a sharp sound and a crack on the face of the shell. These cracks – up to 20 sets for a given question – were then interpreted. Later interpretative manuals list over 50 variations in angle and length. The library of "oracle-bones" produced by this practice gave birth to the Chinese written language, and the attitudes of sacrifice and communion with ancestral spirits it embodies permeate later culture.

ABOVE: Aboriginal warriors painted themselves to resemble bone-men before going to do battle. This is presumed to confer extra powers on them.

RIGHT: A Chinese oracle bone from the Neolithic period. It is inscribed with oracular characters.

ANIMAL SACRIFICES

The sacrifice of animals so that their entrails may be read or their bones consulted was a very important part of the divination process in many ancient cultures and is still practiced in some areas of the world today. Some examples are given below.

RIGHT: A black hen is prepared for sacrifice by Sopono worshipers in Africa. The witch doctor directs proceedings.

BELOW: A goat is sacrificed by Sopono worshipers, its throat cut over a ritual trough to catch the blood.

RIGHT: A copper-bladed Tlingit knife with a hilt carved to resemble a bear. Shamanic knives like this are both symbolic and practical.

BELOW: Bird bones and skulls for sale as charms in a Nigerian street market.

Heard and Overheard

f bones tell of the presence of the dead and need ritual specialists to handle the contact, the *kleidon* or random word omen was available to all. It suggests an atmosphere charged with souls and spirits who express themselves through turning and redirecting "winged words." It appears in virtually all cultures on both a popular and a highly sophisticated level.

On the most basic level, the word omen appears spontaneously. Here is a modern example: a woman was walking down the street, struggling with what to do about a complicated relationship, when she heard a female voice scream from a telephone booth: "All right, then I'll simply take my things and go!" The omen spoke directly to her situation. These omens can also be solicited. In Tibet, a diviner may propose a question, put a bone with a piece of juniper tied to it with white wool in his left pocket, and walk out the door. The first words he hears answer the question. In traditional China, officials would pay very careful attention to the songs that children sang in the streets, seeing them as a direct reflection of coming events.

LEFT: Chinese children at play; in traditional China, the songs sung by children were considered to reflect coming events.

ABOVE: When your mind is focused on a particular problem, it can be useful to open your ears to the conversations of others heard at random. You may hear an omen that will help you decide the direction you will take.

KING SOLOMON'S OMEN

In old Israel, the chance word acts as an omen when it is recognized as containing an oblique other meaning. When a group of captives faced the king, they heard him ask if "he who was my brother" was still alive. They "saw" that the word "brother" was an omen and indicated no harm would come to them. King Solomon sent his commander-in-chief into a sanctuary, chasing after his enemy Joab. The soldier tried to get Joab to come out, but he refused, saying: "No, I will die here." When he heard this, Solomon instantly "saw" it as an omen and ordered the soldier to cut Joab down.

This kind of omen could also be created: when Jonathan was trying to decide whether or not to attack the Philistines, he said: "We will cross over. If they say, 'Stay where you are,' we will stay. If they say, 'Come up,' we will attack. We will take it as an omen that Yahweh has put them into our hands."

ABOVE: King Solomon, enthroned, welcomes the Queen of Sheba. In less peaceful and civilized situations he relied on oracle and augury to support his legendary wisdom.

An Oracle of Hermes

The Greek God Hermes was the friendliest of gods, who mixed easily in the events of life. He was actively involved in business, communication, voyages, and persuasive speech, in border crossings and sudden changes of perspective. He was also a soul-guide who could lead through dreams, difficult crossroads, and the underworld.

The cult of Hermes Agoraeos, or Hermes of the Marketplace, at Pharae is very old. In a small temple on the public square, or agora, there stood a statue of ithyphallic Hermes called kleidonios, or "giver of word-oracles." Near it was an altar, an incense burner, and several bronze oil-lamps. To use this oracle, you would arrive at evening, when the day was changing to night, burn incense in the brazier, fill and light the small bronze lamps, and place a coin on the altar to the right of the god. You then approached him, whispered your question, and, closing your ears, walked out of the temple onto the square. Once outside, you took your hands away from your ears. The first voice you heard was the oracle's answer.

Another kind of word omen – the *sortes* – arose in the cultural crisis of late Mediterranean antiquity, when the great public oracle centers were failing. This practice turns a book into a divinatory instrument and can yield surprising results. Originally, it used the Bible or Virgil's *Aeneid*, which Romans considered to be a holy book. The practice survived for centuries, even though formally forbidden by the Church.

CONSULTING HERMES

If you have this kind of question, try his oracle. Make your question clear, wait for the time when the day is changing – Hermes loves borders – and go to a place where people mix. Choose a place to sit, close your ears, and concentrate on your question. Think about how the power of Hermes helps wayfarers and travelers and opens the way for them. Get up, walk in a direction that appeals to you and open your ears. The first words you hear are Hermes' response. Let them change the way you are thinking about your problem or question.

The method is simple, though in some forms it involved ritual preparation. It consists of posing a question, opening the book you have chosen without looking, and putting your finger on the page. The word or phrase picked out at random is the answer the book gives to your question.

This practice was never successfully suppressed by the Church. It was even used, occasionally, by high-ranking clerics to confirm their choices or decisions. The *sortes* is an example of many of the old pagan beliefs. It sees chance as a revealer of meaning, the world as a language of signs, and the presence of spirit in the events of everyday life.

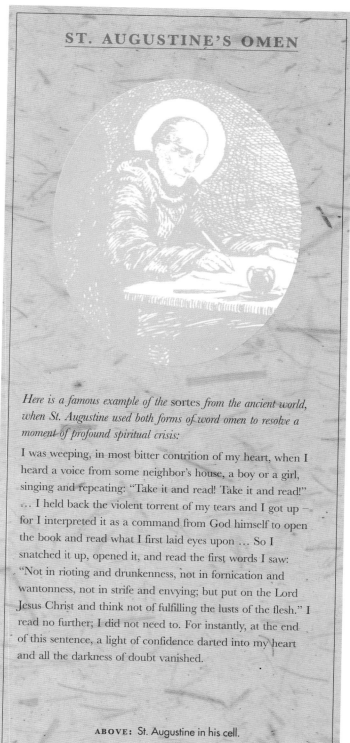

ST. AUGUSTINE'S OMEN

Here is a famous example of the sortes *from the ancient world, when St. Augustine used both forms of word omen to resolve a moment of profound spiritual crisis:*

I was weeping, in most bitter contrition of my heart, when I heard a voice from some neighbor's house, a boy or a girl, singing and repeating: "Take it and read! Take it and read!" … I held back the violent torrent of my tears and I got up — for I interpreted it as a command from God himself to open the book and read what I first laid eyes upon … So I snatched it up, opened it, and read the first words I saw: "Not in rioting and drunkenness, not in fornication and wantonness, not in strife and envying; but put on the Lord Jesus Christ and think not of fulfilling the lusts of the flesh." I read no further; I did not need to. For instantly, at the end of this sentence, a light of confidence darted into my heart and all the darkness of doubt vanished.

ABOVE: St. Augustine in his cell.

OPPOSITE BELOW RIGHT: An Egyptian marketplace; Hermes was considered to be at his most communicative among crowds and bustle.

OPPOSITE TOP: Hermes, the Greek god of thresholds and communication, magic and trickery. The son of Zeus and the nymph Maia, he is considered to be the patron saint of thieves and merchants, the bringer of luck, and the protector of travelers. As his father's messenger, he was in charge of guiding the souls of the dead along the paths of Hades.

ABOVE: Books are a simple way to make random consultations. The Bible was often used as a quick and simple – and spiritually safe – way to ask for divine guidance.

Unnatural Births and Living Statues

The "unnatural" has always been considered a sign, something that must be interpreted and dealt with. Etruscans and Romans called unnatural events and monstrous births "prodigies." They indicated the wrath of the gods and a need for purification. Chief among them was lightning. Etruscans would obliterate the site of a lightning fall. Everything connected with it was ritually cleansed or killed. In Rome, lightning was the sign that whatever was underway must be aborted. In the same way, eclipses, comets, and strange conjunctions of planets in the sky were occasions for rituals of exorcism.

Unusual planetary conjunctions and the unnatural births associated with them became a major concern of European astrologers and theologians, keys to interpreting violent changes in society as a whole. In the Renaissance and Reformation, battles to capture the popular imagination were fought through rival interpretations of these *wunderzeichen*. The books produced by artists such as Albrecht Dürer (1471–1528) and Lucas Cranach (1472–1553) to explain the wonder-signs became the first example of mass propaganda in European history. The Church of Rome interpreted them astrologically. The circle around Luther took on the robes of Babylonian diviners and interpreted the signs

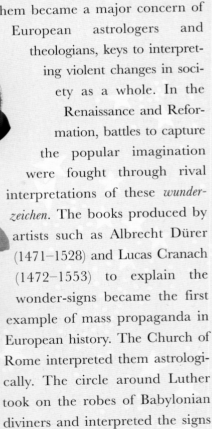

through the old omen-tablets, thus bypassing the very unfavorable position of Saturn in Luther's supposed birthchart. The *T'ui-pei t'u*, a Chinese prophecy book of historical events and prodigies, also presents a potentially subversive vision of history. If you can locate an event that occurred in present time in this series of wonder-signs, you will know what is to follow it in the progression of images and can thus anticipate political changes. The book was officially prohibited on political grounds from about 1200 C.E. on.

Another kind of "prodigy" was the living statue. In Egyptian oracle centers, the statues of the gods regularly nodded or spoke in answer to questions posed to them. A statue would also be carried through a crowd of questioners by special porters who would go into trance. This allowed their movement to be directly controlled by the god, who could indicate answers to the questions of his followers. There is a beautiful literary example of this talking statue in the *Golden Ass* of Apuleius, a late antique romance. The hero, Lucius, had been condemned to wander in the form of an ass, having lost his human shape through being enslaved to his desires. He sees the goddess Isis in a procession rising from the sea, who speaks with him and gives him back his human shape.

OPPOSITE BOTTOM LEFT: A child at the Bun Festival in Hong Kong.

OPPOSITE TOP: Mothers in the Azande tribe pass their newborn babies through purifying smoke to ensure good fortune.

OPPOSITE BOTTOM RIGHT: Turkish astronomers anxiously scan the skies from Galat, a tower in Istanbul, looking for signs and portents.

BELOW: A comet, or "smoking star," warned the Aztec leader Montezuma of the coming of the Spanish conquistador Hernan Cortès to South America in 1519. Comets were considered a bad sign by the Aztecs, and indeed Montezuma lost his family, empire, and life to the intruder from the Old World.

Crossing the Threshold

Any event that occurs at a "threshold" becomes an omen. Traditional peoples are much more aware of borders, thresholds, and liminality, the in-between state where things change shape, than we are. Like a cat approaching a door, they are very careful of the images that emerge from this in-between state, where, literally, anything may happen. The threshold may be the first step out of the door, the beginning of a journey, the passage from one stage of life to another, the transition from sleep to waking, from the known world into an unknown, the beginning of a relationship, the approach to a crossroads. All are a dark door or portal into the unknown. Images that emerge at this time are charged with importance.

Celtic diviners used the augury of the "first thing seen" as a trial or proof of significant events. The diviner would climb a hill or grave mound, consider the question and start down. The first creature he met was the answer to the question. To find the luck of the year to come, an inquirer would walk out of his house on the new year with his eyes closed. When he opened them, the first thing he saw was the omen.

BORDER CROSSING

Here are two practices that may make you aware of the power hidden in the small events of everyday life. The two thresholds we cross virtually every day are the border from sleep to waking and the threshold of the house. Be like an animal, who is very careful about crossing these borders. Take a moment to wake up, and remember the last images you have as you move into the day. Similarly, as you cross the threshold of your house, be aware of any happening or image that reaches out to you, that strikes your attention. Carry these images with you during the day and watch how they connect with the things that happen to you. Entertain the images, and let the connections emerge.

Heads or Tails: A Game of Chance

A basic function of many divinatory practices is to give a yes or no answer to a question or to decide between two alternatives. These "yes and no" oracles are also used to confirm the judgment of more complicated systems. They reflect variations of the idea that there are two basic energies in the universe, one that opens to action and one that closes toward rest and stasis.

Chinese diviners use two comma-shaped blocks of wood with one flat side and one curved side called *chiao pai*. The mysterious *Urim* and *Thummim* mentioned as a portable oracle throughout the oldest parts of the Hebrew Bible is probably the same sort of divinatory tool. If both curved sides fall upward, the answer is yin: rest, stay in place, don't proceed. Two flat sides indicate yang: take action, proceed directly. One flat and one curved is neutral. They are often used in combination with a temple oracle or chim, a set of bamboo sticks with numbers that are shaken out of a cylinder to key divinatory sentences.

OPPOSITE BOTTOM: Silbury Hill, Wiltshire, England, the largest manmade sacred mound in Europe. Burial mounds were seen as one of the thresholds separating life and death.

ABOVE LEFT Chinese divination beans, *pua pou*. These simple divinatory tools were marked with indents or mounds to indicate a negative or positive response to a particular question.

ABOVE: A traditional temple in Kunming in the Western Hills of China. Oracles such as the *I Ching* could be consulted in temples.

LEFT: The yin/yang sign, a symbol of the interdependence of light and dark, negative and positive, masculine and feminine, yes and no. Each polar opposite contains the seed of the other.

EL COCO

Santeria initiates use Biague or El Coço as an oracle. This is a group of four pieces of coconut meat called obinu, with a white side and a shell or dark side. They can produce five possible variations on yes and no. Questions can also be addressed to a specific Orisha, or spirit. The ritual surrounding Biague is complicated, and it is felt that the ashé, or gifts, of the operator play a great part in the result. After invocations, the four pieces of fresh coconut are tossed onto the floor. One of five answers will result:

OTAWE (three obinu white side up, one dark side up): Maybe, there are doubts, hope but not complete assurance, subject to circumstances.

Chango, Ogun, Yemaya, and Oshosi are speaking. Make your question clearer and throw again. If Otawe is repeated, the answer is no. Confirms Alafia, but points at the necessity of a sacrifice.

ALAFIA (all four obinu land white side up): Affirmative, possible.
The spirits Chango and Orunmila are speaking. Happiness and health, peace and prosperity. Things are in proper order. Repeat the question. This reading must be confirmed by Otawe or Eyife.

OCANASODE (one obinu white side up, three dark side up): No, beware, possible tragic consequences, be alert, grave difficulties.

Chango, Babalu-Aye, and the spirits of the dead are speaking. Open your eyes and ears. Ask again if this answer is a simple no or the sign of hidden danger.

EYIFE (two obinu white side up, two dark side up): Yes, absolutely positive.
Elegua, Ogun, Oshosi, and Oshun are speaking. Confirms the throw of Alafia.

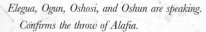

OYEKUN (all obinu dark side up): Absolutely not, death and suffering await.
Chango and Oya are speaking. Cleanse the obinu and consult a Babalawo. You must be ritually purified and consult a priest to find out where this evil influence is coming from.

Bones and Rubbing Boards

South African tribes use a set of four bones called *bola*, a word that means both divination and cosmic power. The ancestors are thought to strengthen these bones, which express the will of supreme power. The pieces, which may be bone, ivory, horn, or wood, are called senior male, junior male, senior female, and junior female. They each have a plain and a decorated side, so there are 16 possible combinations. Each combination has a praise-poem or myth and a general interpretation associated with it. The tradition is oral, and can vary widely from one region to another. An example of a response is *Four Senior Men*. This is a quite negative sign that means strife, illness, witchcraft, quarrels; the dust rises, the ox is loosed, the sun rises in the east.

The Azande *Iwa*, or rubbing-board oracle, is a "pocket oracle" used when a personal problem arises that must be immediately resolved. *Iwa* has two parts, a small oval wooden table with three legs that is female, and a male lid that fits onto its surface. Each person must make his own apparatus. It is then anointed with medicine, bespelled, buried, and dug up before it becomes a usable instrument.

THE POCKET ORACLE

To use *Iwa*, a man sits on the ground, steadies the table with his right foot and squeezes plant sap on the table surface. He moistens the lid, then moves it back and forth on the surface while reciting the question. The male lid will either slide smoothly or stick, indicating yes or no. If it does both, there is something hidden in the matter that invalidates the question.

LEFT: Wood and bone divining sticks from the Transvaal, South Africa.

TOP: An Azande diviner consults a rubbing oracle.

The Universal Compass

eople who lived life without the buffer of technology depended on an acute awareness of "nature" to lead them, a "nature" that included quite a few things we have since relegated to the trash can of superstition. Strange incidents, vivid impressions, sudden appearances of the numinous took hold of the imagination, opening a space and creating a symbolic language. Anything that can be "symbolized" can become part of that language: birds and animals, parts of our body, memento mori, strange events, words and phrases, masks, statues, and emblems, the alternation of yes and no, day and night, male and female, natural processes and patterns. The continuing relevance of these traditional omens is based on the idea that they describe events in the soul, the deep imagination, where we all still travel in an unknown and mysterious world. The perception of significance in these collections of omens fed the development of the great divinatory systems. The purpose is a dialogue with that deep part of your self that is your indwelling spirit or daimon, your fate in its most creative sense.

Part of this process was the creation of a network of associations and a cosmic model that could locate and interpret the signs. Omens are the origin of writing in many cultures. The Runes, which are divining signs, are the origin of northern European alphabets. In both Babylonia and China, the origin of writing is directly associated with recording and understanding omens. The kind of relations used to connect the signs gave the language a grammatical structure.

In Babylonia, this kind of linguistic grid produced the omen tablets, formulaic lists of all sorts of omens and their meanings: birds, events, smoke, noises, animals, physical features, planetary movements. These lists were used by the *barû* priest to provide the rulers and nobles with specific information on the activities of the gods.

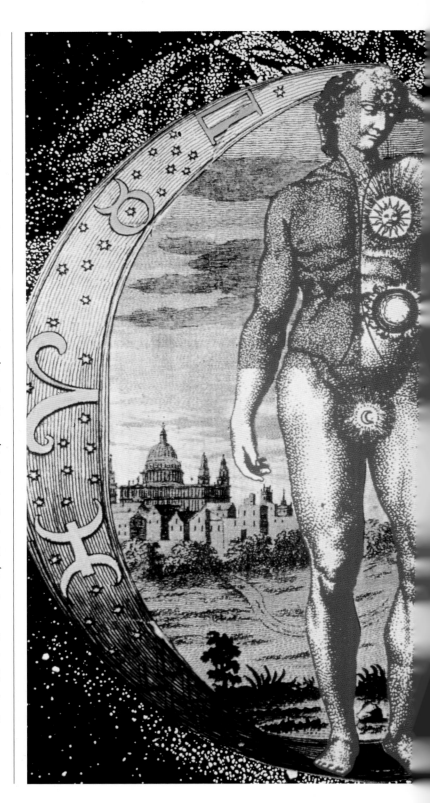

THE CHANTING OMEN

Here are fragments from a Babylonian priest's "physiognomic" list that locates and explains the occurrence of an *umshatu*, a kind of mark on the skin. It moves systematically through the body from above to below, right to left. Like a chant, each phrase has the identical form.

If an *umshatu* occurs on a man's forehead, to the left: unhappiness.

If an *umshatu* occurs on his right eyebrow: he will not seize what is present to his eye.

If an *umshatu* occurs on his left eyebrow: his hand will seize what is present to his eye.

If an *umshatu* occurs on the upper left wing of his eye (eyelid): his oldest son will be taken from the house.

If an *umshatu* occurs on the upper right wing of his eye: his oldest son will be safe ....

If an *umshatu* occurs on the lower right wing of his eye: his children will have no spirit-guardian.

If an *umshatu* occurs on the lower left wing of his eye: his children will have a spirit-guardian.

If an *umshatu* occurs on his nose: he will always be badly spoken of.

If an *umshatu* occurs on the corner of his eye, to the left: he will receive the "gifts of the road."

If an *umshatu* occurs on the lower part of his nose: there will be a year of fertile women in his house.

If an *umshatu* occurs on his lower right cheek: he will lead a slave's life among his sons.

LEFT: A graphic representation of the links between the cosmos and humanity.

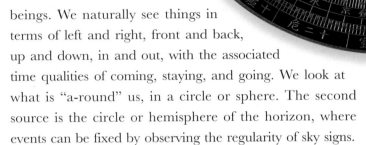

The Universal Compass

Something similar occurred in China, where huge libraries of "oracle bones" cataloged the results of royal scapulomantic divinations. A language was invented in order to transcribe and organize this great collection of signs, oral formulas, and numinous events. The realm of omens became a written world in which meanings could be consistently reproduced. It was the beginning of another kind of sign, the written word.

This language grid is also connected to a circle of "sacred space," a circle of directions, seasons, numbers, elements, body parts, and celestial phenomena. By using this circle of sacred space, you can locate an omen in a network of associations and processes that are thought to duplicate the spiritual structure of the world.

There are two sources for this circle of sacred space. The first is our body. We are erect, bilaterally symmetrical beings. We naturally see things in terms of left and right, front and back, up and down, in and out, with the associated time qualities of coming, staying, and going. We look at what is "a-round" us, in a circle or sphere. The second source is the circle or hemisphere of the horizon, where events can be fixed by observing the regularity of sky signs.

By connecting these two, a universal compass is created, a circle of meanings that links cosmic directions and body orientations, so you can, so to speak, put it on like a set of clothes. This circle connects the four directions, time (the four seasons, hours in a day, or months in a year), cosmic forces (planets, stars, sun, and moon), qualities of experience (birth, growing, maturity, dying), elements (fire, earth, air, water, metal), creatures, body organs, feelings, thought qualities, gods, and spirits.

When this plan of sacred space is located through geomantic divination – when a "power point" is "seen" and fixed, and the plan unfolded through ritual measurement – it produces a city, town, or temple connected through participation to the shape of the cosmos. Body, city, and cosmos are linked through a common pattern. When divinatory symbols are added, the system becomes responsive to individual questions and events.

The Great Celestial Sphere

In Western cultures, the four- or eightfold circle as a cosmic model is found in old divinatory board games, in the astrological chart, and in occult diagrams of the directions and their spirits, diagrams that also contain the human body. This celestial sphere, axis, and circle were associated with specific astrological images in late antiquity. It is the "occult image" that lies behind most Western magical and divinatory systems. The most recent example comes from what is called the "Western Esoteric Tradition," a kind of philosophical and ritual magic descended from the late 19th and early 20th century reimagining of esoteric practices in the Order of the Golden Dawn. Here, associations to zodiacal signs, the signs of the Cabala and Tarot images are projected onto the directions and seasons of the celestial sphere. The diviner can thus locate the significance of an omen directly, or enter the magical processes the progressions imply through a divinatory sign.

The Eightfold Circle

In China, the universal compass was assembled about 200 B.C.E. It uses the eightfold circle to unite the directions; a cycle of time based on the seasons that describes all temporal units; interconnections of yin and yang, the two fundamental energies; a uniquely Chinese cycle called the Five Transformative Processes: wood, fire, earth, metal, water; celestial signs; "orbs" of interconnected organs; emblematic actions, feelings, and colors; and eight divinatory signs or trigrams from the *I Ching*. This schema gave rise to the diviner's compass used in feng shui, a type of geomancy that analyzes geographical situations for a favorable energy flow (ch'i) in graves, buildings, and rooms.

Even more, it was an overall divinatory cosmology.

Thus, for example, in the Chinese version, the color red, heart, summer, fire and the process of combustion, awareness, ovens and hearths, collecting in groups, brightness and light, the middle daughter, the pheasant, the action of disclosing or coming to light, a particular hour of the day, month of the year, and certain heavenly constellations that have symbolic meanings are all connected along one axis. Any sign that occurs on the axis invokes all the other qualities and is thus "located" in that nexus of meaning. At the center of each group is a divinatory sign that can be produced through consultation.

Qualities in these systems also occur in a sequence connected to the circle that organizes them. By locating something, you know what came before it, what comes after it, what it "likes" and what it does not "like." Further, the chain can be reversed, the divinatory net can also become "magical." In the Chinese system, something that is "cold and wet," for example, and thus associated with black, water, midnight, midwinter, north, loneliness, dissolving form, hard work, danger, and obstacles, can be ameliorated by connecting it with something from the "summer" category through an image. Similarly, in Renaissance magical astrology — another universal compass — the "saturnian" qualities of melancholy and depression can be tempered with "jovial" or "venusian" qualities of sun, expansiveness, gold, love, and pleasure.

OPPOSITE LEFT: Ptolemy (c. 100–170 C.E.), the Egyptian astronomer and geographer who codified the ancient concept of interlocking celestial spheres.

OPPOSITE BOTTOM: A Chinese oracle bone from the Shang dynasty.

ABOVE LEFT: A modern Lo-Pan Chinese geomantic compass, based on an ancient design.

Fang-Shih Masters

One of the people who used this universal compass was the wandering diviner-magician called *fang-shih*, who traveled among the various courts to predict the unfolding of personal, social, and cosmic events. The compass he used assimilated an enormous range of signs, from cloud patterns and body organs to dream series and the movements of winds and stars. All of them could be accessed through manipulating the yarrow-stalks, the divinatory procedure used with the *I Ching* (see pages 134–5).

SHOOTING THE BASKET

A prince would test a *fang-shih* through a game called "Shoot the Basket." The inquirer would hide an object under a basket and the diviner would manipulate the yarrow-stalks and mobilize the system of associations in order to "see" it. A very famous *fang-shih* once guessed thirteen hidden objects in a row, ending with a live lizard. Many others predicted the outcome of military campaigns, the fate of political figures, and the date of their own death. Some were summarily executed for indecorous or ill-omened predictions.

The "Rose of the Winds" is an example of the sort of divinatory practice based on such a system. The sponsor of this system was the god of the winds, *Fong-po*. He dwelt in the heavenly house *Ki*, whose sign was the winnowing basket, the mouth and tongue of Heaven and origin of the cosmic breath. It corresponded to the transformative process Wood, the trigram *Hsuan*, and the northwest.

On the first day of the first month of the year, the diviner would "observe" the winds to determine harvests, sickness, wars, or other events to unfold in the year to come. The word "observe" meant to watch the direction, strength, and intensity of the wind. In addition, he would note the sound made by the noise of the surrounding people and determine which note it was on the musical scale. The observations would last the entire day, and required interpretative subtlety. If, for example, the wind was from the northwest and was accompanied by light rain, and the musical tone was *Yu*, there would be an abundant harvest of beans, military troubles would soon be pressing, and there was danger of heavy rains and floods.

Islam and Rome

Islamic culture evolved a "universal compass" based on a large zodiacal circle enclosing other concentric circles for the spheres, the elements, created things, spiritual beings, and sciences. Each circle is divided into sections; the lines or chords dividing each section run to the center. Along each chord are sets of letters that have a numerical value. You can enter this system through the number values of the letters in a question, or through producing geomantic signs (see pages 120–1).

Another form of universal compass, the *templum*, was used in the official Roman method of divination, the auspices or, literally, the bird-signs that were collected by the officials of the College of Augurs. These officials also took omens from thunder, animal appearances, and any "accidents" that happened during the period of official consultation. The taking of the auspices was required to validate any important action. The question was always the same: do the gods approve of the action contemplated by the Roman people?

A templum was laid out by drawing celestial cross-lines and taking a circle from this center to locate the heavenly sphere on the terrestrial surface. This circle was squared to define the templum's sides, a process that imitated the mythic origin of Rome itself. The augur then used a curved wand to define the favorable portion of the heavens to be observed and a tent, a "little templum," was erected to focus on the observed area.

AL-KINDI'S WAGER

The diviner al-Kindi (associated with the court of the Caliph in 9th-century Baghdad) was once challenged by a professional scholar to prove that the universal compass was not worthless by showing that he could guess something the academician would write on a piece of paper. A wager was made, the scholar wrote something on a piece of paper that was put under the Caliph's protection. Al-Kindi used an earth tray to produce geomantic signs, ascertained the ascendant, determined the star positions, and located them on the compass. He then pronounced that what was written was "first a plant, then an animal." The scholar had written "rod of Moses," the prophet's wooden staff that had turned into a snake in front of the Pharaoh.

After this ritual preparation, the augur would specify what kind of omen was looked for and during what period of time. When all extraneous things had been excluded, ritual silence was declared. The omens were taken according to the flight, calls, and the kinds of birds to appear. Another form of auspice was developed for use on military expeditions. The preparatory ritual was brief. The practice was to see if the "sacred chickens" carried with an army in the field would or would not eat grain that was laid out for them. A favorable auspice was, theoretically, required before any military action. One commander, when told the chickens would not eat, remarked, "Let them drink, then" and threw them into the sea. In the subsequent battle he was killed and his entire army devastated.

OPPOSITE: The wandering diviner-magicians of China studied an enormous range of signs and symbols.

RIGHT: An Islamic map of the universe showing the seven stages of the sun, the signs of the zodiac, and the phases of the moon.

The Emperor's New Clothes

The universal compass and its paradigmatic picture of the sacred design of the cosmos evolved at a particular point in the evolution of human culture. It gathered older perceptions and the hoard of omen-lore into a coherent system at a time when the great collective cultures of the world emerged. One of the central features it evolved was a strictly hierarchical relation between what virtually all human cultures have perceived as the "Three Worlds": the heavens, the surface of the earth where human life unfolds, and the underworld of the dead and the seeds of things to come.

At a certain point in many cultures, this hierarchical relation was fixed and projected onto other parts of experience. Heaven possessed ultimate value and was "above"; earth was its servant and its medium "below." This relation became a paradigm for all relations: just as Heaven is above and Earth below, so the king is above, the people below; man is above, woman below; the father is above, the children below; the elder is above, the younger below. Preserving these relations became a religious duty, for it was a direct reflection of the shape of the "sacred cosmos." The signs that appear through divining with the universal compass can and were used to authenticate this structure of power. Once this occurs, however, the power figure becomes involved in a paradoxical attempt to stop the very processes that brought him to the position he occupies, to fix eternally the images of change.

All divination is potentially dangerous, for it accesses an uncertain terrain that is always breaking through to destabilize fixed structures of meaning. The power of omens, words, dreams, numinous events, and significant patterns induces movement in the individual imagination. It changes the awareness of the person who is divining, and focuses him on the significance of his individual fate. The model of sacred space relies on principles of hierarchical connection. When it is enacted socially, certain values come to the fore: "harmony," stasis, duty, and the subordination of one class to another. When it is used as a divinatory instrument, however, these values begin to shift.

In Rome under the emperor Augustus (63 B.C.E.– 14 C.E.), this conflict led to the strict prohibition of private divination, so that the signs that announced his reign could never change. Augustus himself jealously guarded the Sibylline Prophecies as an imperial secret and constantly relied on personal "signs."

Under the christianized emperor Theodosius, all divination was prohibited as a capital crime, for it connected people to "unclean" spirits outside of the circle of the Church, which had fixed the eternal meanings of things. In Han and Sung dynasty China, popular forms of divining were legally prohibited, as was the collection of omen-books that could lead to nonofficial insights.

We encounter this conflict when we, as individuals, move into the divinatory space, a field where our lives are played out subject to fate, destiny, choice, luck, or karma, in search of our own sense of meaning. In this encounter, the collective values that clothe the institutions around us seem to dissolve and, for a moment, the emperor stands naked once more. The people who facilitate this entrance, who look behind collective values to build a working model of individual fate, are the subject of the next chapter. These figures have a history and an identity, but they are also archetypal, a part of each person's inner world.

OPPOSITE: An eclipse of the sun throws astronomers into a frenzy.

ABOVE: The emperor Augustus who outlawed all private prediction and divination, considering them treacherous to his regime.

Shamans, Seers, Mediums, and Guides

The shaman, the seer, the medium, and the spiritual guide take on or are taken over by forces outside their usual range of experience. Contact with these forces enables them to offer healing, insight, warning, and help to the people all over the world who rely on their insight and power.

These figures are also inner guides that help you establish contact with the images and forces of the deep imagination. If you have ever acted and felt the part you were creating take on a life of its own; if you have ever had the feeling that something other than yourself took over in a desperate situation, helped you in your work, or came through you when you wrote, danced, or spoke; if you have ever seen or felt deeply that events were moving in a certain direction, or "knew" that a certain event was a warning of things to come, you have experienced something of this fundamental way of divining.

The Shaman

The shaman is the world's oldest religious figure, a visionary who uses trance and spirit helpers to establish relations with fundamental powers and great souls on behalf of the people he or she serves. His powers come directly from contacts in the other worlds. The word shaman comes from Tungus, a Siberian language, and was chosen by anthropologists who "discovered" shamanism in the 19th century to represent a certain set of beliefs and practices. But the way of the shaman is worldwide, an underlying layer of culture spread throughout Asia, North and South America, Japan, China, Tibet, Australia, and Melanesia. Shamans come from a nomadic hunting and gathering culture.

Though people in such a culture live in close contact with the living world, they are not enclosed in a fixed calendar or cycle of events. Rituals and interventions arise at need, emphasizing the individual's capacity to create and move in the world of myth. Because of this imaginative freedom, this figure has come to represent our individual capacity to make myths and establish contact with spiritual realities.

ABOVE: A corroboree of South Australian aborigines, led by their shaman or medicine man.

RIGHT: A shaman's rattle from the Haida nation of North America. Such rattles were used to summon up the spirits to the shaman's aid.

ABOVE RIGHT: Inuit mask of a hair seal; the face shows that the mask represents the *inua*, or spirit, of the animal.

TRAVELING IN SPIRIT

The shaman voyages in alternative states of consciousness. Shamans establish contact with spirit guides, solicit advice, explain dreams and inner necessities, communicate with spirits, connect people to healing processes, and facilitate spiritual purification. He or she takes on the power of bird and animal helpers through mask, ritual drum and dance in order to travel to archetypal sources of power.

Shamans use a wide range of ecstatic techniques. The awareness they have of a free-soul that can travel outside of the body is usually very painfully earned. They use this visionary capacity to visit the heavenly powers and the realm of the dead, in order to mediate between those powers and the people they serve. Here is a classic description of one such voyage.

Takanakapsalak is the goddess of fate for the Inuit. The sea animals whose meat, skin, and fat make life possible through the long arctic night come from her, created from the joints of her fingers. When she is angry with humans, she keeps the animals hidden in her pool at the bottom of the ocean and sends famine and sickness among the people. One of the shaman's greatest tasks is to visit and tame her when she is angry.

On the eve of the shaman's journey, all the people gather in a darkened hut. All the knots and fastenings on their clothing must be loosened. Then the shaman, sitting in silence on the bare snow, calls on his spirit-helpers to open the way. The people answer in chorus: "Let it be!" As the passage opens and the shaman falls into it, his voice is heard receding until it is lost. He is on his way to the house at the bottom of the ocean. The hut fills with sounds, the sighing of the shaman's dead ancestors and the puffing, blowing, and splashing of sea creatures. The shaman's clothing flies through the air. The people keep singing, reaching out to the woman at the bottom of the ocean.

As the shaman emerges from the passage, he finds himself on a road along a bay. He may encounter obstacles on his way to the house of Takanakapsalak, but he must surmount them. If he arrives there and finds a wall surrounding the house, the goddess is very angry. Nevertheless, he must kick the wall down. When he enters the house he will see her, sitting by her lamp at the side of the pool where she has hidden all the animals. Her back is turned. Her tangled, matted hair hangs down one side of her face so she cannot see. Her body is covered with filth. The shaman must grasp her, turn her face to the lamp and the animals, stroke and untangle her hair, and calm her until she utters the reasons for her anger. Then she will take the animals from the pool one by one and drop them on the floor, where a whirlpool draws them back to the ocean above. This means good hunting.

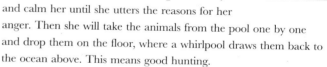

The shaman returns, and the people above hear the rush of his passage through the tube connecting the worlds. He shoots up into the room with a mighty sound, like a sea creature surfacing. Then he calls for the people to confess, to bring out the broken taboos and promises. The cause of the goddess's anger is found and everyone rejoices. There will be abundance among the people once more.

ABOVE LEFT: A soapstone carving of a fish with a woman's head, used by shamans to charm the fish into traps.

ABOVE RIGHT: A seal hunt; Inuit hunters depended on shamanic ritual to help them find their prey, or to lure it into their traps.

Soul Searching

Another of the shaman's major tasks is soul retrieval, finding the soul of a sick person that is held in the underworld and, if possible, setting it free. A modern shaman described this process. Shamanizing for someone who had suddenly become sick with no apparent reason, he drummed and called on his power animals. He visualized the person, then set out in search of her. He found himself floating in a gray place without time or physical feeling. In the distance was a flicker of light. As he went toward the light, he saw it was her face. But it floated away, not responding to his call until he chanted the name over and over. Then the face came closer and became aware of him. It looked lost and confused. He sent out a strong message that it was not time for this soul to leave its body, that it should return. The face faded and he journeyed back. The next day he heard that the patient had come out of coma at the time of the soul retrieval.

ABOVE: An Assiniboine hand drum, painted with scenes conjured up by a shaman after a period of fasting and thirsting.

SHAMANISM AROUND THE WORLD

Shamanism originated in the vast polar region of Siberia, where the shaman is regarded as both a healer and an intermediary with the spirit world. Shamanism spread from the north in all directions, via Tibet down through China to Korea and Vietnam, via North America to South America and even as far as South Africa and parts of Australasia. A few examples of the varying facets of shamanism are shown below.

RIGHT: A Shamanic mask worn to help the shaman summon up the desired animal spirit during a trance.

BELOW: A Tlingit shaman from the northwest coast of America making a healing incantation. Shamans healed by journeying through the spirit world to discover the underlying spiritual reason for the disease.

LEFT: A pottery jar from the Mochica culture, which flourished in pre-Columbian South America in what is now Peru. It shows a shaman examining a woman.

BELOW LEFT: A traditional European witch on her broomstick; this is believed to be a metaphor for shamanic flight, in which the shaman's spirit leaves his or her physical body and travels the world and the realm of the spirits.

BELOW RIGHT: A carved and painted figure of a shaman dressed in ritual robes and headdress from the northwest coast of Canada.

ABOVE: A ritual test undertaken by the men of the Plains Indian tribes. They would gather in a special lodge where they fasted and deprived themselves of sleep until they achieved altered states of mind. Bunches of sage, the purifying herb, were burned to keep away bad spirits.

The Shaman's World

The shamanic cosmos is centered in a great tree or axis that connects three different worlds: a heavenly world of wisdom spirits to which the shaman may fly in ecstatic trance; a lower or underworld of power figures, souls, and soul-devouring creatures; and the everyday reality between them where these things take effect. It is only by entering the other worlds that the real causes of things happening in our particular world can be found.

In the world of the shaman, people have two souls, a body soul that makes physical life possible, and a free soul that can travel outside of the body. The shaman makes use of this free soul in his traveling. In contrast to the medium, who may be possessed by spirit-figures, he always retains awareness and memory of what is going on.

In tribal culture, becoming a shaman is a vocation, and the call often comes through suffering and disease. Shamans are "wounded healers," marked out by the spirits. They are pursued, torn apart, taken on a visionary journey, and given a new body. Through this initiation they acquire the capacity to heal and serve rather than be the victim of their visionary capacity. In the process, they also acquire a tremendous physical energy, endurance, and concentration.

Each shamanic journey, which may be induced through drumming, dancing, or hallucinogenic substances, repeats this initiation. It is a return to the time of the first ancestors and the origins of spirit. The beginning of the journey is marked by the summoning of the shaman's helping spirits. This access to power potentiates his ritual equipment, which may include an altar with divinatory objects or a bridge to the spirit world. He may send his spirit allies to detect the cause of a sickness, locate lost objects, or take him to a specific part of the spirit world. The shaman's ritual objects, drum, and clothing all reinforce the idea of traveling between worlds. They are decorated with bones and skeletons, bird feathers, stuffed snakes, images of sacred and helping animals, the World Tree, sun, moon, and the doors to the underworld.

The shaman is also a skilled actor, stage magician, and ventriloquist. Most of his ceremonies are *performed*, and he relies on the willing support of the audience, who form a kind of chorus. His skill at illusion is part of his ability to open the gates to extraordinary experience. An example of this "healing illusion" is the withdrawal of the "witch-arrows" that cause certain kinds of illness. The shaman will "read" the patient's body then, using his mouth or a special cone-shaped funnel, will "draw" small slivers of bone or crystal from the person's body. This conscious illusion is an effective part of the "magical" healing.

The shaman may use a range of other divinatory techniques to amplify or confirm the results of his travels. They include drawing lots or tossing a drumstick or bone ring, balancing a bow on an outstretched finger and observing its movement while posing questions, or heating a ritually prepared shoulder bone and reading the cracks produced. In these, as in other shamanic practices, the goal is not to achieve enlightenment for the shaman but to help others through finding the answer to a specific problem.

Shamanism Now

Shamans are still active in many parts of the world, with much to say and give, and there has been a series of "new shamans" who attempt to translate the shaman's "way" into modern terms. Perhaps the most fundamental part of this movement is the work of Michael Harner, a former member of the New School for Social Research who was initiated by Cunibo shamans in the Amazon. He was given visions usually reserved for people who were crossing the threshold into death and has been amazingly successful in translating the core experience of shamanic reality into modern terms.

DRUMMING UP

Harner's workshops often use the beating of a large flat drum as a vehicle to travel into the mythic worlds. Participants relax in darkness or with closed eyes and visualize the world tree extending up to the heavens and deep into the earth. They enter a doorway at the foot of the tree and pass into one of the great roots. The root becomes a tunnel with light at its end. Riding the pulse of the drum, they move out into this luminous haze and call for a guide – an animal, spirit, or myth creature – to help explore the realm that is now opened to them. The journey lasts for about twenty minutes, though it may feel much longer. A special drumbeat calls the traveler back, to recall and record as much as possible.

OPPOSITE: A modern African witch doctor casts a spell on behalf of a paying client.

ABOVE: A Binzar shaman or witch doctor from the Dinka tribe of southern Sudan.

The same sort of technique is used in "shamanic counseling," where a counselor helps a client to take a divinatory journey that opens the way to a dialogue with power animals, mythic persons, great teachers, and the spirits of the dead. It seeks to put the individual in touch with sources of guidance in nonordinary reality, where, it is felt, the real counselors exist. The answers that come out of these sessions reflect the "friendship" of the spirit that users of divination systems often experience.

Many doctors who have become aware of Western medicine's "lack of soul" are working with shamanic models of healing and self-help. For many other people, the shaman represents the power to experience the reality of the spirit through their own imagination. This kind of "journeying" solves problems, provides an orientation toward many important matters, and contributes to the creation of a powerful and compassionate personal mythology. The shamanic element in all divinatory acts is a combination of this myth-making power and the dedication to "help and serve," to further the path of the person involved and the transforming world of the spirit.

Seers, Wise Women, and Prophets

Seers, wise women, spirit guides, and prophets all, in one way or another, share the ability to see, hear, and report what goes on "behind the veil" of ordinary reality. This ability to perceive things hidden to normal sight is usually called clairvoyance, or "clear-seeing." Clairvoyance or "seeing" connects you with a moving stream of images where time and space are surprisingly relative. The seer may see a sudden clear vision of a future event, a symbolic portrayal of the present situation or what people are doing in a far away place, an acute insight into motives and feelings or how energy is moving in and through a person's body. These images and events "show the way."

There are many examples of people in the ancient world or in folk culture who had this second sight. It is seen in virtually all cultures, forming the base of most methods of psychic and ritual healing. Seeing or clairvoyance allows the seer to connect the inquirer's problems to psychic sources and prescribe ritual actions and medicines to change them. Though it is a natural ability common to most people, one that can be developed, it sometimes spontaneously forces itself on the seer. Like other psychic powers, seeing was also thought to run in certain families.

The old Greek seers all traced their ancestry to a specific mythical figure. Reincarnate Tibetan lamas will "pass on" their gifts by reappearing in a new body. In matriarchal groups, the sacred gifts of "seeing" possessed by the queen will return in the person of her daughter.

TEIRESIAS THE SEER

The most famous seer and reader of signs in old Greece was Teiresias. This figure was reinterpreted many times as different methods of divination, particularly the cult of the shaman and oracle god Apollo, took over the divinatory function. On the oldest levels, Teiresias could speak the language of birds and snakes, was both blinded and given the gift of "sight" by Athena, the owl-goddess, alternated between being woman and man, and lived through at least seven generations. He was a liminal or borderline figure who could "keep his head" in alternative realities. The hero Odysseus consulted Teiresias in Hades, where he spoke from the realm of the dead to show the hero the way home. He revealed Oedipus' tragic secret identity as parricide and lover of his mother, and counseled Pentheus, the young king of Thebes, to yield to the new god Dionysus before he was torn apart. Teiresias is an example of the seer whose borderline existence – woman and man, human and animal, alive and dead, blind and seeing – gave him access to the hidden significance of things. In some ways, he was older than the gods themselves.

ABOVE LEFT: The traditional image of an Eastern wise man; a priest sits serenely in a meditative yoga pose.

RIGHT: Tibetan monks in Darjeeling; boys enter training in the monasteries when they are very young.

OPPOSITE: A photograph purporting to show the aura or energy field that psychic healers claim to be able to see with the naked eye.

Celtic stories are full of descriptions of the mind that suddenly opens to a moment of vision: "I saw a great flock of black birds," said King Eochaid, "coming from the depths of the ocean. They settled on all of us and fought with us. They brought us confusion and destroyed us." His Druid correctly interpreted this vision and foretold the downfall of the kingdom. What lies behind this "seeing" is the experience that coming events cast shadows in front of them as they move toward us. The ability to see these shadows seems to be connected with innate intuitive ability, feeling, and need, and the capacity to go blank, to allow images to appear spontaneously in the mind's eye. The threshold of consciousness was not as rigidly guarded in pretechnological ages, so it was easier for the images to appear. But the journals, dream diaries, seances, and spontaneous manifestations throughout Europe in the late 1930s, full of visions of the coming holocaust, vividly show the strength of this forecasting.

Psychic healers often maintain that they can "see" the aura or energy field that plays around each person. The changing color patterns of this field indicate emotional states, blocks, and general character. Other psychics can "see" emotional and pragmatic situations through examining an object that someone has used or touched.

Chinese folk stories are filled with tales of wandering Buddhist and Taoist monks, figures outside the social hierarchy who have

totally given up any idea of "face," who have the uncanny ability to "read" a person's fate and to "see" the activities of malevolent spirits. *Hombahomba* diviners in Zimbabwe can spontaneously tell their clients' names, family connections, and problems the first time they see the person. Disciples of a *Tsaddiq*, or saintly master, in Hasidic Judaism frequently tell how their master can "see" a person's soul at the first meeting and recount the course of their past and future lives. The same thing is related about many Hindu *gurus* and spiritual masters.

A Bowl Full of Shadows

The divining or scrying bowl, which links water and the mirror, is a central image for "seeing." This bowl comes in many forms. It is at the center of a cluster of symbols and practices concerned with water sources, reflection, inspiration, seeing, and the world of the dead.

For the Chinese, water is a symbol of the way, or *tao*, mother of all signs and symbols. In old Greece, the first being to know the secrets of the future was Metis, goddess of shifting waters and fluid possibilities. She was swallowed by Zeus, king of a new generation of gods, and lived on inside him, giving him the ability to see the shapes of all things to come.

Seized by the Nymphs

The power of Metis to "see" things in the shifting waters is incarnate in the *numphai*, or nymphs, the spirits of water sources. Someone who was "seized by the nymphs" acquired a poetic exaltation that enabled him to see and sing the past, present, and future. We can see a vestige of their power in the oracle of Limera, a fountain sacred to Ino Leucothea, white goddess of water and the moon. On her feast day, cakes were thrown into the waters and a question posed. If the water took them, the answer was yes; if they were refused, no. The oracle of Demeter and Persephone, Queen of the Dead, was used to see if the dark waters were going to take a sick person. A mirror was attached to a cord and lowered to the surface of the dark pool. After a sacrifice, you could look into the mirror and see the person in question either dead or alive. Similarly, a West African water diviner places a basin of water in a sick person's yard and "sees" the sick person's soul flying around it. He tries to charm the soul into the water. If he succeeds, the person will live. If not, the soul is already on its long journey to the land of the dead. A Jewish water divination was used to find out if someone would survive the coming year. On the eve of Hasha'anah Rabba, water was taken from a well and put into a glass in the center of a room. You could "see" a face in this divining bowl. If its mouth is open, you will live another year; if the mouth is closed, you will soon die.

Liquid Visions

The center of this complex is the bowl filled with liquid, sign for an opening to the other worlds. This bowl could yield symbols in many ways. You could throw melted wax, lead, or hot oil into it and read the resulting shapes. Babylonian diviners had several omen-tablets devoted exclusively to the interpretation of these signs. In Uganda, diviners cast powdered herbs onto the waters and "read" the shapes. They would "see" tiny fishlike spirits moving among them.

Other diviners pour a few drops of a clarifying liquid into pots of muddy water and read the shapes in the clearing water. An unbroken star shape is a good augury; irregular and broken shapes bode ill.

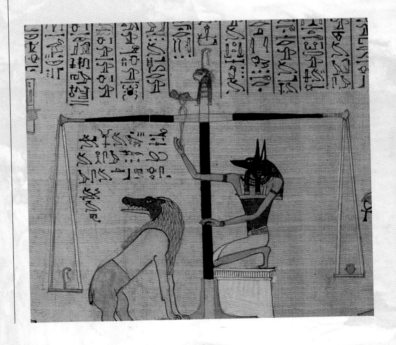

The divining bowl was one of the symbols of the end-product of alchemical transformation. It was often used to work magic. Nectanbo, an Egyptian prince of the 4th century B.C.E., wrought magic with a bowl of water, wax figures, and an ebony rod. He would put wax figures of enemy soldiers and ships into the water, recite spells, and touch them with the rod, whereupon they came to life and quickly sunk to the bottom. At the same time, the literary source says, the hosts of his enemies were destroyed.

In Egyptian myth, the bowl is connected with Anubis, dog-headed god of the dead. This connection with the dead lurks behind most forms of "seeing," for in old cultures the images we see in dreams and visions and the souls of the dead are virtually synonymous. Bowl diviners were thought to be necromancers, capable of calling ghosts and demons into their troubled waters. Odysseus, sent by the sorceress Kirke to gain knowledge from the dead, was told to dig a ditch and fill it with milk, wine, and, finally, water. He was to turn his attention to the flow of the underground stream of images welling up in this water and he would see the souls of the dead flocking toward him. Only then could he distinguish the great soul of Teiresias, with whom he needed to speak.

In Haiti, one of the two souls of a dead person will live temporarily underwater. After a certain period, it can be called home and conjured into a vase or bowl where it can be questioned. Melanesian dream-diviners are often called on to find and free people's souls who have been caught by underground water-spirits.

The souls of the dead reflected in the divining bowl were also seen as guiding spirits, or *daimones*. In Hellenistic Alexandria, a particular kind of spell was evolved to "fix" these spirits as an oracle. They could confer success in love, wealth, health, knowledge, and freedom from constraint. Consultants could "see" these spirits through ceremonies at the tomb, ritual ventriloquism, in dream, and, above all, in the diviner's bowl. This led to a kind of theater. We are told that certain magicians would stand a basin of water in the middle of a dimly lit room with a blue floor, whose color made the surface of the water seem like the sky above. The bowl was made of stone, but had a glass bottom with an opening onto a hidden room beneath, full of people dressed as gods and daimones who would be "seen" at the magician's directions. This is a great theatrical metaphor for the act of scrying.

OPPOSITE: The Egyptian god Anubis weighs the soul of a dead person against the feather of truth. In Hellenistic Egypt, dead souls were considered to have oracular powers.

ABOVE: A simple bowl of water focuses the seer's eye. Melted wax dropped onto the surface forms random shapes that can be "read."

The Witch Hunt

he seer and the divining bowl are also connected with one of the darker uses of divination, finding the source of black magic, witching, and sorcery. The wandering exorcist who can "see" malevolent spirits and deal with them through ritual practices was a familiar figure in Chinese and Greco-Roman culture. In African societies, there was a widespread belief that unexplained misfortune is a direct result of people's hidden anger, greed, envy, and malice. "Witchcraft" is the result of those negative feelings, conscious or unconscious. Its hidden malice brings people into relation with events in such a way that they are injured. Because they could lead to the death of an accused witch, witchcraft divinations were outlawed by Africa's white colonizers. They survived underground and flourish today in both rural and urban environments.

The ground for these divinations is something we are often afraid to think about, that our anger, hatred, envy,

greed, and desire to hurt, acknowledged or unacknowledged, can do others literal harm. Though "black magic" was certainly used in tribal cultures, these negative feelings can also cause harm without a conscious focus. A witchcraft divination asks the people found responsible for harm to "own up to" their own shadows and take responsibility for their feelings.

The divining bowl and the divining basket were often used to "see" the source of trouble. Some diviners used a large shallow bowl carved from a single piece of wood, with a cowrie shell set in the center that represents the mother-spirits. There are designs around and in the bowl representing key mythic figures and kinds of human relations. The bowl was filled with water and several seeds or small pieces of wood set floating on the surface of the water. Their movement on a symbolic journey enables the diviner to "see" the history of the sickness and pose

conflicts that surround the society's values. The story they tell explains suffering as a breakdown in human relations.

A consultation is usually made by a group of relations on behalf of a sick person. After an invocation, the diviner will go into a light trance, showing the same sort of symptoms that characterized his initiatory sickness. He fills the basket and shakes it, "seeing" the situation through the relations of the figures that repeatedly come to the top. On the basis of these figures, he begins to question the people involved with the sick person. He establishes the person's name, and the relationship of the force attacking him or her, and how it manifests itself. He moves deeper and deeper into the social, psychological, and physical nexus of the attacking force until he can "see" the witch, ancestor, or spirit causing the trouble and can level an accusation. If it is a person, they are asked to take back their poison; if an ancestor, the kin-group is told to correct the oversight or neglect that is offending him; if a spirit, a major community healing ritual will be enacted.

pertinent questions to the people involved in order to locate its source. In another tribe, two people hold a bowl of water between their fingers and go into light trance, while a list of names is recited. When the name of the person responsible occurs, the bowl twists and falls.

Nedembu diviners "shake the basket" to "cut a trail" to and from the dark springs of malice, hatred, and the desire to hurt and control. These diviners are usually marginal men themselves, whose experience as outsiders gives them a clairvoyant insight into the malice of others. They have usually been picked out and haunted by a very angry ancestral spirit and have been forced to turn this anger into "seeing" through a long initiation ritual. The basket diviner uses a winnowing basket and a set of 20–30 small objects that he makes or finds. These tell the story of misfortune, loss, and death, and the revengeful motives responsible for them. They articulate the disturbances and

OPPOSITE LEFT: A scrying ceremony from *The Thrice Holy Triniosophie* by the Comte de St. Germain. A bowl of liquid is used for the ritual, and occult symbols decorate the room.

ABOVE CENTER: The fearsome faces of witchcraft in Mexico.

ABOVE RIGHT: A witch doctor from Cameroon.

Speculating with the Wise Woman

The figure of the wise woman – seer, priestess, witch, and crone – lurks behind many religious and divinatory traditions. It is a reminder of an old spiritual way devoted to the Great Goddess, a blend of clairvoyance, ritual action, and psychic healing. In many cases these wise women became the mediums and pythias in oracle shrines of a later generation of gods. We see traces of the wise woman and her ability to see things at a distance in time and space in the preclassical Greek *numphai*, or nymphs. These far-sighted figures, who were simultaneously young and old, were associated with water sources. They gave a kind of inner "frenzy" that allowed the person they possessed to see and sing of the past, present, and future. In old China, female shamans known as *wu* called the spirits to tell of events past and future and brought them together to bring rain. European witches not only wove spells but also used their clairvoyant abilities to "see" into the web of the future as it was being woven.

The Icelandic *volva* was such a figure, a guiding force in her culture and repository of oral tradition and knowledge. When the people needed guidance or information, they would construct a special platform and "raise" the *volva* on it, while chants were sung. Going into trance, she would "see" into the nexus of coming events and search out the answers to the problems confronting her people. In the central poem of the Icelandic tradition, Odin, a younger god of prophecy and wisdom, seeks out the volva. He listens to her sing of the origin of the worlds, the gods, and the inevitable return of primal chaos.

In a time without any forms of long distance communication, the wise woman's ability to see beyond her literal situation was of great value. It reflects an inherent ability to watch over loved ones and children even at a distance. The gypsy woman, gifted with both second-sight and the evil eye, and the country woman who is weather wise and an animal friend inherited something of this tradition.

CRYSTAL GAZING

In order to scry, your attention must be diverted, directed away from the normal flow of events. The speculum, ball, or cup is treated with respect, and both it and the place of seeing are set off from everyday things. Begin by centering your breathing and opening the heart-space. Focus attention gently on the ball; if your attention drifts away, gently bring it back. Eventually the ball will become hazy, full of a swirling "astral" mist. The direction and colors of these clouds can themselves be a sign. If you persevere, a darker area will open in the mists, a window in the mind or tunnel in time through which images will flow. These images do not appear in the ball itself, but in the "mind's eye" that has been opened. They may be literal events, symbols, or sudden personifications of your own hopes and fears. As you work with the symbols, a language will open up.

Reading the Tea Leaves

Much of any wise woman's ability to "see" involves the use of a *speculum*, a reflecting surface of some sort that allows them to "cross over" into another kind of space and time and thus "scry" into the stream of images that tells of coming events. A piece of polished stone, a pool of still water, a glass filled with wine, or a blackened bowl filled with water are examples. In Europe since about the 16th century, the object of choice was a ball made of rock crystal or, in later times, glass.

Reading tea leaves, scrying from the shapes and position of the leaves left in the bottom of a teacup, is a more domestic form of the wise woman's cosmic mirror. It has been used in Europe since the introduction of tea in the 18th century, and is also practiced with coffee grounds, or *marc de café*. The gypsy woman who called at the door to "read" for the women of the house was a popular Victorian figure. This art still revolves around the kind of questions asked over a cup of tea: love, family, home, partnership, career.

ABOVE: A playing card depicting the witch from an 18th-century German card game called "Bird's Play."

ABOVE RIGHT: A teacup, the humble arena for tasseomancy, or reading the patterns left by tea leaves or coffee grounds when the liquid has been drunk or poured off. The shapes the leaves make determine the kind of symbolism the patterns carry. Some of the shapes can indicate good or bad fortune depending on their form.

SIGNS IN THE CUP

The ritual begins with whole-leaf tea brewed in a pot without a filter. It is poured into a shallow-bowled cup and drunk while considering the question. When the tea is almost gone, the questioner swirls the cup three times with her left hand and empties it into the saucer. The reader then looks at the patterns made by the dregs remaining in the cup. There is a varied repertoire of symbolic meanings for patterns such as the heart (the love in your life), snake (treachery), moon (waxing, full, or waning may indicate increase, romantic fulfillment or an end to delays), broom (brushing out difficulties), dagger (sudden attack and jealousy), and saw (breaking old relations or isolation). If the symbol is placed near the rim, it is near in time. Perceiving the patterns and their relations, however, is a very individual thing. When the cup is seen as a universal compass, the different parts can indicate areas and elements of your life, while the clarity of the symbol in the area gives a sense of its intensity and importance.

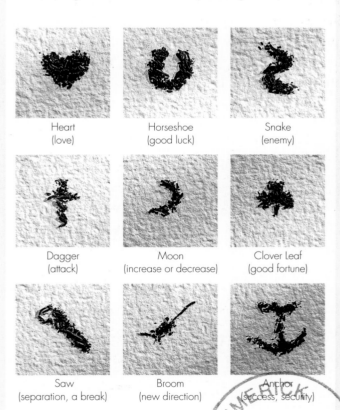

Heart (love)	Horseshoe (good luck)	Snake (enemy)
Dagger (attack)	Moon (increase or decrease)	Clover Leaf (good fortune)
Saw (separation, a break)	Broom (new direction)	Anchor (success, security)

The Lake of Visions

ibetans call this kind of seeing through signs and visions *tra* divination. Normally, it is felt you must acquire the ability from someone who has it, and not everyone has the gift. Some are able to call up the visions but not able to read or see them. The tra diviner focuses his attention on a reflecting surface, empties his mind, and calls on the divine protectress Palden Lhamo. As his trance concentration deepens, a current of images begins to flow and a vision appears. A common practice was to use the ball of the thumb, painted red and dipped in soft wax, as a speculum. The divination occurred in a darkened room with a single lamp burning. The *tra-pa* holds up his thumb and it seems to grow large, becoming a screen on which the images appear.

The greatest speculum for tra divination is the sacred lake Lhamo Lhatso, recognized for several hundred years as a divining site. It was used to locate the new incarnation of the Dalai Lama, head of traditional Tibet's religious and political life. The 13th Dalai Lama was found through a series of visions visible to hundreds of people: three letters from the Tibetan alphabet, a great three-storied, gold-roofed monastery, and a road from the monastery to a house with a blue roof and a spotted dog in the courtyard. The visions appeared at the request of lamas who were seeking the new leader. They led to the place where he was found.

Tra divination was often used by refugees fleeing the Chinese in order to find their way through the mountain and forest wilderness to the Indian border. In response to need, clear visions of the path ahead would appear. Though such divinatory practices speak the language of dreams and symbols, they can be an ever-present help in times of danger.

Our innate intuitive or visionary capacity can be developed so that it will respond to our particular needs by producing a guiding image.

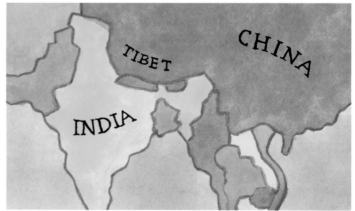

OPPOSITE: A map showing how China, India, and Tibet relate to each other, meeting at the point known as the "roof of the world." It is easy to see how cultural influences spread and flow through this region. In 1951, the Chinese took control of Tibet, and in 1965 it became an autonomous region of China. The Dalai Lama, the religious leader, is forced to live in exile.

ABOVE: Nam Tso Lake in Tibet. Tibetan lakes are considered to be the mirrors of visions.

RIGHT: Visions in the sacred lake Lhamo Lhatso led to the discovery of the 13th Dalai Lama. They included a spotted dog, a blue-roofed house, a golden-topped monastery, and three letters from the Tibetan alphabet.

Guides, Interpreters, and Fire-Gazers

The spiritual guide or advisor uses divinatory practices to give and receive guidance, often – but not always – in terms of a particular spiritual tradition. By acting as an intermediary, these guides can activate and channel the flow of spirit in the imagination, helping people connect with their own sources of inner guidance. The spiritual practice of a Tibetan lama, for example, may be at times directed through divination, indicating the deities and practices to which he should attend or explicating karmic patterns. He will use his ability to connect with specific deities and qualities to empower divinatory procedures in order to be of help to others. Thus he fulfills two tenets of his spiritual practice: realizing the "interdependent arising" of all things, and giving compassionate service to others for the "happiness of all sentient beings." In the same way, a *houngan* or *mambo*, leader of a *vaudou* community, will use divination to direct an initiate to his or her "guiding and teaching" *loa*. One of the basic functions of African *Ifa* divination, root of many New World spiritual practices, is to help an individual find his "head," his individual identity, and to serve and feed it rather than work against it.

This dedication is a powerful part of most divination. Many traditional people believe that divination does not work without specific ritual invocations and empowerments. The contemporary revisioning of these divinatory ways, making their symbols and methods available to all, may be one of the great gifts of our "postmodern" age. It is when the divination is dedicated to helping or serving that the power of the images opens up. Divining helps people to live their lives in connection with the inner flow of images that guides them, their *daimon* or guiding spirit. Paradoxically, it is when we are most fully ourselves that we can contribute to the happiness and well-being of others. A spiritual guide will use divinatory images to further this paradoxical goal.

ABOVE RIGHT: An engraving of an Aztec calendar stone.

ABOVE: A Tibetan monk preparing butter lamps for ritual ceremonies.

OPPOSITE TOP: Carl Gustav Jung, father of the archetype.

OPPOSITE BOTTOM: King Arthur (in armor) in company with St. Michael and Joseph of Arimathea.

The King and I

The diviner as advisor, with access to hidden knowledge of the gods and the stars and secret ways of "seeing," was a familiar figure in the centers of culture in the ancient world. But whom did the advisor advise? We think of each person as a separate being, an individual, but this is a recent development. In earlier times, the only fully individuated person was the king or queen. Everything they did had a symbolic value. The Babylonian *barû* priest, with his hundreds of omen-books established over generations; the Chinese bone-diviner, whose engraved tablets were a synthesis of a long shamanic tradition; the *Ifa* diviner's aristocratic lineage and many ritual initiations; the Celtic Druid's secret language and occult studies; Mayan and Aztec omen-readers and star-gazers with their carved circles of signs – all these figures put their accumulated knowledge and clairvoyant abilities at the service of the ruling power. They focused on giving advice to the being who maintained the connection between heaven and earth, the individual whose actions would have an effect on the world, for good or evil. It was only in times of social breakdown and change that these elaborate systems became a source of "wisdom" divination available to private individuals.

We have redefined what an individual is, and we no longer feel that all good flows through a single powerful figure at the head of the state. But one of our fascinations with the ancient art of divining comes from this old quasi-magical sense that the actions of the individual make a difference, they "count" in the spiritual economy of the universe. C. G. Jung, the depth psychologist, saw this as an important characteristic of our time, which he called a *kairos*, or critical moment, when our fundamental beliefs are changing. In such a time the individual is the "make-

JUNG

Carl Gustav Jung was the father of modern depth and archetypal psychology. Deeply concerned with the way mythic, magical and divinatory images reflect the deep structures of the soul, his central concern was the individual's attempt to find a spiritual and imaginative life in an age that had rejected all mythical thinking. Jung's thought is one of the major ways we can connect traditional myth and modern psychology.

weight" in the change, the place where transformation occurs. The diviner as advisor's job is to articulate the time and the challenges as they play into the weave of each person's life. In that sense, each of us is king of our own realm, for it is in the crucible of our individual awareness that the monumental changes will be carried through.

Staring into the Fire

If seers gaze into water and the moving stream of images, prophets stare into the fire. This is not divination by fire, of which there are many examples. Bedouin diviners used the sounds of the fire to affirm or deny their divinatory narrative spoken in a trance state. Tibetans studied the flame of a butter lamp on the 8th or 10th day of the month, or on a half or full moon night. They would pose a question and read the answer in the shape, color, behavior, and smell of the flame. The prophet, however, stares into the fire and is transported, raised into an exalted "transpersonal" state. He feels impelled to speak with the voice of the highest god and the highest realm of the spirit, revealing its message and will. In monotheistic cultures, we can see the figure of the prophet actively taking over divinatory functions from other methods of knowing.

The prophet differs from the seer or the medium in that he is exclusively concerned with the ascent of the soul to a heavenly place. He speaks in terms of universal values. The prophet gives prescriptions for the spiritual health of a nation, warnings of imminent disaster, and God's demand for right living. His utterance is revolutionary; he seeks to demolish an old order and replace it with a new vision. His language includes destruction, God's wrath, apocalypse, judgment, and the hope of radical renewal. Those who speak about prophecy generally oppose it to divination and seeing, which are concerned with the problems of individuals. Prophecy speaks in terms of great general truths; in the scheme of the three worlds, it connects exclusively to the highest realms of pure spirit.

Jewish tradition produced a long line of prophets, whose direct connection to the High God eliminated other forms of divining. "If there is a prophet among you," said The God, "I will make myself known to him in vision."

These Biblical figures are what usually comes to mind when we think of prophecy. They challenged the political order with their demands for righteousness and spiritual reform and relayed the messages of the High God. Over the centuries, they sought a vision of Him, to give the unknowable an image. Their challenging apocalyptic tone reached its climax in the early Christian prophet John of Patma, "author" of the Book of Revelations, which told of the end of the world, the last things and the final judgment of God.

This "millenarian" aspect of prophecy is another common feature. It is a call for a renewal of the world based on the thousand-year reign of joy, peace, and justice proclaimed in Revelations. Joachim of Fiore, for example, redefined the apocalypse for medieval Europe, dividing history into the Age of the Father, or Law; the Age of the Son and the Gospels; and the Age of the Holy Spirit, soon to appear on earth. Thousands of people were caught up in the vision, wandering throughout Europe to await the new age. In the same way, at the end of the 19th century, Karl Marx proclaimed an apocalyptic vision of history that would end in the establishment of a Worker's Paradise through the destruction of the existing corrupt society. At several times in Chinese history, prophetic movements associated with Taoism and the return to an agrarian Golden Age have swept the country, leading to major political conflicts and repression. This millennial vision is very strong in prophetic utterance, from the return of the "Sleeping King" in British prophetic myth to current prophecies of the "Return of the Goddess."

OPPOSITE: Moses communed with God through the medium of the Burning Bush.

LEFT: A steady candle flame is a focus for divinatory meditation.

Prophetic Books and Flying Rolls

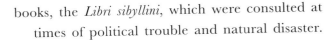

Prophets are thought of as *en-theos*, or "full of god." In Greek and Roman culture since the time of Plato, intellectuals have sought to draw a firm line between such "inspired" prophecy, which is pure and high, and the mundane arts of divining with lots, images, and signs. The inspired prophet was the real medium of the gods, while other, more popular methods were both pedestrian and fraudulent. Much of our current attitude stems from this Platonic perspective. One of the results was the evolution of the late Antique figure of the sibyl, a priestess of Apollo who evolved into a prophetess. The pronouncements of the sibyls were collected in oracle books, the *Libri sibyllini*, which were consulted at times of political trouble and natural disaster. Augustus, Rome's first great emperor, outlawed all forms of private divination, burned any divination books in private hands, and carefully guarded the Sibylline Prophecies as an imperial resource. The association prophecy makes between politics, reform, and the highest spiritual authorities, as well as its disconnection from individual affairs, has made it particularly susceptible to being used as propaganda. Roman and Chinese emperors, Reformation clerics, and German fascists have all manipulated prophecies of the coming of the Golden Age and the wonder-signs associated with it to legitimate their rule.

LEFT: A Nazi rally in Nuremberg in 1938. Hitler, an archpropagandist, based his expansionist ideas on the prophesied coming of the Golden Age.

ABOVE CENTER: A sibyl, a prophet-priestess of the god Apollo.

ABOVE RIGHT: A 16th-century Chinese emperor.

OPPOSITE LEFT: Aleister Crowley, author of the "found" *Book of Law*.

OPPOSITE RIGHT: Nostradamus, probably the best-known European prophet.

Found Books

Prophecy is also connected with the Sacred Book. The idea of finding a sacred book occurs in the Jewish Prophet Zachariah, who "saw" a "Flying Roll" that was the "curse of The God going forth over the face of the land." The literary tradition of the Sibylline Prophecies was interpreted by Christian apologists as predicting the coming of Christ. Tibetans have the idea that past spiritual masters have written texts that they left to be discovered much later when the world has need of them. In our own time, Joseph Smith, prophet of the Mormons, said that he found the Book of Mormon, the founding document of the Church, engraved on golden plates. Members of the Theosophical Society and ritual Magicians of the Order of the Golden Dawn also received written messages from their guides in the form of books that were to change the world. Aleister Crowley's *Book of Law* is, according to its author, an example of such a found or dictated book.

Nostradamus (1503–66) is probably the most famous nonreligious prophet in European tradition. An astrologer, doctor, and magician, Nostradamus composed 100 quatrains of prophetic verse or "perpetual vaticinations" that covered the history of the world until the year 3797. About the same time he was elaborating his enigmatic prophecies, John Dee, a British magician who sought to be the prophet of a Third Rome established in London, was using his scrying glass to contact angelic powers at his library at Mortlake, Surrey, England.

Nostradamus felt himself filled with a divine vision that connected with the actions of the "nocturnal and celestial lights" that governed the natural world. Sealed in his secret study, he would concentrate on a brass tripod until a "slender flame issued from the emptiness." He would make passes with an ebony rod until a trembling voice was heard, a voice that inspired great fear. In this moment, "the God sat near" and the prophecies appeared. This "subtle spirit of flame" dictated the quatrains, a résumé of history past, present, and to come.

Few of us are prophets in this high Biblical sense, and our age has learned to distrust great visions for the reform of the world after one of history's bloodiest centuries.

Prophecy lies outside the realm of divination proper, for it has no direct connection to the questions of soul, fate, and individual destiny that form the purpose of most ways of divining. The myth of the Golden Age, however, a time when humans, gods, and spirits freely interact, is something that they share. We have seen the destruction inherent in trying to realize a millennial vision. But divination shows that we should not forget the possibility of personally experiencing the "care and friendship of the gods."

Mediums, Oracles, and Body Diviners

ediums use a variety of techniques in order to become the vehicle of gods, ghost voices, and spirit guides. They may be able to speak with their spirits, like African body diviners who use light trance and a contact with an inner "heart-spirit" to read the conflicting voices possessing a sick person's body. They may reflect a series of different voices, like the spirit-medium through which people could talk to the dead that became a major religious force in the late 19th and early 20th century. They may be completely inspired by a god and go through radical changes of voice and physical presence.

A medium is someone who is in one way or another "possessed" by a spirit. They offer their bodies, voices, and creative intelligence to the "others," who may be dead ancestors, gods and demons, or split-off parts of people's souls. By putting themselves in the middle, they become a means of expression for these forces. This mediates relations with spirit-energies in an individual personality and in the body politic.

There are many different descriptions of the relation between spirit and medium: the spirit is thought to "mount" the medium who then becomes the "horse" of the god; the spirit can enter, take possession of, haunt, inhabit, seduce, invade, or have sexual intercourse with the medium.

Possession in its most severe form is marked by complete trance, but this is not characteristic of all mediums. As they develop the ability to handle contacts with the other world gracefully, they can often move in and out of trance or create a "double" awareness.

In most cultures, when a person is possessed by a spirit, the resources of the group or tribe are mobilized to help them understand and deal with the invasion. If the invader is seen as a malignant force, it may be ritually exorcized. More often, ritual, initiation, and instruction are used to help the "possessed" person gain control of the situation rather than be its unconscious victim. He or she becomes a full-fledged medium, a means of communication and mediation between the spirit and the group.

Mediumistic divination is common in Africa, South America, the Caribbean, and the Far East. In Christian Europe, it was usually associated with witchcraft and being "possessed by the devil," like other divinatory practices. But the medium is a part of our common imagination, representing the process of "making things conscious." It is based on the idea that there are voices and perspectives outside our immediate awareness that might know more or see things differently than we do.

The simplest answer to this question is that the medium's voices articulate a self, a divine other that mediates the world and the spirit. Much of what we routinely see as "inside" is, in other cultures, part of an "outside" that is not directly subject to our conscious control. A deep look at your own "inside" will convince you that there is a lot to this viewpoint, for there are forces, figures, and feelings within each of us that have a real independence, a will, and a wisdom of their own. Mediums contact these forces and can give them a voice. "Mediumism" has also been a metaphor for the poet and artist, who acts like an antenna for contact with unknown voices in the culture. This connection shows us how both receptivity and art or craft are involved in developing a mediumistic relation with an inner voice. The spirit-world, its movements, inhabitants, and evolutionary processes, is a powerful image of the mind and the deep imagination. Being connected to the spirits is a creative act, and it brings the possibility of living in a world that is imaginatively alive rather than simply enduring what seems like a series of meaningless events.

What do mediums talk to? Who or what speaks through them? Like a radio receiver, mediums may articulate the inner conflicts and tensions in another person's body, perceiving them as voices and images. In traditional cultures a medium may be possessed by an angry ghost or offended spirit who seeks revenge for injuries, an ancestral spirit that seeks recognition through ritual and attention, or a spirit guide that he or she must come to grips with. The process of turning "spirit possession" into a creative relation with one of these guides can turn you into a healer or a seer. The "call" is often announced through sickness, and resisting the call can result in depression, extreme alienation, uncontrolled dissociation, and fugues or blackouts. Entrance to the liminal world of the medium is often actively sought, through drumming, chanting, and sensory overload or deprivation.

OPPOSITE: A Nepalese man consults an oracle astrologer. The belief in the power of mediums is a worldwide phenomenon.

ABOVE: Mediums can find themselves in more than one world – or body – at once.

RIGHT: A North Vietnamese medium enters a trance to communicate with the spirit world.

Mediums as Oracles

he other familiar image of a medium is that of the god Apollo at the oracular shrine at Delphi in ancient Greece, the Pythia. Classical Greece and the Mediterranean had several oracular shrines, the oldest being the temple of Zeus at Dodona, but none was as important as Delphi. People came from all over the Hellenic world to question Apollo, god of light and prophecy, through his medium.

The Pythia or "snake-woman" was an older, often uneducated woman traditionally chosen from a small group of peasant families. She was the living embodiment of the sky-god Apollo's conquest of an older culture and an older way of divining associated with the snake, earth, and water sources. Like the "sun that uses the moon," Apollo would possess his medium at certain times of the year and speak with her voice.

Private citizens, statesmen, religious leaders, poets, and philosophers consulted the oracle of Apollo. In later years, an extensive, idealizing literary myth was built up around the practice. A series of philosophical questions posed to an Apollonian oracle became the base for the *Chaldean Oracles*, a magico-mystical form of meditation, sun-worship, and transcendence, an oracle in a book. In the later Hellenistic magical papyri, the process of consulting the oracle was transforming into a magic spell, through which the god or daimon could be summoned and subsequently questioned in the privacy of the study.

ABOVE: Apollo, the god of divination, prophecy, music, and the arts, natural death, and healing. He established an oracular shrine at Delphi in Greece, the most important in the ancient world.

LEFT: Pythia, the priestess of Apollo, in a trance. She was named for the Python, a gigantic female serpent and powerful prophetess, whom Apollo had killed in order to found his own shrine.

CONSULTING APOLLO

To consult Apollo at Delphi, you would climb the heights to the sacred site, a staggeringly beautiful place. Particularly on the 7th day of *Byzious* (February-March), the sacred way would be filled with purified pilgrims. You were received into the statue-filled antechambers amid a flurry of wings, as the flocks of birds that surrounded the temple rose into the air. Hermes smiled down on you enigmatically and proclaimed: "Know thyself." The priest called out to the pure at heart to approach, and you walked down the long colonnade filled with statues and votive gifts, carrying an offering of honey-cakes and an animal sacrifice. Great doors of wood and ivory swung open and, at the bottom of the inner room, you saw the altar, bathed in light, and the entrance to the divinatory grotto beneath it.

The animal was asperged, sacrificed, and burned. Then the Pythia entered, a mysterious old woman dressed in white and crowned with laurel, Apollo's plant. Throwing grain and laurel leaves on the smoldering brazier, she descended into the grotto and took her place on the sacred tripod. As you followed the priest and the scribe into this underground cavern, you saw the huge laurel tree that grew here under the earth and the stone that marked the "navel of the world." Golden statues of Dionysus and Apollo looked down and, as the Pythia went into full trance, an exquisite aroma filled the air. The priest posed the question and the Pythia's voice rang out in answer, haunting and vibrant.

LEFT: The father of Psyche sacrifices to Apollo before consulting his oracle.

A similar practice takes place twice a year at Dharamsala, where the Tibetan government-in-exile and the Dalai Lama reside. In traditional Tibet, many laypeople were parttime mediums and healers and many monasteries had protective deities who would be periodically embodied by a monk who had devoted himself to the task. The greatest of these oracles is the Nechung State Oracle. Its medium, or *kutan*, incarnates the great protector of the people and advisor to the Dalai Lama known as *Pe Har* or *Dorje Drakden*, a pre-Buddhist demon tamed and converted by the guru Padmasambhava. The prophecies of the Nechung State Oracle have played an important part in Tibetan history. The oracle's advice is always sought on important political questions, and it prognosticates and warns about the future each year.

The present medium is a 33-year-old monk named Thubten Ngodrub who is the 14th *kutan* of the Nechung Oracle, which was established in 1642. He joined the monastery at age 14, following the lamas into exile in India after the Chinese takeover. In 1987, after the death of the previous medium, he spontaneously went into trance during a ceremony at the Nechung Oracle site. After questioning and testing, he was officially enthroned as the 14th *kutan* in 1987.

The Nechung Oracle conducts public trances twice a year, and private consultations at need. The medium, who spends his time in prayer and meditation, goes into deep, physically active trance. Wearing a costume and headdress weighing over 100 pounds, he dances, jumps, and runs through the temple at the onset. As the trance calms the medium's activity, the voice of the oracle emerges. Accompanied by twitches, strange yelps, and convulsions, it delivers political advice and practical guidance that is recorded by monastery scribes. The medium will often remain in trance long enough to bless participants, giving each a red cord of protection.

Turning the Tables

The most common image we have of the spirit-medium probably comes from the Spiritist and Theosophical movements that swept over North America and Europe in the 19th and early 20th centuries. Table-turnings, séances, and seers provided people with first-hand evidence of an after-death existence and an opportunity to talk to loved ones on the "other side." Automatic writing, where conscious control is turned over to "voices within," was used by surrealist poets to break the rigid bonds of conscious thought. At the same time that the first psychologists were investigating hypnotism, sleepwalking, clairvoyance, and hysteria, people would gather around a table, hand-in-hand, pass into a light trance and watch the table begin to move, produce noises, and apparently answer questions put to it in code.

The séance is an elaboration of this contact with the unconscious. A medium, almost always a woman with "inborn psychic gifts," would go into full trance and be inhabited by souls of the recently dead: they would appear in response to the presence and questions of their living relations or loved ones. The spirits would tell of existence on the "other side" and offer advice to the living based on their ability to see farther into the future than those still in the material world. Some mediums built an entire world of spirits and souls, with special languages, interplanetary origins, and messages for the living.

Continual spiritual evolution was a central idea in these spiritist circles. It was believed that human experience was a result of good and bad actions in past lives; that humans and spirits themselves were constantly moving toward the source of light and love in the universe, passing through a purgatorial process to reach their goal. The active compassion and insight into this process gained through spiritist practices was the tool through which you progressed on the long voyage of the soul.

RIGHT: A Western séance; holding hands is thought to concentrate whatever psychic power is generated by the group.

OPPOSITE: Monks are called to prayer in a lamasery in Qinghai, China.

Feeding the Ancestors

he shared meal, where human and spirits eat and drink together, is the most basic form of Chinese religious practice. The *Ding*, a bronze vessel that was used on high ceremonial occasions to cook the offering and thus connect the worlds, is a symbol of this meal. Such shared offerings mark the passage over the thresholds of life, such as birth, marriage, and death. In the oldest ceremonies, one person was chosen by divination to become the *Shi*, the Incorporator or Embodier of the Spirit. He would mediumistically incarnate the Ancestral Spirit at the ritual meal. The Embodier would prepare carefully through fasting, ritual, and a detailed visualization of the last departed ancestor, who was the key to the chain that linked humans to the founding spirits. At the ritual meal, he would eat and drink nine cups of a dark, fragrant millet wine, entering into a trance state through which the ancestor was visibly present. At the height of the ceremony, it was announced that "the spirits are drunk." Humans and ancestors were bound together in an ecstatic kind of love and benevolence. This old relation to the spirits is echoed in two enduring practices: communal meals at gravesites, and placing shrines and tablets on a table full of food offerings that are then eaten by family members.

ABOVE: A Taoist spirit-medium in a trance.

RIGHT: A communal meal at an ancestral gravesite.

OPPOSITE ABOVE: Food set out for the ancestors in a Confucian temple.

Mediums for the People

The public use of mediumistic divination was banned at several points in Chinese history as a threat to order and morality, but temple mediums and "wise people" who could speak for a spirit always had a great place in popular culture. The *wu*, one of the "shamans" of old China, was more a spirit-medium than a shaman. He or she could induce the spirits to dance with humans in ritual ceremonies, or could call the rain spirits to descend.

One typical mediumistic practice is the *Fu Chi*, a kind of automatic writing device. It was used to ask questions about the welfare of departed relatives in the afterworlds or to allow a spirit that is present the opportunity to speak. The use of this planchette also played an important role in private Confucian political circles in the early part of this century.

The other common form of medium was associated with a temple. Virtually every temple in old China had a medium who could answer questions on behalf of the deities who resided in the images. Even today, whenever government restrictions are lifted, these spirit-possession cults flourish. Singapore and Taiwan

offer a wide range of examples. Most of these mediums are women, and they are consulted about a wide range of problems, from marital discord to finding a lottery number. The medium, who is often under the supervision of a temple master, has cultivated a specific spirit, something like a Western witch and her familiar. When confronted with a question, the medium will go into trance and take on the voice and personality of the spirit, who will answer or advise her client.

FU CHI WRITING

The *Fu Chi* was originally a sieve or winnowing basket with a short stick attached, sign for "sifting the grain from the chaff." It was held over a bed of sand or ashes by two people, who went into light trance in order to act as mediums. It was traditionally said that the gods procure the assistance of the spirit of the men to effect communication. This reflects an old belief that the *shen*, or spirits, that confer intelligence and intensity on the mind lack a language. It is the job of humans to put a language at their disposal. As the mediums go into trance, the stick moves in circles. Then it begins writing characters at a quite rapid pace.

The communications may be banal, or of startling beauty and originality. A son who inquired about his departed mother in an ancestral temple received this answer:

> *This is a woman who lived up to her virtues;*
> *She entered the spirit world without tortures,*
> *Passed through the festival where all spirits are judged.*
> *She was honored and is bound to heaven:*
> *She has already departed for the Western Paradise.*

ABOVE: The Chinese character for peace.

"Tell my Horse..."

Africa offers what is perhaps the archetypal image of spirit possession, combining an ecstatic experience of the spirits and the desire to move the soul through the circle of its journey. Virtually all African tribal cultures recognized and valued "spirit possession" as a call, an imperative posed by an unknown force. The tribe or family mobilized their resources in aid of a possessed person, providing the means to elaborate the possession as dance or ritual. The possessed person, often someone who is troubled or marginalized, becomes a means of communication with the spirit world for the whole group. As a diviner, his insight into spirit allows him to cut through illusion and reveal the hidden workings of disease, sorcery, hatred, and greed. This response directs a community's attention to its trouble spots, and can turn that trouble into a source of insight. It is a way that the community "thinks," how it may deal with new, strange, or repressed material.

Vaudou, or voodoo, the Haitian religious form of spirit-possession, has roots in old African cultures and New World experience. It has enabled its supporters to survive long years of oppression, bringing depth, joy,

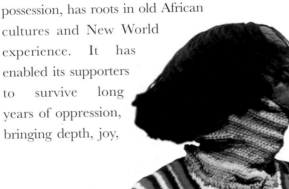

and meaning to experience. *Vaudou* is an extremely articulated practice filled with symbols and ritual practices that seeks to put its participants in direct contact with the spirits – *loas*, *mystères*, or *orisha*. The center of the practice is the *cérémonie*, a rich combination of symbols, dances, incantations, and drumming. It induces possession in a prepared initiate, who becomes the "horse" or medium of the *loa*. But the *loas* – Dambala, the rainbow snake; Erzulie Fréda Dahomey, erotic spirit of love and laughter; Legba, seducer, messenger, and god of crossroads; La Sirène, voice of the open seas; Guédé or Baron Samedi, lord of death; Ogun, iron warrior; Papa 'Zaca, peasant spirit of growing – will choose their own horses. Once chosen, a *loa* will lead a person into a life-long dialogue, instructing, guiding, and demanding attention.

The way a spirit expresses itself, its walk, voice, likes, and dislikes, are learned through the initiation process. The moment of possession or crossover, when the *loa* mounts its horse, is practically instantaneous. The person falls, passes through a curtain of convulsion or stupor supported by the attendants, and emerges as someone different, with a different voice, walk, and amazing energy. The *loa* will have messages for the medium and the congregation: "Tell my horse...," it begins.

ABOVE: A modern Voodoo altar painting showing Guédé Mazaka. This is one of the facets of Baron Samedi, the lord of death, whose attributes include a skull and a top hat.

LEFT: A Zambian dancer placates the god of fertility by dressing as a woman.

OPPOSITE: Worshipers in a trance after a ritual.

The Seeing Body

The body-medium, another characteristic African type of diviner, locates the sources of sickness or psychic conflict through the images they induce in his "seeing heart." It has many forms. In the simplest form, the diviner sits side by side with the client, holding hands, and goes into light trance. He poses a series of questions, asking who or what is causing the trouble, where it is located, and what might be done about it. When he hits on the source, both arms will slowly but irresistibly rise. Other diviners, with an established relation to an inner guide, will go into trance and "read" the client's body, producing images and voices that represent quarrels, hostile relations, or blocked points.

The Yaka body-diviner is chosen, possessed, and made sick by a spirit. Through coming to grips with his illness and isolation, his awareness of reality is profoundly changed. He is said to acquire the ability to "see behind things" and "scent" the presence of conflicts and hidden troubles. The diviner begins with an object that has been in contact with the troubled person, on the navel, heart, or left shoulder. He smells this object "like a hunting dog" to begin the process. He will take this awareness into dream. When he encounters the person or his representatives the next day, he will be watching a current of dream-images set off by the olfactory search. Listening to "the heart that sees the dreamlike images," he asks a series of questions, the answers to which set the inner images in motion. He translates their appearance and combination into a revelation of where the illness is located in the body of the client and in his relation to the "social body."

The Dedicated Medium

In Afro-American cults such as *Umbanda* and *Candoblé*, mediumistic consultation is of central importance. It is a spiritual path for the mediums and a source of advice, help, and counsel for members of a community. In these cults, which grew out of a fusion between African worship and 19th-century spiritism, mediums are dedicated to a particular spirit who visits them in dreams and in ritual. Through a process that may stretch over several years, they develop the ability to go in and out of trance gracefully and to regulate creatively their relation to their guide. The mediums go into trance in order to give their clients specific counsel. They diagnose and cure illness, locate the source of witchcraft and black magic, propose purifying and "luck-changing"

ABOVE: A sacred water ewer in the shape of a leopard, from Benin.

ABOVE CENTER: A cult head from Benin, West Africa

RIGHT: A *gulukoshi*, a divining instrument from Zaire, which is held in the diviner's lap and springs out at the mention of a wrongdoer's name.

OPPOSITE TOP: A *Candoblé* priest in full ritual robes.

OPPOSITE BOTTOM: A Zulu chanter from Durbak.

rituals, and help to solve the personal, marital, and professional problems of their community members.

Rites are performed at *centros* or *terreiros* that may serve hundreds of people. The mediums are supervised and guided through the learning process by a *mai* or *pai de santo* or *babalorixa*, a mother or father of mediums who leads the daughters and sons in the spirit. Each cult has its own ritual cosmos, and each medium is consecrated to a particular guide: an *orixa*, or African deity; a *santo*, or saint; one of the *prêtos velhos*, or souls of African ancestors; one of the *caboclos*, or Native American souls; or a *criança*, a dead child. *Exus*, trickster figures linked to the African spirit trickster *Legba* and his consort *Pomba Gira*, a sexy, devilish woman, also make periodic appearances.

The *consulta*, or consultation, is the most important ritual in these cults. It takes place in an "embodying room" in front of an altar arrayed with ranks of images. Through drumming, dancing, chant, and suggestion, the mediums go into trance. Dressed in ritual garments, they then take their place on the consultation seats, surrounded by those who seek answers to their questions.

BLOWING BAD LUCK AWAY

The *Candoblé* may prescribe rituals as well as give advice. One of the most significant is the *ponto de desarregar*, a procedure that blasts away the effects of serious misfortune. It is an unfolding of benediction, confidence, and shared spirit. The client stands within a circle drawn around him in sacred white chalk, marked with spirit signs that invoke peace and protection and activate guardian spirits. Four piles of gunpowder and a connecting circle of alcohol are placed at points representing the entrances to the person's life. When they are set off, the explosions blast away the aura of stagnant energy and awaken spirit at these key points, while the flame encloses the person in a circle of protection. He is then led through another series of spirit images, or *pontos*, in order that his relation to the fundamental powers be changed. There are prayers for protection; his body is bathed in handfuls of cascading coins; he is given a children's drink and blessed so that he will be cared for as a mother loves a child.

The Medium's Gift

For many people, the phenomenon of spirit possession is not the product of demons or mental disorder, but a gift that can unfold a world of care and contact. It is related to those times when we have the feeling "something else" is working in us, bringing moods, strange happenings, or sudden insights. Not all the "voices" in what we now call the unconscious are the great spirit-guides, but they are all worth talking to. The medium's experience is that there is a great wealth of spirit hidden there.

Another mediumistic practice was developed by people who work with Tarot images as divinatory tools. It is a sort of oracular "co-counseling," and involves taking on the character of one of the Tarot's Major Arcana, archetypal figures that articulate the persons of our soul and the spiritual process of moving through the world.

LENDING A HAND

One way to contact these voices is to allow them the use of your powers of speech, writing, and imagining, things that you usually feel are in your conscious control. When something is bothering you, when you feel the presence of an "other" hanging around you, try offering this mood or feeling your voice. Relax, breathe into the heart-space, diffuse your attention and consciously offer your voice and your attention, to whatever is floating just outside of awareness. Then wait, listen, reproduce what simply "comes in," as a voice in your ear or words forming on paper. Make no attempt to censor it. If you respond as if it were a fully independent being, a dialogue will soon develop in which you learn quite a bit about things normally hidden from your sight.

ABOVE: Image of Wagner's music made under clairvoyant influence.

RIGHT: The psychic gift comes easily to some people, but we can all test our powers by relaxing in a meditative position and simply letting images and thoughts flow through us. Just as our ears learn to adjust to a particular voice in a crowded room, so mediums learn to focus on one particular message or feeling in the vast sea of psychic information that floods them.

THE TAROT ORACLE

This practice involves two people, who may alternate roles. The inquirer will form a question, shuffle the cards, and pick one of them at random. The other person, who acts as "medium," enters the world of this card through visualizing it. If you are the medium, you concentrate on the image, then enter the frame of the card and greet the figure, visualizing the landscape from within. You then turn in imagination to face the outside world. As you make this turn, you will feel the figure enter you. There will be a distinct change in body posture, feeling, and voice. When this occurs, signal the inquirer who poses the question. Answer with the words that "fall" into your awareness. They will usually be quite surprising.

As the session ends, reverse the imagining process. Put off the spirit, turn, thank it, give and ask for a gift. Take the gift with you as you retreat over the threshold of the card and return to normal awareness and everyday existence.

ABOVE: Cards from the Major Arcana represent archetypes and can be used to help focus on a particular aspect of the unconscious mind to help solve a problem or ask a question that is bothering the conscious self.

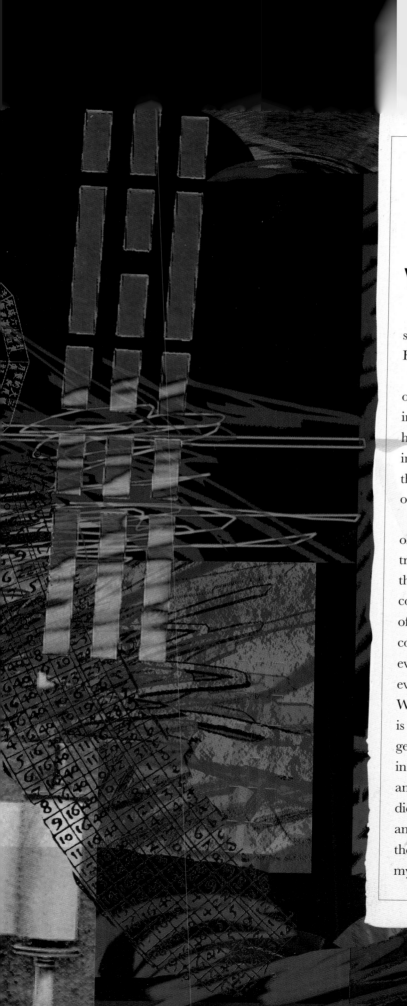

Opening the Book of Fate

What is happening? Why is it happening? What should I do? Is the way in front of me open or closed? What does this situation mean to me; what part does it play in my life? How can I choose?

These are the kinds of questions posed to the great oracle systems. They imply something that we all intuitively sense, that time – this moment, this "now" – has a shape and a meaning. Oracle systems tap this intuitive flow of meaning. They put you in touch with the spirit of the time, what the Greeks called *daimon* or fate.

Creating and using an oracle system reflects a very old and deep image of life that interweaves spiritual truths and pragmatic advice. They help people live their lives and search for happiness in a more conscious and connected way. European culture officially outlawed this type of divination, though it continued on in the shadows. Other cultures, however, evolved complex and fertile ways to see through the events of daily life to the forces moving behind them. We can see this in the *I Ching*, the *Classic of Change*, that is the basis of Chinese philosophy and magic; in geomancy and African *Ifa* divination, reading the "stars in the earth"; in the Runes that embody Scandinavian and Germanic myths; in Tibetan *Sho Mo*, or dice-divination, used to connect spiritual forces and practices to everyday events; and in Tarot, the divination system linked with the underground myths of European culture.

Archaic, Archetype, and Identity

t was C. G. Jung who remarked that every so-called civilized human, no matter how evolved his or her consciousness, remains "archaic" at the deep levels of the soul. This "archaic" level is made of myths and symbols that can move us in many directions. "Archaic" means both "old" and "originating." It is something shared, something that unites people, at the same time that it separates each of us into our personal encounter with fate. This is the paradox of the archaic imagination.

These archaic or primary parts of our imagination are often called *archetypes*. The word means a basic pattern from which impressions are taken or "struck." Archetypes are ways in which we are ready to act, inherent structures of our mind and body. These structures are at once very conservative and very adaptable, the leading edge of change. They are fields of possibility, ideas, feelings, and ways of acting all at the same time.

When an archetype appears, when it is "constellated" by a particular situation, it automatically seeks to arrange things in certain characteristic ways of thinking, feeling, and reacting. If we can *reflect* on this instinctual process, we become aware of a spiritual drive or goal behind it. This goal is something toward which we are all striving: happiness, connection, spirit, identity, a "fullness" or wholeness of being. The goal is something everyone must experience for themselves, but we all share the desire and the need continually to reimagine the quest we hold in common.

We do not know where the divination systems described in this chapter come from. They are a sample, for producing such a system reflects a basic human drive. They grew out of archaic levels of the soul, were re-formed and focused over centuries of collecting omen-lore and, at some critical moment, became independent of the cultures that gave them birth. They image a level of our being we cannot cut free of without making ourselves sick, a gift and

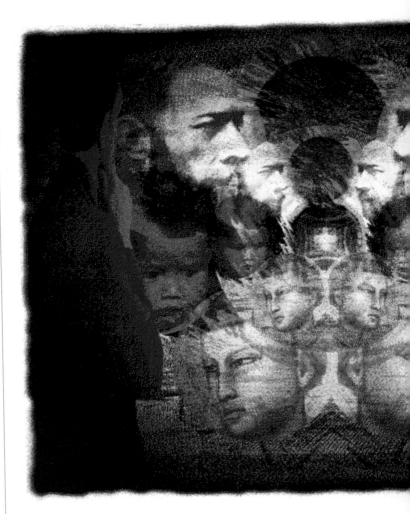

inheritance we are continually seeking to reimagine, to "dream the myth onward."

The symbols we meet with in these divination systems are at once simple and complex, "nothing but your imagination," and enormously fascinating. They are dynamic representations of actions, types, and situations that continually draw our attention. They are surrounded by a protean cluster of meanings, feelings, and ideas that can mirror our individual situation and connect it to that quest for happiness, meaning, and identity. Depth psychologists have often speculated that any collection of archetypal symbols will ultimately lead you through a process of transformation that confronts you with the unconscious

parts of yourself: the *shadow* (what you do not want to admit about yourself); the *anima* and *animus* (the part of yourself that is of the opposite sex); the *Wise Woman* and *Wise Man* (inner guides that can direct you); and the *Child* (at once young and old, an image of rebirth). The encounter with these figures occurs any time you turn to the "unconscious" for help and advice.

Whatever the process may be, divinatory systems give us a model through which we may interact with the way the world is shaping itself. The symbols in these systems are continually changing. They have the capacity to adapt to many new and different situations. They can give you the experience of connection through their fields of many meanings. They can protect you by giving signals about where potential dangers may be concealed. They present the archaic imagination as it relates to you at a particular time, in a particular situation. This lets the time move you toward the experience of meaning and connection. Altogether, they offer an image language, a way to describe the events in your life in terms of imagination, spirit, and transformation.

CENTER: According to Jung, human souls are composed of complex layers teeming with myths and symbols born of a shared archaic imagination.

TAKE A CHANCE

Very early people became aware that "chance" occurrences at critical moments can reveal the way time is moving. We can see this perception in the English word "lot": a sign that represents fate; the act of selecting something through chance; something that happens to you that is beyond your control; a symbol, type, or kind of thing.

In traditional thought, the combination of a symbol, chance, and a critical situation is a basic image of fate. You reproduce this act of picking a fate each time you cast the lots. The most common meaning for the word "oracle" is "a word given in response," both where you go to ask, and the answer you receive. Older symbols for "oracle" show how this response was originally given. They portray a stick, leaf, bone, or stone marked with a sign – a lot or token chosen by chance. By reproducing the process through which "chance" occurrences become symbols, oracle systems let you interact with fate. They introduce you to the experience of a guiding or helping spirit.

ABOVE: Leaves marked with an agreed sign were one of the earliest forms of "lots." Sticks, stones, and bones were also used to consult the ways of fate.

The Web of Time and Fate

An oracle system is a set of open-ended symbols that reproduce deep structures of the imagination. It is consulted through a chance procedure, throwing, choosing, casting, or calculating, in which your body often plays an important part as the voice of an unconscious knowing. The symbols produced by this process indicate what kind of activities, ideas, and perspectives are in harmony with the time. They involve you in a dialogue with its creative potential.

Modern quantum physics gives one model of this process. In quantum physics, events can occur only through a process called transactional interpretation, an interaction of two probability waves. One wave comes from "now," the current situation or problem. It is a range of possibilities that spreads from "now" like ripples from a stone dropped into the water. For an event to occur, this wave must be met by a responding or resonating wave that comes *from the future*. The interaction of these waves produces the probability field in which an event can occur.

Historically, there are many symbols of this perception that our life is continually being woven on a web of fate whose meaning we can perceive and influence. Poets have seen our lives as the product of great hierarchical figures playing cards, or as a child throwing dice on a checkerboard floor. Myth-makers and mystics have seen it as the Three Sisters or Three Fates weaving a fabric in which each of our lives is a thread; as the Veil of Maya, a constant dance of illusions; or as the Wheel of Fortune, an ever-moving play of happiness and suffering. Our personality has been imagined as the product of the great interlocking movements of the spheres of the planets, the continual coming together and dissolving of two primal powers, or the journey of the soul weaving its way through a forest of transformations from one form of life to another.

The basic purpose of an oracle system is to give you advice on these points of interaction and the decisions you face in life by making you aware of the imaginative possibilities. It does this by creating a symbolic language, a place where you can interact with the forces that are shaping time and fate. This interaction can bring joy, happiness, a sense of well-being, and awareness of spirit, as well as some very pragmatic help. It is a navigational aid on the mysterious voyage of life.

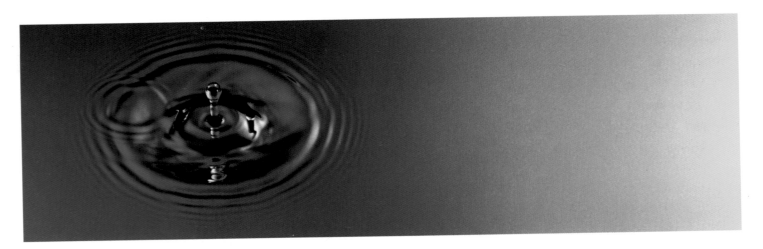

The Moment of Choice

Anything that has symbolic value may become a "lot" or token at a critical moment. This is the most archaic method of making a decision and may be used in various ways. Arrow divination, for example, relied on the symbolic power of the arrow as a "lot" connected with bird-signs, destiny, and death. It was practiced throughout the Mediterranean, the Near East, Asia, and the Americas. An arrow might be symbolically marked and shot at random; its trajectory, flight, and landing place "read" as an answer to the question that was posed by its launching. It might also represent psychic movement. Tibetan arrow-divination, or *Dah-mo*, used two arrows marked to indicate the fundamental polarity of the powers: dark and light, negative and positive, yin and yang. They were thrust into a pile of barley in front of the diviner, who concentrated his attention through breathing and mantra exercises until he went into trance. The arrows would then begin to move, and the diviner would interpret their patterns.

The connection between a symbol, a "charged object," and chance reveals how our personal identity is linked with things we might take as accidents, puns, coincidences. These things can suddenly open to an old, archaic level of meaning. A divining bowl full of these symbols was the sign for the goal of the alchemical process of the transformation of matter.

Similarly, the shrine of Preneste in Roman times offered a fate taken from life and speech, reproducing the awe of the omen. The *sortes* at Preneste were connected with an old Pelasgian cult of the goddess, "issued from the guts of earth and the gates of dream," *Fortuna Primagenia*, mother of the gods and guardian of the destinies. To obtain a reading, you made sacrifice to the goddess, obtained her favor through a nod of her image, then employed a virgin child to draw the lots for you. A single poetic line gave you an orientation. The prophetic power of these lots was passed on through a technique called the Prenestine Fortune. It used laurel-wood dice on which the letters of the alphabet were written. The dice were tossed into an urn and drawn out at random. Each letter keyed a series of possible words through which the diviner produced an oracular sentence.

In late Mediterranean culture, these old "oracles of chance" became "street oracles," a process repeated in many cultures as divinatory techniques became accessible and the "oracle books" developed. Street oracles used dice and lots to replicate very old divinatory practices. They proliferated at the expense of the major oracle centers. Similar oracles are in use today throughout the East.

A DEMOCRATIC ORACLE

In a Mediterranean street oracle, a questioner would invoke the god, throw a set of five or seven dice, and read the answer in a Book of Fate. Five threes, for example, might mean: "Zeus and Athena, now is the time! The gods will fulfill your intentions ...." An alphabetic oracle offered readings like: "You are fighting the waves, looking for a fish in the sea. Forget it, rest in peace and wait for the time to change." These oracles were available to anyone who wished to consult them, a radical spiritual democracy. They offered their user a relief from confusion, a spiritual connection, and a direct answer to practical problems, which was often lacking in more élitist philosophical practices.

ABOVE: A Tibetan Mo die of the kind used in dice divination.

OPPOSITE TOP: The wheel of fortune, one of the oldest symbols for the mutability of fate. This Tarot card is from the Visconti-Sforza deck.

OPPOSITE BOTTOM: The ripples from a stone cast in a pond, an elegant image for the possibilities and probabilities that proceed from a single event.

An Oracle of Zeus

The oracle of Zeus is an example of this way of making decisions. Zeus is the father god of the Greek pantheon, an executive and ruler who made important decisions that affected the lives of others. Though humans might analyze to the best of their ability, Greeks felt there was always more unknown than known in the choice of a chief, a champion, or an important public figure. This "unknown part," the unknown destiny to be fulfilled, was called Zeus and he spoke through the lots. Each person considered for a post would make his mark on a stone, a mark known only to him. The stones would be put into a helmet or urn and shaken until one jumped out. This marked the person chosen. Later, Athenians used this procedure to fill public offices, opening the choice to Zeus in order to evade the question of jealousy and influence.

DOUGH BALL DIVINATION

We see another example of the sacred lottery in Tibetan "dough ball" divination. This method was practiced in the monasteries when there was a particularly important decision to be made. The possible answers – for example, the names of candidates for an office – were written on slips of paper and encased in equal-size balls of dough. The balls were then put into a bowl that was sealed and placed on an altar. The deity presiding over the altar was requested to aid in making a decision. The monks fasted and prayed for three days. On the fourth day, the bowl was opened by a senior monk who rolled it until one ball spontaneously fell out. That ball indicated the answer chosen by the deity who had been invoked.

CONSULTING ZEUS

You can use this oracle when you have to choose between several alternatives and you are beset with conflicting emotions. Make a lot or symbol for each alternative, laying it out as fully and clearly as you can. Put all the lots into a container. Mix thoroughly. Think about the fact that Zeus knows all the ways the situation will unfold in the future and that he speaks through chance. Close your eyes and select one of the lots. Whether you take the advice or not, meditate carefully on why this lot was chosen.

OPPOSITE LEFT: Zeus, the king of the gods, whose powers were thought to range through every aspect of life.

LEFT: The Garden of Zeus. Buildings at Dodona, Greece, associated with the ancient site of the sanctuary and oracle of Zeus.

ABOVE: A homemade oracle for informal consultation with Zeus.

The Power of Numbers

For many ancient people, numbers were fate. The nine single whole numbers and the mathematical forms that you can build from them expressed a fundamental mystery of the cosmos. Numerological divination and "magic squares," number charms to draw and control spirit energies, are found in India, Greece, Egypt, China, and old Europe. A number gave shape to things; it "set the gods and demons in motion." If you knew your number, you knew who you were and what would be the challenges and blessings you faced in this life.

Modern numerologists use their systems to produce analyses of personality traits and behavior patterns, and describe the potential for compatibility. They can help explain why certain people may have difficulty understanding each other and point at areas of possible communication. They investigate the powers of names, fortunate numbers and dates, and their effect on identity and individual happiness.

ABOVE: The sun is the heavenly body associated with the number 1, the number of uniqueness and individuality.

RIGHT: Blue is the color associated with the number 5, the number of fecundity, sensitivity, and sensuality.

OPPOSITE TOP: The Moon is associated with the number 2, the number of intuition, emotions, and duality.

OPPOSITE BOTTOM: The Priestess from the Major Arcana of the Tarot is associated with the number 2, and Strength is associated with the number 8.

THE NINE NUMBERS

The symbolic meanings that surround the nine whole numbers are the center of numerological divination. They play a part in many other divinatory methods. They can represent stages in the unfolding and infolding of any process, and can be keyed to planets, days, colors, qualities, character types, and Tarot images. They are also keyed to letters of the alphabet, so words and names can be analyzed. Here are some of the central associations in Western tradition:

1 Unity, the divine presence; thesis; opportunity, new beginnings; will and focused consciousness, ability to use personal resources; the Sun, the Magician, Sunday, red.

CHARACTER: The Individualist; *independent, resourceful, self-reliant; clear self-identity and values; resolute, capable, ingenious; desires action, seeks new paths, takes on responsibility;* also: *intolerant, inconsiderate, stubborn, self-satisfied.*

※

2 Duality, polarity; antithesis; dilemmas, choice, ambivalence: good/bad, either/or, light/dark, joy/sorrow, love/hate, rich/poor; ability to feel and use emotions; balance, harmony, concord; balanced judgment through intuitive awareness; the Moon, the High Priestess, Monday, orange.

CHARACTER: The Silent Knower; *calm, just, giving, considerate, intuitively aware; gives things form; peacemaker; harmonious, social;* also: *irresolute, indifferent, weak, avoids responsibilities.*

※

3 Creative action; synthesis; triad: heaven-human-earth, past-present-future, thought-word-action; ability to use personal creativity, demonstrate love through creative imagination; comprehensive, dynamic, fulfilling; Mars; the Empress; Tuesday, yellow.

CHARACTER: The Maker; *free, strong, frank, forceful; capable organizer, inspires action, moves others; cheerful, flexible, creative, enthusiastic, brilliant;* also: *indifferent, impatient, lacks stamina and concentration; spectacular rise and fall; mania, mood swings.*

4 The world; completion; root of all concrete things; practice, repetition, realization of power; stable, square; ability to use practical thinking; basic form of order: four elements, directions, seasons; consolidate, complete, prepare for renewal; practical intellect, instinctual knowledge; Mercury, the Emperor, Wednesday, green.

CHARACTER: The Stabilizer; *solid, loyal, tenacious; honest, steady, capable; can undertake difficult or unpleasant tasks; deep, faithful friend; capacity for focused will and self-sacrifice; aware and accepting; creates order; also: clumsy, dull, unadaptable, conventional.*

※

5 Body, sensuality; conflict; the five senses, fingers and toes; able to learn and teach from direct experience; health, expansion, prosperity, fecundity; grounded in the world; challenges faced in learning from experience; Jupiter, the Hierophant, Thursday, blue.

CHARACTER: The Adventurer; *courageous, vivacious; passionate, responsive, quick to grasp and learn; optimistic, encouraging, sympathetic, inspiring; great traveler or explorer; also: rash, fickle, thoughtless, endlessly distracted.*

※

6 Connects above and below; reconciliation; intellectual creativity; discrimination, imagination, union, love, perfection; ability to use imagination and intellect; relatedness, taking responsibility for choices; beauty, harmony; Venus and Uranus, the Lovers, Friday, indigo.

CHARACTER: The Idealist; *seeker, strives for harmony and beauty; honest, careful, tolerant, unselfish, loving; cheerful, energetic; free of compulsive attachments to money and success; also: disconnected, unaware, hypocritical moral superiority; weak, impractical, flabby.*

※

7 Limits; manifestation in time and space; stability, endurance; ability to set limits and endure in time; complete in itself; the world's governor, good fortune; wisdom, evolution, balance, completion; Saturn, the Chariot, Saturday, violet.

CHARACTER: The Thinker; *wise, discerning; philosopher, writer, ascetic; rigorous, long-sighted; ahead of the time, thus often in conflict with the present; able to bear hardship; deep seeing, deep thinking; love of knowledge; also: morbid, misanthropic, resentful, self-righteous; unwilling or unable to share ideas.*

8 Resolves dualities; expansion, dissolution, dimension of the timeless; good and bad, right and wrong, day and night; ability to see and relate to eternal dimension; balance between forces, connects spirit and matter; developing confidence to follow a vision; breaks down barriers to transformation; reality, courage, strength, self-esteem; North Node of Moon (individual fate), strength, silver.

CHARACTER: The Boss; *practical, powerful drive to succeed; organizer, decision-maker; intensely active, seizes opportunity, takes control; wants security, success; also: unimaginative, tactless, domineering, greedy, sneering.*

※

9 Ability to see; integration; the three worlds: physical, intellectual, spiritual; last symbol before return to unity; ability to understand inborn talents and compulsions; introspection and personal integrity; unity, truth, perfection, concord; dissolves ego-attachments; challenges faced in looking for your own wisdom; South Node of Moon (karma, residue of past lives), the Hermit, gold.

CHARACTER: The Artist or Seer; *intelligence, understanding, brilliance, artistry, intellect; good advisor, high moral sense; also: disconnected, dreamy, lethargic, unable to concentrate.*

What's Your Number?

Birth date, Psychic Number, and Fate Number

Numerology can also give a deeper sense of how your personality and fate are working together, and where your problems and challenges may lie. Most of these practices start from your birth date and name. Here is one way to find out what number or numbers you are.

Your birth date gives you a psychic or soul number and a fate or destiny number. The psychic number shows the way you see and imagine yourself, your "self-image." The fate number shows what fate has in store for you. The contrast between these two can be very interesting.

Your soul number or self-image comes from your day of birth. Reduce the day of the month to a single whole number by adding the digits together. If you were born on October 24, 1960, your soul number is 2+4=6.

Your fate number is the single whole number obtained when you add day, month, and year together. For October 24, 1960 it is: 2+4+10+1+9+6+0=32=3+2=5. Here, you see yourself as a 6, an idealist striving for beauty and harmony, while fate has 5 in store for you: learning through the body, adventure, passion, and change.

The personal number comes from your first or personal name. This is calculated by assigning numbers to the letters of the alphabet, as shown in the box, right. Martina Sasse's personal number would be 4+1+9+2+9+5+1 =31=3+1=4. Her name number, which comes from both numbers, would be 4+1+9+2+9+5+1+1+1+1+1+5=40= 4+0=4.

By adding the fate number and the name number together, you get yet another overall character index, the number to which you respond as a whole, your deeper goal or affinity. Martina Sasse's goal or affinity number would be 5+4=9.

NAME AND NUMBER

Your name provides two other numbers: a personal number showing how you relate to others, and a personality number indicating how you tend to act and react in general. For this, convert your name to numbers through the following table:

1	2	3	4	5	6	7	8	9
A	B	C	D	E	F	G	H	I
J	K	L	M	N	O	P	Q	R
S	T	U	V	W	X	Y	Z	

DEEPER MEANINGS

To see more deeply into the dynamics behind the personality number, note the number of times each whole number occurs in the separate digits that add to make the name number. This will identify areas of major concern and strength, areas of lower awareness, and hidden areas, where a number is not represented. The hidden powers will draw energy from surrounding numbers, tend to express themselves in wild or compulsive fashion, or indicate a lack of awareness. They are keys to inner work and challenge, a kind of karmic goal. Tally the numbers in your name, note the strong and weak points, and try to see how they manifest in your life. Make a phrase for each, starting with either "I have at my disposal..." or "I need to develop..."

1 will/ability to use personal resources and assert identity.

2 connection to emotions.

3 ability to take creative personal action.

4 practical thinking, ability to proceed step by step toward a goal.

5 body sense, ability to learn through experience.

6 abstract thinking, intellectual processes, imagination; ability to follow an ideal.

7 sense of limits, ability to set limits and endure in time.

8 spirit, ability to see and participate in spiritual values.

9 karma, ability to recognize inborn talents and compulsions.

CALCULATING YOUR NUMBERS

This example shows how to calculate the various numbers for Martina Sasse, born October 24, 1960.

$$2+4=6$$

Your *soul number* is calculated by reducing the
day of birth to a single digit; in this case 24 yields the number 6.

$$2+4+10+1+9+6+0=32$$
$$3+2=5$$

Your *fate number* is calculated by adding all the digits of the birth date
(day, month, and year) together and reducing the result to a single digit.

$$4+1+9+2+9+5+1=31$$
$$3+1=4$$

Your *personal number* is calculated by adding the alphabetical code
numbers of the letters of your first name and reducing the result to a single digit.

$$4+1+9+2+9+5+1+1+1+1+$$
$$1+5=40$$
$$4+0=4$$

Your *name number* is calculated by adding your *personal*
number to the sum achieved by adding up the alphabetical codes
of the letters of your second name and reducing the final sum to a single digit.

$$5+4=9$$

Your *goal number* is achieved by adding your
name number to your *fate number* and reducing the sum to a single digit.

Gematria and Magic Squares

There are many other ways to use numbers. Chinese diviners calculate the favorable and unfavorable aspects of a venture or a relation by analyzing the number of strokes in the characters that make up its name. Magic squares, in which the numbers add up to the same total in any direction, were considered to be talismans that could attract and focus the energy of specific gods. *The Sphere of Demetrius* was a late antiquity and medieval way to predict if a sick person would recover. It had two groups of numbers, one above and one below the center line of a square. You would take the number of the day in the moon-cycle on which a person fell ill, add the numerical value of his name, and divide by thirty. If the resulting number occurred in the top half of the square, the person would recover; if in the bottom half, prospects were not good. Similar squares with a series of letters were set up to answer questions with a group of encoded phrases. You would frame the question, put your finger at random on a letter, then write it and every eighth following letter down to receive an answer.

ABOVE: The Chinese characters for "Chinese medicine."

ABOVE RIGHT: Magic squares were used to predict whether a person who was sick would recover or not.

RIGHT: A magic letter square, consulted by means of a special code.

OPPOSITE TOP: A magic number square; the figures add up to 15 in all directions.

OPPOSITE CENTER: The relationship between numbers and letters was considered to reflect the structure and interdependence of the cosmos.

Letters and Numbers

Gematria was a highly developed occult science in late antiquity. It assigns number values from 1 to 800 to the letters of both Greek and Hebrew alphabets. These alphabets were seen as an expression of the sacred structure of the cosmos. Any word that has the same number value is in the same "series" and shares a spiritual identity. Thus "Christ" the Savior; "Pan," god of the "all" who links humans and animals; and the infamous "Beast of Revelations" (with the number 666) all have series of things interconnected to them through number.

By finding the number of your name, and identifying which gods and heroes have the same number, you could see to whom you were related. The numerical equivalents open the hidden connections between things and allow you to ascend in contemplation toward the sources of spirit. The use of number connections induces a contemplative or imaginative state that not only sees hidden connections but, makes awareness fast and fluid, disconnecting it from specific concrete things. This geomatric numerology was particularly developed in relation to the Hebrew alphabet and the mystical and magical practices known as *Cabala*.

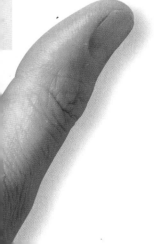

Writing on the Earth

eomancy is one of the fundamental Western divinatory systems. The word comes from *gaia-manteia*, literally, "earth-seeing." It is used to describe two different divinatory methods, one oracular and one locational.

Wind and Water

Locational geomancy or *geo-location* is concerned with finding the best sites for human constructions. The best example of this kind of divination is the Chinese system called *feng shui* or "wind-water." It relies on an elaborate universal compass, the *Lo P'an*, and a series of ideal landscape forms to determine the optimum flow of *ch'i* or positive energy for any particular construction. The ideal is to produce an environment that brings peace of mind, happiness, health, and prosperity.

Good *feng shui* relies on the relation of the building site to "dragon lines" of energy that move over the earth, and to the free flow of *ch'i* energy within the building. *Ch'i* naturally flows in curving lines, like water. It should flow through an entire building effortlessly. If it is confined, it stifles and stagnates. If it is drawn away, the energy of the people in the building goes with it.

The geomancer may propose a site in an optimum relation to hills, open spaces, and running water. He will then read

the site using his compass, which includes lucky and unlucky directions, times, days, qualities (the Five Transformative Processes), and celestial constellations. The square base is aligned with the shape of the building, and the movable compass adjusted so its needle faces south. The diviner then reads the favorable times, directions, and qualities for the building, including where to place entrances and exits. Within the building he will adjust the flow of *ch'i* by insuring it has a free path. He may place mirrors decorated with the eight trigrams of the *I Ching* to help direct the flow. He will above all seek to break up straight lines that draw *sha*, a negative energy that can produce accidents, illness, and a bad atmosphere.

This practice, in which buildings are adjusted to coincide with an idea of sacred space, has parallels worldwide. Early European geo-diviners would "see" psychic patterns or "earth lights" produced by electromagnetic and geothermal configurations in order to site temples and cities. These geo-locators would then unfold their ideal pattern of "sacred space" through a ceremony called "killing the dragon," driving a central stake into the ground to symbolically fix the flux of underworld forces.

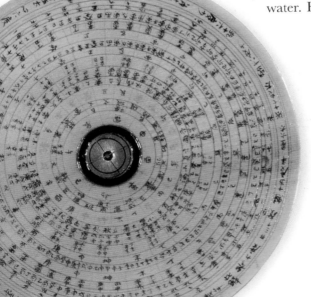

The Earth Oracle

Oracular geomancy is quite different. This system relies on 16 signs that were originally produced by making and counting random marks made in the earth or sand. Though its precise origins are uncertain, geomancy grew out of the same "Alexandrian atmosphere" that gave birth to alchemy, individual astrological charts, hermetic magic, and "the occult image of man." According to late antique sources, the presiding genius of this system is Hermes Trismegistus ("Thrice-Greatest Hermes"), mysterious father of all things erudite and magical.

The first concrete evidence of the system emerges about 800 C.E., in the Arabic "sand-science" called *ilm al-raml*. It was carried into North Africa by the Islamic wars of conquest, to be completely re-invented in Nigeria as *Ifa* or *Fon* divination and in Madagascar as *Sikidy* or *Vintana*. At the same time, like many other "pagan" practices, it was reintroduced into Europe through translations from Arabic between about 900 and 1100 C.E., where it became a popular part of the underground divinatory tradition. It was, in the poet Dante's view, a false image of truth and its practitioners were assigned to deep circles of hell. Along with alchemy and hermetic magic, it formed part of an outlawed complex of practices associated with intellectual paganism: bird-signs, animal oracles, lots, dream-divination, moon-magic, attention to random words and sounds. In the 16th century, primarily through magicians and alchemists such as Cornelius Agrippa, it was associated with astrology and the chart of the houses. It became a way to manipulate astrological images and enabled magicians to make an "instant horoscope" of an event without recourse to either books or calculations.

Geomancy was carried into the Americas primarily in its African form, *Ifa* or *Fon*, by slaves. It was associated with spirit possession cults and the determination of a person's "head" or in-dwelling spirit. It remains a vital force today throughout Black America.

The system was magically reinterpreted as a form of "earth" divination by the Order of the Golden Dawn in the late 19th century. At the same time a shortened version enjoyed widespread popular use throughout Europe as *Napoleon's Book of Fate*.

OPPOSITE BOTTOM: The *Lo Pan*, or Chinese geomantic compass.

OPPOSITE TOP: A Doric temple in Segusta, Sicily; the propitious orientating and siting of temples was the responsibility of the geo-diviner.

ABOVE: Heinrich Cornelius Agrippa von Nettenheim (1486–1535).

RIGHT: Dogon geomancers from Mali study the earth for signs left by the Pale Fox, the divinatory animal of their system.

The Geomantic Signs

Geomancy relies on 16 basic signs that have names, meanings, and a wide range of associations. These signs are often used by ritual magicians to produce *sigils*, offensive charms that reach out to grasp the quality invoked, and *amulets*, charms that protect against that specific quality.

ABOVE: A metaphorical image for the alchemical process of the transformation of matter. Geomantic signs have a strong affinity with alchemy.

THE SIXTEEN SIGNS

This is the European and Mediterranean version of the signs, grouped in pairs.

POPULUS: *The People and their Assembly*; society, crowd, union or reunion; a city, a judge, an assembly of notables; democracy, abundance; amass, gather up, without visible order; all kinds of news; speaking, rumors, gossip; the spirits of the dead. Populus can be positive or negative, depending on the question and what surrounds it.

VIA: *The Way and the Wanderer*; path, street, highway, journey, direction; ways and means; solitude, dispersion, nomads; news from outside; river, route; leave, wander; a guide, language; a hearse; sign of good trips, successful voyages; good for solitary people. Via can be positive or negative depending on the question and what surrounds it.

CARCER: *The Prison*; cell, confinement, servitude, binding, delay; public punishment, exercise of authority; despair, melancholy, egotism, lies, diabolical possession; *also*: boundary, resistance; shut in, conserve, protect; good for vagabonds, protects secrets. It is connected with the alchemical operation called the *nigredo*, or blackening. Carcer can be negative or positive depending on the question and the position of the inquirer.

CONJUNCTIO: *Union and Marriage*; connection, recovery, gathering, reunion; contracts and public recognition; hope, renewal of hope; teaching, protection, participation, sympathy; encounter and join; an obstacle is destroyed; friendship, love; weights and measures. It is connected to the alchemical operation called *conjunctio*, the marriage of the opposites. Conjunctio is a positive sign that brings friendship and connection.

FORTUNA MAJOR: *The Great Fortune*; victory, good luck, success, safety and security; recognition, entrance, glory, health, happiness; union, defeat of enemies, accomplishment; fertility, return, loyalty; light and fire. It is associated with the alchemical operation called *multiplicatio*, spreading the products of transformation. Fortuna Major is the most positive sign.

FORTUNA MINOR: *The Lesser Fortune*; success and good fortune to a lesser degree; assistance from others, protection from harm; success for the wanderer and the individual; voyages, dispersion. Fortuna Minor is a positive sign, especially for solitary endeavor.

※

ACQUISITO: *Acquiring*; gain, profit, financial success through property, investment, and investigation; great benefits, riches, rise to power; a closed grip, take, gain, grasp, seize, protect; a successful group; healing wounds, lightness of spirit. Acquisito is a very positive sign.

AMISSO: *Losing*; take away, lose, fail; illness, loss of force, theft, financial problems, deception in love; a superior external force, a stranger, dispersion; the opening hand, let fall, let go; tears, heaviness, earth; dilapidated; *also:* escape, liberty for prisoners. Amisso is a negative sign unless you are a captive, in which case it can signal escape.

※

LAETITIA: *Joy*; delight, gladness, beauty, grace, release, laughter; balance, health; peace, concord, generosity, liberation; goods, acquisition; bond, connection; a king, a bearded man. Laetitia is a very positive sign, particularly for marriage and foundations.

TRISTITIA: *Sadness*; misery, mourning, humiliation, decrease, poverty, anguish; melancholy, death, shadows, obscurity; inflexible, stubborn, fixed; good sign for pregnancy. Tristitia is a very negative sign unless it relates to a question of pregnancy.

ALBUS: *The White One*; beauty, illumination, wisdom, clear thinking, fairness; profit, positive for business and entering into a matter; judicious, careful; pure, calm, slow, peaceful; spiritual elevation. It is related to the alchemical operation called the *albedo*, or whitening, of the imagination. Albus is a definitely positive sign.

RUBEUS: *The Red One*; Attention! Stop! passion, vice, destructive temper, violent outbreak; anger, rage, power, violence; war, blood, fire, capture, kill; excite, stimulate, turn upside down. It is related to alchemical sulfur, raw emotion and compulsion. Rubeus is a negative sign telling you to stop what you are doing.

※

PUELLA: *The Girl*; daughter, wife, nurse; a girl given in marriage; pure, clean, pleasant, graceful, soft, kind; love affairs, good for purchases; *also:* deception, rotten inside, false appearances. Puella is a positive sign with a warning of possible deception or hypocrisy.

PUER: *The Boy*; son, servant, employee, young man; the inquirer; rash, inconsiderate, aggressive, combative; a man asking for something, an unknown enemy; danger. Puer is a negative sign unless it relates to romantic love or combat.

※

CAPUT DRACONIS: *The Dragon's Head*; fate, entry, the upperworld, the heavens; marry into a group, cross the threshold; interiorization, depth, mystic development of the soul; something that comes to you. Caput Draconis is a positive sign.

CAUDA DRACONIS: *The Dragon's Tail*; karma, the way out, the underworld; calamity, fraud, illusion, danger, bad magic; exteriorization, something that leaves you. Cauda Draconis is a negative sign that advises you to change direction.

Questioning the Oracle

 hen elaborated by ritual magicians, geomantic divination can be quite complicated. The basic system, however, is straightforward and amazingly effective. Use geomancy primarily for pragmatic questions that reflect the quality of earth, stabilizing and practical affairs.

First, make the question clear. For example: "Will this enterprise be successful?" Focus yourself and clear a psychic space. The most traditional method of obtaining an answer is to make marks with a wooden rod in a box of earth or sand. The more modern alternative is making marks on a piece of paper.

The signs are produced by making 16 horizontal lines of random marks, then counting the marks to determine if the total in each line is even or odd. An even number produces two dots; an odd number produces one dot. Each four of these sets of marks produces a geomantic figure. These four geomantic figures are then manipulated to produce a reading.

Take a sheet of paper and divide it into 16 horizontal rows. Make a random number of marks in each row. Do not count while you are doing it. When you are finished, count the number of marks in each row. If the number is even, make two dots side by side. If odd, make one dot. Each group of four dots makes a figure. In all, you will have four original figures or *Mothers*. Note them from right to left.

Then make the *Daughters* from the Mothers. The first Daughter is made from the top lines of the four Mothers. The second Daughter is made from the second lines of the four Mothers in the same way. The third Daughter is made from the third lines, and the fourth Daughter from the fourth lines. Enter these figures below the row of Mothers, again from right to left.

Begin by drawing up 16 horizontal parallel rows of marks or dots on a piece of paper.

Do not think about the number of marks you make across the line; the number should be completely random.

When you have finished, count up the number of marks in each row and note the figure.

When you have done all the additions, translate the figures into a code; one dot for an odd number, two for an even number.

When you have coded the figures from your rows, you can interpret the code, using each four of the 16 sets of marks.

Mothers

4	3	2	1

Caput Draconis Albus Amisso Via

Daughters

8	7	6	5

Carcer Puella Carcer Fortuna Minor

Nephews

4	3	2	1

Albus Acquisito Acquisito Caput Draconis

Witnesses

2	1

Caput Draconis Albus

Judge

Acquisito

Now produce the *Nephews* from the Mothers and Daughters. The first Nephew is made by adding the corresponding points from the first two Mothers. If the total is odd, make one point; if even, make two points. The second Nephew is made in the same way from the third and fourth Mothers. The third Nephew is made from the first two Daughters, the fourth Nephew from the last two Daughters. Enter these figures on the next line, beneath the Mothers and Daughters.

This is the geomantic Household, four Mothers, four Daughters, and four Nephews. If you were doing astrological geomancy, these figures would be entered into the houses of the chart, through a variety of methods. Now we are ready to determine the outcome.

Combine each set of Nephews in the same way you combined the Mothers and Daughters. This will produce the two *Witnesses*. Then combine the two witnesses to produce the *Judge*. The Judge gives you the outcome, the answer to your question, modified and influenced by the two witnesses, particularly if it is a neutral sign. If the result is doubtful or unclear, you can generate a *Reconciler* by adding the Judge to the first Mother. This will give a further perspective on the outcome. Do this only if the final result is not clear.

In the case of our example, the enterprise in question stands a very good chance of success. The Judge, Acquisito, is the sign of profit, gain, and great expansion. It is witnessed by Caput Draconis as the place of entry to upperworlds, and by Albus, clarity and insight.

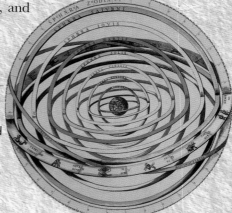

LEFT: A simple geomantic oracle.

RIGHT: Astrological geomancy is based on the Ptolomaic worldview, with the Earth as the center of the universe.

Feed Your Head: Ifa Divination

*If*a divination represents another of the major variants of geomancy. It is an oracular system of belief and worship at the center of traditional Yoruba culture in what is now Nigeria. *Ifa* is an extremely sophisticated imaginative and spiritual practice that remains a vital part of life in Nigeria, Benin, and Togo. It traveled to the Americas, becoming an integral part of many of the new Creole religious practices. A variant called *Dilogun*, which counts groups of cowrie shells to produce the symbols, plays an important part in the religious and magical practice called *Santeria*. *Ifa* diviners and priests, called *Babalawo*, or "Father of Secrets," practice throughout the Caribbean, Brazil, and Bahia, and Black North America.

Ifa is an oral system, though some of its material has been recorded. It uses the geomantic signs to organize and key a vast and continually evolving range of stories, myths, and ritual actions. In *Ifa*, these signs are called *Odu*, a word that means both goddess and container.

ABOVE: A Yoruba ritual figure known as an *Ibeji*.

THE MAJOR ODU

The 16 major signs in particular are thought of as spirits with an independent existence and will. In *Ifa* the geomantic signs are doubled. When the 16 major signs are mixed and recombined they produce 240 minor variations, for a total of 256 *Odu*. Each of these *Odu*, major and minor, is the center of a circle of myths, stories, and ritual actions. It is a "book" in the memory library of the culture, housed in the imagination of the *Babalawo*.

Here are the 16 major signs, or Odu, *ranked in their usual hierarchical order:*

1 EJIOGBE

2 OYEKU MEJI

3 IWORI MEJI

4 ODI MEJI

5 IROSUN MEJI

6 OWONRIN MEJI

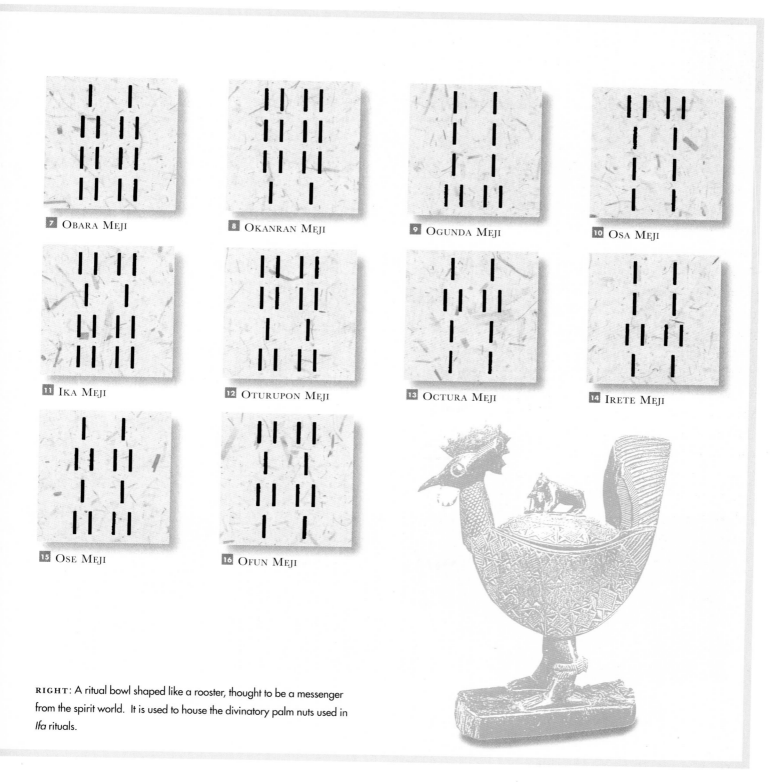

7 OBARA MEJI

8 OKANRAN MEJI

9 OGUNDA MEJI

10 OSA MEJI

11 IKA MEJI

12 OTURUPON MEJI

13 OCTURA MEJI

14 IRETE MEJI

15 OSE MEJI

16 OFUN MEJI

RIGHT: A ritual bowl shaped like a rooster, thought to be a messenger from the spirit world. It is used to house the divinatory palm nuts used in *Ifa* rituals.

Opening the Space

Ifa is a way of connection. It does not tell the future, but seeks to dissolve resistances in the present between the individual's inner self, social being, and the spirit world. One of the central ideas of this divinatory way is that each person chooses a "head," an inner personality and a potential path in life, as they come into the world.

Consulting *Ifa* teaches you to recognize and "feed" your head rather than fighting against it. By observing ritual obligations and sacrifices and "telling yourself" into the stories the oracle proposes, you dissolve obstacles blocking the flow of spirit between your head, your place in the world, and the realm of the spirits.

Ifa myth says that this way of divining originated in a time of trouble and disorder, a rupture between generations. *Orunmila*, the active "fathering" spirit, fought with his son and withdrew from the world into the heavens. This produced chaos on earth. People lost *ela*, the spirit that preserves and cares. In response to their appeals, *Orunmila* sent the *Odu*, the signs, to make a new order. The key to this order is *Elegba*, the Trickster and messenger. He connects the *Odu* with people's lives through creating difficulties, and he carries their offerings and sacrifices to the ancestors and gods.

Ifa divination is the property of its diviners, who spend their lives learning its stories. It is surrounded by ritual practices and special objects. The diviner will use either 16 consecrated palm nuts or a divining chain made of eight seed halves to produce the figures. In front of him will be a wood divining tray, bordered by carved images of *Elegba* and the serpentine path of life. He will mark the figure obtained in wood dust sprinkled on its surface. He uses an ornately carved wand to tap the tray and open the ritual space. Other carved and covered bowls hold the paraphernalia and a set of small objects, including a bone and a pair of cowrie shells that are used to pose specific questions that clarify the basic reading.

Initially the inquirer presents his problem to the system, not the diviner. He whispers the question to a shell or coin and places it on the divining tray. The diviner taps the tray with his wand and invokes the *Odu*, then uses either the palm nuts or the divining chain to produce a figure. This

CONNECTING WITH THE ODU

  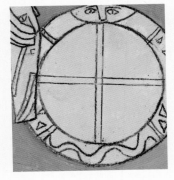 

The Ifa diviner with his divinatory tray, wand, wood dust, and sacred palm nuts.

The tray is sprinkled with wood dust and a cross drawn, from top to bottom and right to left.

The diviner taps the tray gently with his wand as he recites invocations to the Odu.

Water is sprinkled over the 16 palm nuts and they are picked out of their container one at a time.

figure is the frame or setting for the problem, a window open to the forces that are creating it.

The diviner will then praise the particular *Odu* that has been created and begin to recite the stories associated with it. Each story is about someone – a person, god, animal, tree, tool – who consulted *Ifa* and received this answer. The inquirer recognizes himself in one of these stories and reveals his situation to the diviner. The diviner will then ask a series of more specific questions about the connections to the inquirer's life, using the divining chain and the series of small objects to produce answers. Through this procedure, the story becomes a specific road the inquirer can follow, and a mirror for deeper implications. He will be given specific ritual actions and sacrifices to carry out and will receive a herbal medicine connected with the *Odu* he has received. These instructions and remedies work over a period of time to change the way he sees the situation and activate the help of the spirits involved.

LEFT: A Nigerian witch doctor wearing magic stones as a necklace.

Holding the palm nuts in his left hand, the diviner presses one against the inquirer's forehead.

With both hands clasped, he touches the cardinal points on the tray, then smooths the wood dust.

With his right hand he takes as many nuts as he can from his left hand. If none remain he starts again.

If there is one nut left he makes a double mark; if two, a single mark. The process is repeated seven times.

The Classic of Change

The *I Ching* or *Chou I*, the Chinese *Classic of Change*, is the oldest continually used divination system in the world; the classic example of what we call wisdom divination. Its three-thousand-year-old roots connect it with shamanistic practices, while its symbols are the origin of philosophical thought. It is a cosmology, a cultural institution, and the core of a traditional science. It has had a seminal influence on the development of Western ideas of synchronicity and the structure of the imagination. All these are directly connected to its use as a tool for personal guidance and transformation.

The *I Ching* is composed of 64 basic symbols, usually called hexagrams. These symbols open a universe that ranges from popular magical practices to the most abstruse philosophical speculations. Divining with these symbols gave birth to the fundamental ideas of Eastern thought: the *tao* or "way," the flow, harmony, and source of things that is at once universal and individual; *yin* and *yang*, two primal forces of shadow and light, receiving and initiating, giving form and providing inspiration; seeing the world as a never-ending series or dance of interlocking processes; and the ideal of the *chün t'zu*, the person who uses divination to live his life in accord with the way.

This version of the great Book of Fate has two basic premises. The first is that the book itself, by virtue of the way it is made, the symbolic elements it contains and the way it is consulted, directly participates in the "ongoing process of the real." It is a double of the *tao* or "way" in action. The second premise is that we experience the "way" not through bliss, stasis, or eternal order, but through change. Change is the interplay of chaos and order, a continual return to the fertile beginning of things.

From a human perspective, it has a purpose, the creation of a certain kind of awareness called *shen ming*, bright spirit, or the light of the gods. This is a continual dance between chaos and order, the experience of which we call meaning. It indicates that you have become a conscious participant in the "ongoing process of the real."

For at least 2,500 years, people throughout Asia, Japan, and Southeast Asia, and more recently, Europe and America, have turned to divination with the symbols of the *I Ching* as a source of practical and spiritual guidance. Old Chinese shamans, nobles seeking the "mandate of Heaven," scholars and philosophers searching for a way to understand how people interact with the world, bureaucrats navigating the dangerous seas of imperial preferment, ordinary people seeking a meaning and a creative strategy to deal with the difficulties they face in life have found in it access to the "way," the hidden heart of things and the guidance of heaven.

ABOVE: An ancient Chinese coin marked with the eight trigrams of the *I Ching*. Coins such as this can be used to consult the classic Oracle of Change.

ABOVE CENTER: A glazed pottery *Lohan* from Chili province, China. A *Lohan* is a Buddhist monk who has attained *nirvana* or enlightenment.

OPPOSITE: A splendid dragon, a powerful and positive symbol in the Chinese tradition. Auspicious energy, or *ch'i*, is known as *Sheng Ch'i*, or "dragon's cosmic breath."

Just Call Me Trouble

The *I Ching* is a collection of 64 divinatory figures, or *gua*, along with suggestions about how to use and think about them. The word *gua* literally means a "pile" of lines, words, possibilities, and perspectives. Each "pile," somewhat in the manner of a collage, gives you the picture of a *shi*, an archetypal moment of time, and *tao*. The *gua* or hexagrams consist of a six-line figure, made up of two elemental three-line figures, and a collection of different texts, whose words define a special oracular language. These divinatory figures act like a mirror for the unconscious forces that move and change things, forces that are shaping any particular situation. In traditional language, the *I* "provides symbols" that "comprehend the light of the gods." When you ask it a question, it produces an answer that "reaches the depths, grasps the seeds, and penetrates the wills of all beings under heaven."

I Ching means "*Classic of I*." This is an honorific title given to the book in the Han Dynasty, when it, along with four other ancient collections of texts, was officially recognized as a canonical book. It is more frequently called *Chou I* or "*Changes of Chou*," the dynasty in which it was first assembled, or simply "The *I*."

The key to the book and the "way" it represents is the cluster of meanings that surround the word "*I*." This word is usually translated as "change" or "changes." The book's symbols incorporate the systems of regular change, such as the change from day to night or the alternation of the seasons, as well as the change of form that occurs, for example, when ice changes to water or a caterpillar to a butterfly.

The word "*I*" means something different. It indicates a particular kind of change, when something unexpected or out of the ordinary occurs. The earliest recorded uses of this word refer to sudden disastrous storms or unpredictable political changes. One old version of the character portrays a lizard or chameleon; another portrays the sun and a negative sign that also means moon. It was also used to mean "give a gift to someone" or "barter or exchange one thing for another."

I is both trouble and the answer to trouble. It makes you aware of what is moving in the moonlit world of the soul. This is a gift to humans. Through it you can move and change, quickly and fluidly. You do not have to get stuck in your problems. *I* connects you with the creative imagination that lies behind these states of change. It keeps you in touch with the "way."

ABOVE: The Chinese characters representing the *I Ching*, or *Classic of Change*.

LEFT: The spiritual cosmos of Taoism, with the 8 core trigrams in the center encircled by the 12 animals of the Chinese zodiac.

OPPOSITE: Consulting the *I Ching* in the traditional way, with yarrow stalks and a copy of the book. Yarrow stalks are seen below.

History and Soul

Like other divinatory ways, the origins of "*I*" divination are rooted in an archaic level of the imagination. It undoubtedly began as a way to speak with the *shen*, or spirits, natural and ancestral, in order to know what they wanted. Its symbols helped you attract or become the vehicle of a *shen*.

At the edge of recorded history in China, a collection of these symbols emerged as a major strategic tool in a political struggle to "renew the time," to connect human institutions with the power of heaven. This struggle between the last tyrants of the Shang dynasty and the heroic founders of the Chou dynasty became a major Chinese myth. As the Chou institutions fell apart in their turn, something very important happened. The oracle became a way for individuals to navigate social and spiritual chaos.

With the reestablishment of order and the emergence of China's first imperial state about 200 B.C.E., the collection of material previously known as the *Chou I* became a *Ching* or "Classic." It was used to organize a vast range of magical and cosmological material. It also acquired a set of philosophical commentaries that sought to fix the moral meaning of the symbols. The culmination of this moral commentary occurred in the Sung Dynasty (c. 1200 C.E.). The oracle unites both of these levels. It is the property of intellectual and street corner diviner alike. It proposes individual transformation as the only hope for political and moral change.

In the first part of the 20th century, the *I Ching* entered Western culture. Though there had been previous translations, Richard Wilhelm, a Protestant missionary who had worked and studied in China for many years, was the first to translate the book as a "living document" rather than a historical curiosity. His German translation was published in 1924 at Jena. Though it sold very few copies, it attracted the enthusiastic attention of the depth psychologist C.G. Jung, who immediately recognized its importance. Jung set one of his associates, Cary Baynes, to work on an English translation, which was published along with his Foreword in 1952. With Jung's insights acting as an entrance, the Wilhelm/Baynes translation sold several million copies and has been retranslated into over 40 Western languages. Divination with the *I Ching* has become part of the Western "wisdom" tradition.

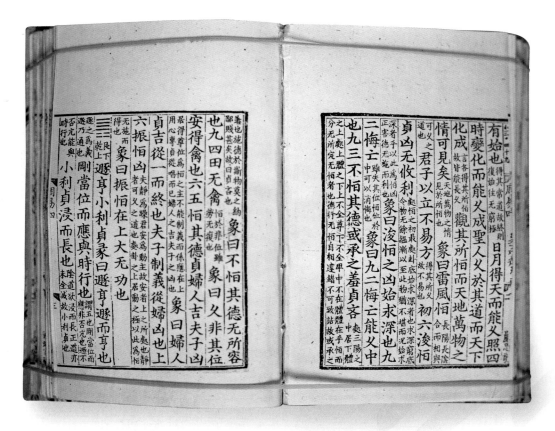

These different historical layers are reflected in the book itself, like levels in the imagination. The oldest parts go back to an oral, shamanistic tradition that first began to be recorded about 1500 B.C.E. This layer is made up of groups of short phrases called *t'uan*, or "heads," that describe a spirit of the time – Augmenting, Diminishing, Sprouting, Returning – and associate it with key actions. They are full of divinatory formulas that indicate what leads to or away from connection with this spirit. The oldest layer also includes the *yao*, or "line texts." These are short oracular phrases that describe specific variations on the basic theme.

These phrases are connected by two kinds of lines, *whole* or *opened*, that are either *stable* or *transforming* into their opposites. These four possibilities translate as "the way is open (or opening)" and "the way is closed (or closing)." We can imagine these words and lines as a pool of divinatory images, floating on the borderline between oral and written; emblematic signs that keyed sets of songs, chants, and magical practices.

Somewhere around 1100 B.C.E. there occurred a revolution equivalent to the modern production of a third-generation computer. Someone, and there are several versions of the legend, used the lines and the numbers to put all the texts together. He piled the lines on top of one another and connected each figure with a "head." He invented or organized a way to produce the numbers that keyed the lines by counting sticks rather than cracking bones, going into trance, or watching birds. Here, for the first time, divination was "easy" – another meaning of the word "*I*." The oracle became portable and acquired a complex visual component, the "pile" of six lines. Individuals could use it whenever they wanted, without the help of an intermediary diviner or priest.

The clarification of the oracle, the selection of heads and lines, and the ordering of the six-line piles was complete by about 750 B.C.E., when the world began to fall apart again. From about 500 to 200 B.C.E. (the Warring States Period), China went through an "axial age" that combined social chaos and violence with great imaginative fertility. The basic texts of Chinese culture were created in this period, among them a series of interpretations and instructions on the personal use of the *I*. This is the next layer of the text. It takes for granted that the hexagrams exist and that they are in a particular order. It contrasts, compares, and analyzes the central features of the older texts from several different perspectives, all of which are more logical, analytical, and individually oriented than the original. It begins to analyze the six-line figures in terms of the tension between two three-line figures or trigrams, one of which represents the "inner world" and the other the "outer world." In this discontinuity we see the gradual emergence of the individual.

The Han Dynasty restored order to a violent and chaotic world. Part of this restoration was the establishment of the *Ching* or Classics, texts they felt embodied ancient wisdom from a golden age "before the fall." The first classic they established was the *Classic of I*,* collecting and transcribing a series of oral traditions and assembling them into a coherent work. The text they established in 200 B.C.E. is virtually identical to the text we have today. It was reproduced in a series of "classic" or imperially sanctioned versions, the last of which was the *Kang Hsi*, or Palace Edition, of 1715.

OPPOSITE BOTTOM: Consulting the *I Ching* with yarrow stalks; other forms of consultation include bamboo twigs, coins, marbles, or colored stones.

OPPOSITE TOP: An open page from the 10th-century blockbook edition of the *I Ching*.

ABOVE: The eight trigrams, the *yin/yang* symbol, and a protective demon's head decorate an amulet designed to protect a Chinese household far from home in Bangkok.

Questioning the Oracle

sing the *I Ching* can give you access to a wide range of transformative symbols that reproduce the fundamental way energy moves in the imagination. They not only give you warning and advice, but they can also change the way that you look at things.

The first step in this process is defining a question, something you cannot deal with in ordinary ways. Think about it, search out what you feel is at stake, why it seems to bother you. Come to a tentative idea of what you want to do and state it as a question: What about doing X? What is happening in this situation? What should I do about this problem?

To get an answer you make a hexagram by producing six lines. There are various ways to do this. The most traditional is counting out a group of 49 yarrow stalks in groups of four. This produces the numbers 6, 7, 8, or 9 six times. These numbers can also be produced by throwing three coins six times, giving "heads" a value of 3 and "tails" a value of 2, but the mathematical odds are different for this procedure.

A modern method uses 16 stones or marbles of four colors to represent the four kinds of lines in the old ratio (1:3:5:7). It is as fast as the coins, but preserves the odds of the yarrow stalks and the dynamic relation of *yin* and *yang*. Whichever method used will produce one of four kinds of lines six times. The "piling up" of these lines reflects the interaction of the two primal qualities as they generate a moment of time. The basic qualities are the stable lines. These lines may be turning into their opposites, a transformation that indicates a particular point of change.

BUILDING A HEXAGRAM

You build a hexagram from the bottom up. When one or more of the lines is transforming (from yin to yang or yang to yin), it produces another hexagram called the Relating Hexagram. This can indicate future developments. Even more, it is the perspective that relates you to the basic answer, the "window" on the situation.

The basic answer to your question is the name or "head" of the hexagram you made. This describes the quality of time that connects your situation to the flow of the tao. These names, in fact all the words or characters in the oracle texts, are symbols for a whole complex of meanings. The actions they describe go in all directions. They are verbs, nouns, adjectives, and adverbs all at the same time. To focus them, you must feel the part you play in the situation.

1 To start your consultation, take 50 yarrow stalks (these were hand picked in Italy) or 50 bamboo stalks. Take one stalk from the pile and put it aside.

2 Divide the remaining stalks into two random piles. Take one stalk from the left-hand pile and put it between the fifth and fourth fingers of your left hand.

3 Pick up the pile on the right and count it into groups of four until one, two, three, or four stalks remain.

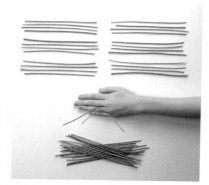

4 Put these leftover stalks between the fourth and third fingers of your left hand and keep them there. Pick up the remaining pile (on the left) and begin to count them out into groups of four.

5 At the end of this operation you should have one, two, three, or four stalks left over and rows of stalks grouped in fours in front of you.

6 Put the leftover stalks between the third and second fingers of your left hand. Take the stalks from between your fingers and put them aside. They are no longer necessary for this line of the hexagram.

7 Keeping aside the stalks from your fingers, heap together all the stalks you have grouped into four and repeat the entire process, putting the stalks between your fingers aside once more. Repeat a third time.

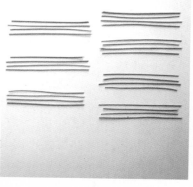

8 Count the number of groups of four stalks on the table. There should be six, seven, eight, or nine. Each number signifies what kind of line you have divined. Six is transforming *yin*, seven is *yang*, eight is *yin*, and nine is transforming *yang*. Repeat the operation five more times.

THE TRIGRAMS

Each hexagram is seen as being made up of two of eight possible trigrams, *or three-line figures (also called* gua*). Each of these figures has a name and a set of qualities associated with it. Though these figures evolved later than the hexagrams, they became the eight mythical persons or processes of virtually all Chinese thought. Here are the eight trigrams:*

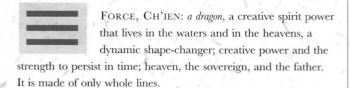

FORCE, CH'IEN: *a dragon*, a creative spirit power that lives in the waters and in the heavens, a dynamic shape-changer; creative power and the strength to persist in time; heaven, the sovereign, and the father. It is made of only whole lines.

FIELD, K'UN: *the womb that gives birth and nourishes everything*; the power to give shape to things, make thoughts and images visible; the earth that yields and serves; work undertaken together, sowing and harvesting a crop; earth, the mother, and the minister or courtier. It is made up of only opened lines.

SHAKE, CHEN: *frightening and inspiring thunder spirit*; arouse, excite and disturb; stirs things up and brings them out of hiding; plants bursting forth from the earth; shock; the strength to undertake and move heavy things, energetic and protective force; the first or oldest son, who began the new generation and provided for the parents and ancestors. The stirring whole line that emerges below two dormant opened lines.

GROUND, SUN: *penetrating and nourishing spirit of wood and wind*, subtle, gentle; permeates things and brings them to maturity; mating, coupling, and marriages, creating and spreading new seeds; growing trees, moving air; an "atmosphere" that influences how you think and feel; establish and nourish things; the first or oldest daughter, who is given in marriage and presides over the new house. The opened line that nourishes two whole lines from below, subtly penetrating and influencing them.

GORGE, K'AN: *the impetuous and adventurous spirit of water flowing in rivers and streams*; taking risks, like water falling, filling the holes in its path and flowing on; difficult but worthwhile labor. It dissolves things, carries them forward and cannot be stopped; focuses energy at a critical point, confronts and overcomes obstructions; the middle son, courageous and venturesome, who must take chances, leave the house, or establish a new concern. It is the single whole line between two constraining opened lines, flowing on without hesitation or reserve.

RADIANCE, LI: *the spirit of fire, light and warmth*, the hearth fire, and the power of awareness, warming and illuminating. A shape-changing bird with brilliant plumage that comes to rest on things. Radiance clings to what it illuminates, warming it and making it visible; the power to see and understand things, to articulate ideas and goals; the middle daughter, mature, supportive, and dependent. It is the single opened line that holds two whole lines together, uniting and illuminating them.

BOUND, KEN: *the mountain spirit*, fixes limits and brings things to a close; encloses and marks things off; the end that prepares a new beginning. It suggests the Palace of the Immortals, the eternal images that end and begin all things; the power to articulate what you have gone through and make your accomplishments clear; the youngest son, the limit and end of the family. It is the single whole line that stops two opened lines beneath it.

OPEN, TUI: *the spirit of water accumulating and spreading*; rising mists that stimulate, fertilize, and enrich; gathering place, stimulating words, profitable exchange, free and cheerful interaction, freedom from constraint; the harvest has been gathered and you are sure of the winter ahead; persuasive and inspiring speech, the ability to rouse things to action and create good feeling; the youngest daughter, light-hearted, whimsical, and magical. It is the single opened line that leads two whole lines forward.

A Sample Response

uppose you had asked about an important relationship that was stuck, blocked, and going nowhere. You didn't know what to do, but you felt called on to do something because the relation had real value in your life. You received in response to your question about what to do Hexagram 59 Dispersing. The basic answer to your question would be this field of meanings:

Disperse, *Huan*: scatter clouds, break up obstacles; dispel illusions, fears, and suspicions; clear things up, dissolve resistance; untie, separate; change and mobilize what is rigid; melting ice, floods, fog lifting and clearing away. The ideogram portrays water and the sign for expand. It suggests changing form either through expanding or scattering.

This can mean many things in different situations. Because you are the one who wishes to act, and you feel something of value in the relationship, you would take it as an imperative: dissolve the illusions, disperse the obstacles, make fluid what is rigid, scatter the clouds so the sun breaks through. If you had asked about a situation in which you felt yourself to be confined or imprisoned, this advice to separate and dissolve things would take on a quite different meaning.

The other texts of the head tell you that Dispersing is the quality that will bring success and growth. This is a time when the king approaches the temple to make great offerings, so you are invited to participate in this by imagining the things that unite people, that dissolve the barriers between them. This is the time to step into the River of Life with a purpose. Putting your ideas to the trial now will bring you profit and insight if you proceed through the quality of Dispersing.

In our reading, we see that the inner world is connected with Gorge, water flowing on and dissolving the old forms of experience. It encourages you to take a chance and leave old ways of thinking behind you. It is coupled with gentle penetration and understanding in the outer world. Together this gives another picture. This is a time to let go of old forms of thought and to let this fluidity gently penetrate the outer situation. Another text tells us that when this happens, Radiance will emerge – light, warmth, and awareness.

The Relating Hexagram

If there is a transforming line, it will key another kind of text, one that describes the precise point of change. If you had a "9," a transforming *yang* line, as the second line of this hexagram, for example, the line text would link the quality of Dispersing to the act of "fleeing your bench," leaving what you normally lean on. In this way, any cause for sorrow vanishes and you acquire what you desire. Because this line is in the center of the lower trigram, and thus in the center of the inner world, it indicates a shift in awareness. If you leave the way you usually think about things, the forms you depend on, the situation will shift of itself. There is the obstacle and the place you can dissolve it.

The Relating Hexagram, created when this line transforms, is 20 *Kuan*, Viewing. It reinforces the idea of looking at things and divining their meaning as the agent of change. Viewing emphasizes lifting repression and letting everything come into consciousness. It describes the moment in a religious ceremony just before the appearance of the spirit that has been invoked. It tells you that you can trust in the efficacy of inner attention. Looking at the situation in a new way will, of itself, attract the spirit.

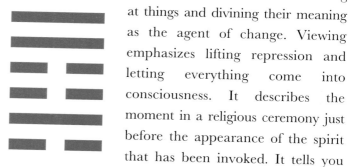

ABOVE: Hexagram 59 of the *I Ching*: Huan, Dispersing. It advises dispersal of obstructions to awareness.

The Sixty-Four Spirits of Time

THE HEXAGRAMS

Here are the 64 divinatory symbols or hexagrams of the
I Ching *in their usual order, with the hexagram graph and name.*

 1 FORCE/PERSISTING, CH'IEN: spirit power, creative energy; forward motion; dynamic, enduring; firm, stable; activate, inspire; heaven, masculine, ruler; exhaust, destroy, dry up, clear away; *also*: strong, robust, tenacious, untiring.

 2 FIELD/YIELDING, K'UN: the visible surface of the world; concrete existence, the fundamental power to give things form; earth, moon, mother, wife, servants, ministers; supple strength, receptive power; welcome, consent to, respond to an appeal; *also*: yield, give birth, bear fruit; agree, follow, obey; nourish, provide, serve, work for, work with.

 3 SPROUTING, CHUN: begin or cause to grow; assemble, accumulate, amass, hoard; establish a base of operations, establish troops at the borders; difficult, painful, arduous; the difficulties at the beginning of an endeavor.

 4 ENVELOPING, MENG: cover, hide, conceal; lid, covering; dull, unaware, ignorant; uneducated; young, undeveloped, fragile; unseen beginnings; *also*: a parasitic and magical plant.

 5 ATTENDING, HSÜ: take care of, look out for, serve; necessary, need, call for; provide what is needed; wait for, hesitate, doubt; stopped by rain; know how to wait, have patience and focus.

 6 ARGUING, SUNG: dispute, plead your case, demand justice, contend in front of the ruler or judge; lodge a complaint, begin litigation; quarrels, wrangles, controversy; correct, reprimand, arrive at a judgment, resolve a conflict.

 7 LEGIONS/LEADING, SHIH: troops, an army; leader, general, master of arms, master of a craft; organize, make functional, mobilize, discipline; take as a model, imitate.

 8 GROUPING, PI: join together, ally yourself with; find a new center; order things in classes, compare and select; find what you belong with; harmonize, unite; neighbors; equal, identical; work together, work toward.

 9 ACCUMULATING SMALL: SMALL, HSIAO: little, common, unimportant; adapt to what crosses your path; take in, make smaller; dwindle, lessen; little, slim, slight; *yin* energy. ACCUMULATE, CH'U: gather, collect, take in, hoard, retain; control, restrain; take care of, support, tolerate; tame, train or pasture animals; raise, bring up, domesticate; be tamed or controlled by something.

 10 TREADING, LÜ: walk, step; path, track, way; shoes; walk on, walk in the tracks of, follow a path; act, practice, accomplish; conduct, behavior; salary, means of subsistence; happiness, luck; the paths of the stars and planets.

THE HEXAGRAMS

 11 PERVADING, T'AI: great, eminent, abundant, prosperous; peaceful, fertile; reach everywhere, permeate, diffuse, communicate; smooth, slippery; extreme, extravagant, prodigious. Mount T'ai was where great sacrifices were made that connected heaven and earth.

 12 OBSTRUCTION, PI: closed, stopped, bar the way; obstacle; unable to advance or succeed; deny, refuse, disapprove; bad, evil, unfortunate, wicked, unhappy.

 13 CONCORDING PEOPLE: CONCORD, T'UNG: harmonize, bring together, unite; union, concord, harmony; equalize, assemble, share, agree; together, held in common; the same time and place. PEOPLE, JEN: human beings; an individual; humanity.

 14 GREAT POSSESSING: GREAT, TA: big, noble, important; able to protect others; orient your will toward a self-imposed goal; the ability to lead or guide your life; *yang* energy. POSSESS, YU: there is; to be, to exist; have, own; possessions, goods; dispose of; arise, occur, events.

 15 HUMBLING, CH'IEN: think and speak of yourself in a modest way; voluntarily give way to others, polite, modest, simple, respectful; yielding, compliant, reverent.

 16 PROVIDING FOR/RESPONDING, YÜ: ready, prepared for; take precautions; arrange, make ready; happy, content, rejoice, take pleasure in; carried away, enthusiastic, respond immediately, ready to explode.

 17 FOLLOWING, SUI: come or go after in an inevitable sequence; conform to, according to, come immediately after; in the style of, according to the ideas of; move in the same direction; follow a way, school, or religion.

 18 CORRUPT/RENOVATING, KU: rotting, poisonous; intestinal worms, venomous insects; evil magic; seduce, pervert, flatter, put under a spell; disorder, error; business.

 19 NEARING, LIN: approach, behold with care and sympathy; commanded to come nearer; look down on sympathetically, confer favor and blessing; inspect; arrive, the point of arrival, make contact; honor or be honored by a visit.

 20 VIEWING, KUAN: contemplate, look at from a distance or height; examine, judge, conjecture about; divination; idea, point of view; instruct, inform, point out, make known; *also*: a Taoist monastery, an observatory, a tower.

THE HEXAGRAMS

 21 GNAWING AND BITING: GNAW, SHIH: bite away, chew, eat; nibble, bite persistently; arrive at, attain; reach the truth by removing what is unessential. BITE, HO: unite, bring together; close the jaws, bite through, crush, chew; the sound of voices.

 22 ADORNING, PI: embellish, ornament, beautify; elegant, brilliant, ornamented; inner worth seen in outer appearance; energetic, brave, eager, passionate, intrepid; display of courage.

 23 STRIPPING, PO: flay, peel, skin, scrape, slice; remove, uncover, take off; reduce, diminish; reduce to the essentials; prune trees, slaughter animals.

24 RETURNING, FU: go back, turn back, return to the starting point; come back, reappear; resurgence, rebirth, renaissance; reestablish, renew, renovate, restore; again, anew; an earlier time and place; the very beginning of the new time.

 25 WITHOUT EMBROILING: WITHOUT, WU: devoid of, not having. EMBROILING, WANG: caught up in, entangled, enmeshed, involved; vain, rash, reckless, foolish, wild; lie, deceive; idle, futile, without foundation, false; brutal, insane, disordered.

 26 GREAT ACCUMULATING: GREAT, TA: big, noble, important; able to protect others; orient your will toward a self-imposed goal; the ability to lead or guide your life; *yang* energy. ACCUMULATE, CH'U: gather, collect, take in, hoard, retain; control, restrain; take care of; support, tolerate; tame, train, or pasture animals; raise, bring up, domesticate; be tamed or controlled by something.

 27 JAWS/SWALLOWING, YI: mouth, jaws, cheeks, chin; eat, take in, ingest; feed, nourish, sustain, bring up, support; provide what is necessary; what goes in or out of the mouth.

 28 GREAT EXCEEDING: GREAT, TA: big, noble, important; able to protect others; orient your will toward a self-imposed goal; the ability to lead or guide your life; *yang* energy. EXCEED, KUO: go beyond; pass by, pass over, surpass; overtake, overshoot; get clear of, get over; cross the threshold, surmount difficulties; transgress the norms, outside the limits; too much.

 29 REPEATING GORGE: REPEAT, HSI: practice, rehearse, train, coach; again and again; familiar with, skilled; repeat a lesson; drive, impulse. GORGE, K'AN: a dangerous place; hole, cavity, pit, hollow; steep precipice; snare, trap, grave; a critical time, a test; take risks; *also*: venture and fall, take a risk without reserve at the key point of danger.

 30 RADIANCE, LI: spreading light; illuminate, discriminate, articulate, arrange, and order; consciousness, awareness; leave, separate yourself from, step outside the norms; two together, encounter by chance; belong to, adhere to, depend on; *also*: brightness, fire, and warmth.

 31 CONJOINING, HSIEN: contact, influence, move; excite, mobilize, trigger; all, totally, universal, continual, entire; unite, bring together the parts of a previously separated whole; come into conjunction, as the planets; literally: a broken piece of pottery, the two halves of which were joined to identify partners.

THE HEXAGRAMS

 32 PERSEVERING, HENG: continue in the same way or spirit; constant, stable, regular; enduring, perpetual, durable, permanent; self-renewing; ordinary, habitual; extend everywhere, universal; the moon when it is almost full.

 33 RETIRING, TUN: withdraw, run away, escape, flee, hide yourself; disappear, withdraw into obscurity, become invisible; secluded, antisocial; fool or trick someone.

 34 GREAT INVIGORATING: GREAT, TA: big, noble, important; able to protect others; orient your will toward a self-imposed goal; the ability to lead or guide your life; *yang* energy. INVIGORATE, CHUANG: inspire, animate, strengthen; strong, flourishing, robust; mature, in the prime of life (25–40 years old); *also*: damage, wound, unrestrained use of strength.

 35 PROSPERING, CHIN: grow and flourish, as young plants do in the sun; advance, increase, progress; be promoted, rise, go up; permeate, impregnate.

 36 BRIGHTNESS HIDING: BRIGHTNESS, MING: the light from fire, sun, moon, and stars; consciousness, awareness, human intelligence, understanding; illuminate, distinguish clearly; lucid, clear, evident; *also*: a bright bird, the golden pheasant. HIDE, YI: keep out of sight; distant, remote; raze, lower, level; ordinary, plain, colorless; cut, wound, destroy, exterminate; barbarians, strangers, vulgar, uncultured people.

 37 DWELLING PEOPLE: DWELL, CHIA: home, house, household, family, relations, clan; a business; a school of thought; to be master of a skill or art; to hold something in common with others. PEOPLE, JEN: human beings; an individual; humanity.

 38 POLARIZING, K'UEI: oppose, separate, create distance; different, discordant; antagonistic, contrary, mutually exclusive; creative tension; at the opposite ends of an axis, 180° apart; astronomical or polar opposition; squint, look at things from an unusual perspective; strange, weird.

 39 LIMPING/DIFFICULTIES, CHIEN: walk lamely, proceed haltingly; difficulties, obstacles, obstructions; the feeling of being afflicted, unhappy, and suffering; crooked, feeble, weak; poverty; pride.

 40 LOOSENING/DELIVERANCE, HSIEH: divide, detach, untie, scatter, sever, dissolve, dispel; analyze, explain, understand; free from constraint, dispel sorrow, eliminate effects, solve problems; discharge, get rid of; take care of needs.

 41 DIMINISHING, SUN: lessen, take away from, make smaller; weaken, humble; damage, lose, spoil, hurt; blame, criticize; offer in sacrifice, give up, give away; let things settle; concentrate.

 42 AUGMENTING, YI: increase, advance, add to; benefit, strengthen, support; pour in more, superabundant, overflowing; restorative, fertile; useful, profitable, advantageous.

 43 RESOLUTION/PARTING, KUAI: decide, declare, resolve on; resolute, prompt, decisive, stern; certain, settled; open and cleanse a wound; water opening a path through a barrier; also: separate, fork, cut off; flow in different directions.

THE HEXAGRAMS

 44 WELCOMING/COUPLING, KOU: meet, encounter, open yourself to; find something or someone on your path; the encounter of the primal powers, *yin* and *yang*; copulate, all forms of sexual intercourse; magnetism, gravity, mating of animals, gripped by impersonal forces; fortuitous; favorable, good.

 45 CLUSTERING, TS'UI: gather, call or pack together; tight groups of people, animals, and things; assemble, concentrate, collect; reunite, reassemble; crowd, multitude, bunch; dense clumps of grass.

 46 ASCENDING, SHENG: mount, go up, rise; climb step by step; advance through your own efforts; be promoted, rise in office; accumulate, bring out and fulfill the potential; distil liquor; an ancient standard of measure, a small cupful.

 47 CONFINING/OPPRESSION, K'UN: enclosed, encircled; restrict, limit; punishment, penal codes, prison; worry, anxiety, fear; fatigue, exhaustion, at the end of your resources; afflicted, disheartened, weary; poverty.

 48 THE WELL, CHING: a water well; the well at the center of a group of nine fields; resources held in common; underlying structure; nucleus; in good order, regularly; communicate with others, common needs; the water of life, the inner source.

 49 SKINNING/REVOLUTION, KO: take off the skin; molting; change, renew; revolt, overthrow; prepare hides; skin, leather; armor, soldiers; eliminate, repeal, cut off, cut away.

 50 THE VESSEL/HOLDING, TING: a caldron with three feet and two ears, a sacred vessel for cooking offerings, sacrifices and ritual meals; founding symbol of a family or dynasty; receptacle; hold, contain, and transform, transmute; consecrate, connect with the spirits; found, establish, secure; precious, well-grounded.

 51 SHAKE, CHEN: arouse, inspire; wake up, shake up; shock, frighten, awe, alarm; violent thunder clap (thunder comes from below in Chinese thought), earthquake, put into movement, begin; terrify, trembling; majestic, severe; *also*: excite, influence, affect; work, act; break through the shell, come out of the bud.

 52 BOUND/STABILIZING, KEN: limit, boundary, obstacle; still, quiet, calm, refuse to advance; enclose, mark off, confine; finish, complete; reflect on what has come before; firm, solid, simple, straightforward; the mountain as a limit and a refuge; *also*: stop, bring to a standstill.

 53 INFILTRATING/GRADUAL ADVANCE, CHIEN: advance by degrees, little by little, slowly and surely; reach, pour into, flow into; moisten, permeate; influence, affect; smooth, gliding.

 54 CONVERTING THE MAIDEN: CONVERT, KUEI: come back to, go back to, return to; change form, turn into; restore, revert, become loyal, give back; belong to; to give a young girl in marriage. MAIDEN, MEI: a young girl, a virgin; the younger or second sister.

THE HEXAGRAMS

 55 ABOUNDING, FENG: abundant harvest; fertile, plentiful, copious, numerous; exuberant, prolific, at the point of overflowing; fullness, culmination; ripe, sumptuous, luxurious, fat; exaggerated, too much; have many talents, friends, riches.

 56 SOJOURNING/QUEST, LÜ: travel, journey, voyage; stay in places other than your home; temporary; visitor, lodger, guest; a troop of soldiers on a mission; a group (of travelers) that holds things in common or have a common goal; a stranger in a strange land.

 57 GROUND/PENETRATING, SUN: support, foundation, base; penetrate, enter into, put into; supple, mild, subtle, docile, submissive; submit freely, be shaped by; *also*: wind, weather, fashion; wood, trees, plants with growing roots and branches.

 58 OPEN/EXPRESSING, TUI: open surface, interface; interact, interpenetrate; express, persuade, stir up, urge on, cheer, delight; pleasure, pleasing, enjoy; responsive, free, unhindered; meet, gather, exchange, barter, trade; pour out; the mouth and the words that come from it; *also*: mists, vapor rising from a marsh or lake; fertilize, enrich.

 59 DISPERSING, HUAN: scatter clouds, break up obstacles; dispel illusions, fears, and suspicions; clear things up, dissolve resistance; untie, separate; change and mobilize what is rigid; melting ice, floods, fog lifting and clearing away.

 60 ARTICULATING, CHIEH: separate, distinguish, and join things; express ideas in speech; joint, section, chapter, interval, unit of time, rhythm; the months of the year; limits, regulations, ceremonies, rituals, annual feasts; measure, economize, moderate, temper; firm, loyal, true; degrees, levels, classes.

 61 CENTER ACCORD: CENTER, CHUNG: inner, central, calm, stable; put in the center; balanced, correct; mediate, intermediary, between; the heart, the inner life; stable point that lets you face outer changes. ACCORD, FU: accord between inner and outer; sincere, truthful, verified, reliable, worthy of belief; have confidence; linked to and carried by the spirits; take prisoners, capture spoils, be successful.

 62 SMALL EXCEEDING: SMALL, HSIAO: little, common, unimportant; adapt to what crosses your path; take in, make smaller; dwindle, lessen; little, slim, slight; *yin* energy. EXCEED, KUO: go beyond; pass by, pass over, surpass; overtake, overshoot; get clear of, get over; cross the threshold, surmount difficulties; transgress the norms, outside the limits; too much.

 63 ALREADY FORDING: ALREADY, CHI: completed, finished; mark of the past tense; thus, that being so. FORD, CHI: cross a river, overcome an obstacle, begin an action; give help, bring relief; succeed, bring to a successful conclusion, complete.

 64 NOT YET FORDING: NOT YET, WEI: incomplete, doesn't exist yet; has not occurred (but will occur in the course of time). FORD, CHI: cross a river, overcome an obstacle, begin an action; give help, bring relief; succeed, bring to a successful conclusion, complete.

The Goddess of Compassion

Divining with the *I Ching* inspired many other oracle practices. One such system, widespread wherever Chinese is spoken, is called *Chien Tung,* and is sponsored by the Goddess of Compassion and Mercy, *Kwan Yin.* Like divining with the *I Ching,* the basic purpose of this divinatory way is to give you advice on how to deal with the crises and decisions you face in life. This protects you and, over time, deepens your understanding of the way spirit plays through your life. It can free you from obsession and compulsion by opening the imaginative world.

The oracle of *Kwan Yin* is a temple oracle. To use it, you would enter the temple dedicated to this goddess, light sticks of incense, make a prayer for guidance before her altar, then pick up a hollow wooden cylinder, often the joint of a large bamboo. In this cup are 100 thin slats of bamboo, painted red on one end – sign of riches and luck – and marked on the other with a number and a character. You shake this cylinder with your right hand until one stick jumps out. You then look up the text corresponding to this number in *Kwan Yin*'s book.

Here is an example: A woman was engaged to oversee the export division of a large firm. To do well was important to her in many ways. But she experienced great difficulties with her immediate supervisor who, though about to retire, insisted on maintaining strict control and dominating his employees. The woman did not know whether to challenge him openly, or to wait out the time. There were issues of character as well as profit at stake, but they hinged on whether or not this was the right *time* to make a move.

The oracle replied: *When you climb a mountain together with a tiger, your heart trembles every minute with the fear of danger.*

In Business Matters: The situation is not favorable; take no risks at present. If you don't want your life to be profoundly disturbed, you must take conscious precautions to protect yourself from danger. Look to the future in everything you do, so you will not be taken by surprise. Do not insist on your supposed rights!

The image proved to be accurate. By avoiding conflict she not only acquired the place she wanted after the "tiger's" retirement, but she avoided the serious harm that was done to others in similar positions who directly challenged the mountain of difficulties.

The oracle's answer achieved two things. It gave the woman an image of the situation, and it gave her a sense that there was a spirit looking after her welfare. This creates foresight and compassion in the person who has received the answer – the long-range goal of the Goddess of Compassion.

OPPOSITE BOTTOM: A serene Buddhist lamasery in China. *Kwan Yin* is associated with *Tara*, the Buddhist Bodhisattva of active compassion.

OPPOSITE TOP: *Kwan Yin* , the Goddess of Mercy and Compassion. Originally she was a pre-Buddhist mother goddess. Now she is regarded as the female guardian of humanity and the patron saint of mothers.

ABOVE: A 19th-century engraving showing the ritual consultation of the oracle of *Kwan Yin*. The person seeking enlightenment or guidance shakes the bamboo cup of numbered sticks; when an individual stick emerges, its number is noted and its meaning interpreted by consulting *Kwan Yin's* book.

RIGHT: Chinese New Year celebrations in Heilongjiang province. Each year is associated with a special animal whose spirit and attributes characterize that year.

The Book of Light and Shadow: Tarot

The 78 symbols of the Tarot deck open the mythic underworld of western Europe. Tarot is in many ways the quintessential divination system of the postclassical world, carrying a whole series of myths about what divination is and does. It first appeared as a game of images in the courts of northern Italy, set amid the reimagining of pagan mysteries we call the Renaissance. It has shown an uncanny ability to fascinate the imagination and catch the shadow of individuals and culture ever since. It has been associated with gypsies, witches, and the shadow side of popular culture. Its imaginative process has been "explained" in terms of all of Europe's underground magical traditions and romantic visions: Cabala, Hermetic Magic, Egyptian mysteries, Gnosticism, Chaldean oracles, Rosicrucianism, astrology, Celtic shamanism, and the Great Goddess. It has been called a great philosophical machine, the universal key to all religions, simple fortunetelling, a map of the imagination, a machine to tell stories, superstition, charlatanism, and the devil's workshop.

Tarot practices have also informed much of the modern reinvention of lost divinatory ways. They offer a way of personally connecting with a great variety of myths and visions. Much of this ability to collect and organize projections lies in the Renaissance spirit of this divinatory way. It affirms the value of imagination, suffering, and the underworld journey and the possibility of personally experiencing the friendship of the spirit, the sacred aspect of experience.

The Triumphs of the Gods

Card games, long associated with divinatory practices, entered Europe from the Arabic East in the 13th and 14th centuries. They were part of a great wave of old manuscripts, magical beliefs, and practices that reentered Europe through Arab translation, a real "return of the repressed." Tarot, *tarrochi, les tarots* – the meaning of the word is unknown – first appeared as a game of cards in northern Italy of the Quattrocento. It is still played in southern Europe and French North Africa, using a French deck from the late 15th century called *Tarot de Marseilles* that standardized the order of the cards.

The first historical mention of a game that used painted cards called *trionfi,* or "triumphs," comes from the court of Ferrara in 1442. From the beginning, it was the subject of much clerical recrimination. According to the priests, there was nothing so hateful to God as this game of triumphs. The 21 symbols contained everything that was evil in Christian eyes. They were 21 steps of a ladder to hell.

The first decks were beautiful hand-painted creations that appeared in the ducal courts of the "golden quadrangle" of Venice, Milano, Firenze, and Urbino. The earliest surviving deck was painted by the artist Bonifacio Bembo for a wedding that linked the Sforza and the Visconti families. By 1500, printed decks appeared and the game became a popular pastime. The "game" was played in many ways, including a kind of "psychodrama" that allowed people to imagine themselves as characters from the cards. This practice was associated with the "magical symbols" of neoplatonic art. It was a hidden "way" that made witty, ironic, yet profound comment on the cultural and religious situation of the time.

The word "triumph" and the association with the courts that sponsored the great magical works of Renaissance art give a particular clue to Tarot's nature. Games and divination are associated in most cultures, but the word *"trionfi"* had a special meaning in Italy of the 15th century. It referred to a pagan practice of "carrying the god," a kind of procession that displayed the virtues and power of the divinity. It was a theme of contemporary art and poetry and was particularly used to talk about the profound mysteries of love. The Palazzo Schiffanoia, or "chase away ugliness," in Ferrara was painted with these *"trionfi"* of the gods. They are a central theme of the poetry of the time, connected to the experience of love, beauty, death, and the garden of the gods, the world reimagined as a golden age.

The particular attractive power of the Tarot lies in a cluster of imaginative and magical practices that sought to reinvent and radically reimagine the religious practices of late paganism, seeing them particularly through the mysteries of love, beauty, and the underworld journey. The symbols propose the events, people, myths, and images of Renaissance Italy as archetypal keys to this journey.

OPPOSITE LEFT: Tarot cards; the Two of Cups is from the Minor Arcana, and The World is the last card in the Major Arcana.

OPPOSITE RIGHT: Zodiacal pictures decorating the Palazzo Schiffanoia.

ABOVE: Japanese playing cards, related to the Tarot tradition.

The Key to the Mysteries

In the following centuries, Tarot divination became associated with the "gypsies," the wandering Romany peoples who entered Europe in the course of the 15th century. This association provoked a series of highly romantic myths about Tarot's "Egyptian" origins.

Tarot first became Key to the Mysteries; however, in 1781, Antoine Court de Gébelin, a French Protestant clergyman and student of mythologies, concluded that this "simple game of trumps" was actually the lost Egyptian *Book of Thoth*, key to the hidden mysteries of a vanished civilization. It reflected what Renaissance Hermeticists had called the *prisca theologia*, the pure knowledge of the gods descending from ancient Egyptian sources. The symbols of this game of cards, Court de Gébelin maintained, were allegories of all life, capable of unlimited combinations, for they contained an ancient way of transformation.

Even more influential in the occult definition of Tarot was the work of Eliphas Lévi (born Alphonse Louis Constant). A renegade priest and journalist turned magician, he, like most 19th-century occultists, was passionately searching for the "key of keys" that could unite all magical practices and systems.

He found that key in the Tarot. He used the key to open the mysteries by identifying the 22 Tarot Trumps with the 22 letters of the Hebrew alphabet, the core of an enormously influential mystical system that was known as the Cabala.

Cabalists view the 22 letters of the Hebrew alphabet as the language of God. Each has a mystical meaning and a magical power of transformation. The letters are organized through a complex symbol called the Tree of Life, composed of ten fundamental stations or powers called *sefiroth*. The paths between these *sefiroth* represent the way in which the world was created and the way in which we can return to an experience of the godhead. They are a way to organize all mystical experience.

The ten *sefiroth* are connected by 22 "wisdom paths," each describing a particular spiritual and psychological process. These wisdom paths are represented by the letters of the Hebrew alphabet. After Lévi, they were connected with the Tarot cards. This let magicians use the Tree of Life as a divination system. Further, it suggested that the overall structure of the Tarot deck and its organization of symbols was the Key of Keys, the "*clavicle*," which could open the ruined temples, make the dead speak and solve the enigma of every sphinx. It was the key to all mythologies; a magical synopsis of an age-old secret religion that was revealed only to initiates.

The definitive reworking of Tarot as High Ritual Magic came through the Order of the Golden Dawn. The members of this Hermetic Order set out to create a magical system of hierarchical "initiations" that synthesized all Western forms of magic and myth, from alchemy and astrology to magia and Cabala.

One of their particular specialities was to give astrological associations to all the systems they encountered.

Linked to this network of associations, rituals, and initiations, Tarot became a "gateway" to the "Western Esoteric Tradition" assembled from the ruins, shards, and shadows of *magia* and myth.

The two most influential modern Tarot decks came out of this milieu. The "Rider" deck, named for its publisher, was created by the Christian occultist Arthur Edward Waite and the theater designer and painter Pamela Coleman Smith. It has sold millions of copies worldwide and profoundly influenced the way everyone thinks about the Tarot. It is commonly regarded as a "basic" deck to which other versions are compared.

One of the great reasons for its popularity is a radical innovation in divinatory technique. The traditional Tarot was composed of the 22 Trumps or Major Arcana, and 56 number cards or "pips." The Major Arcana have images, while the number cards have only the correct number of signs in the suit that each represents. Pamela Coleman Smith changed that. She painted a scene for each card, a practice that has been followed ever since. This let diviners and inquirers interpret these situations through images as well as formulaic meanings.

The second "modern" deck was the *Book of Thoth* created by the "Great Beast" Aleister Crowley and artist Lady Frieda Harris. The Crowley-Harris deck is darker, more complicated and provocative than the Waite-Smith deck. It introduces a wide range of radical scientific speculations to the repertoire of magic that was unique in its time. Both of these creators, though wrapped up in the myth of a "hidden elite" or "elect minority," presented the modern view of the cards. They insisted that the Tarot symbols present basic structures of mind and imagination,

and it is in this sense that they contain a "secret doctrine." The literal origin of the cards was irrelevant. The processes they describe lie outside what were considered normal categories of time and space.

In the years since the creation of these modern decks, Tarot's system of symbols has demonstrated an amazing ability to assimilate and redefine a wide range of other mythologies, from Mayan, old Greek, and Native American to contemporary goddess culture. Whether this assimilation is historically accurate or not is another, and perhaps ultimately irrelevant, question. The Tarot symbols remain true to their basic nature, reproducing what Jung called *Archetypes of Transformation*. They figure forth a process of imaginative hope and transformation that has haunted European culture for the past 1,500 years.

OPPOSITE LEFT: Hermes Trismegistus, the inspirer of the Order of the Golden Dawn. They attributed great importance to the Tarot and inspired the design of the Rider-Waite tarot deck.

ABOVE LEFT: A winged caduceus, one of the attributes of Hermes, used in the *Stella Matutina*, the temple belonging to the Order of the Golden Dawn. This Hermetic order redefined the Tarot system as a magic ritual.

ABOVE: Madame Lenormande, a fashionable French cartomancer consulting the Tarot on behalf of Empress Josephine at Malmaison.

The House of Cards

ike other divinatory systems, Tarot is a way of imagining and a literal artifact – the cards. The deck has two parts, the 22 Major Arcana and the 56 Minor Arcana or "pip" cards. The Major Arcana or Triumphs are full-size pictures with a name and a number. These cards are the "gods." They suggest archetypal worlds, with a rich set of associations. Each is an image of existence, a perspective on existence and a set of ideas and feelings. Many people who work with the cards see the Major Arcana as the journey of the soul from birth through experience to enlightenment. They divide the series into three sets of seven cards that express the stages of this process: the basic challenges of life and the formation of an ego; the inner journey to an independent self; and the confrontation with universal forces and the creative experience of the world.

The Minor Arcana consists of four suits of 14 cards each. The suits – Wands, Swords, Cups, and Pentacles in most modern decks – correspond to the four elements Fire, Air, Water, and Earth. Each typifies a kind of experience and a quality of perception. A suit has ten number cards, beginning with the Ace that epitomizes its quality, and four Court cards – Page, Knight, Queen, and King – that represent the diversity of temperaments, ages, positions and genders. The Minor Arcana is seen as an encyclopedia of experiences, the events and concerns that make up daily life. They connect the "gods" to everyday experience. Through the systems of correspondence developed in the Golden Dawn, all of these cards are also associated with astrological and numerological meanings and letters of the Hebrew alphabet.

The Minor Arcana or "number" cards entered Europe as early as 1200, probably from the Near East. By 1400, their use as a popular card game was widespread. The Major Arcana, however, were created in the courts of Renaissance Italy between 1420 and 1450. The cards appeared in Venice, Ferrara, Urbino, Bologna, Florence, and Milan almost simultaneously. Called *trionfi*, or Triumphs, they connect with the religious and courtly processions of allegorical figures that were so much part of the Renaissance art and literature, the "processions of the gods." The Triumphs or trumps represent characters well known in Renaissance culture. They reflect all the major strands of Renaissance magic and myth: memory systems, gnosticism, neoplatonism, magia, and art as a carrier of the mysteries.

We have texts on Tarot divination from about 1526. But the cards of the Major Arcana were also quite controversial to contemporary churchmen. These *trionfi* were a ladder to the depths of hell, whose names were given by the Devil. Their use was later forbidden by the Spanish Inquisition.

The Marriage Deck

Shown on the next three pages are the Major Triumphs in their usual numerical order, along with a brief description of the traditional core image and a few of the associations. These images come from the oldest surviving tarot deck, the Visconti-Sforza deck. It was probably painted by the artist Bonfacio Bembo in about 1441 for the marriage of Francesco Sforza and Bianca Visconti, daughter of Fillipo Maria, Duke of Milan.

LEFT: The first known appearance of Tarot cards was as a 14th-century game from northern Italy.

THE MAJOR ARCANA

Here are the Major Triumphs in their usual numerical order, along with a brief description of the traditional core image and a few of the many associations.

2 HIGH PRIESTESS: *a seated, robed woman. Silent Knower.* Intuition, hidden secrets, mystery; the power of the unconscious.

4 EMPEROR: *an older man seated on a throne. Father.* Structure, reason, order, authority, society; peace.

0 FOOL: *a young man walking an unknown path. Adventurer.* Quest, journey, the leap of the spirit into the world; chaos; naive, unaware.

1 MAGICIAN: *a man before a table full of ritual objects. Maker.* Focused will, creation, change, manipulation; trickster; bringing the dead to life.

3 EMPRESS: *a seated woman robed as a queen. Mother.* Passion, material creation, nature, sensuality; the Great Goddess.

5 HIEROPHANT OR POPE: *a man in religious robes. Teacher.* Wisdom, teaching, established religions, morality, tradition, orthodoxy.

THE MAJOR ARCANA

6 LOVERS: *man and woman with angel. Lover.* Attraction, soul, connection with divine; choice; erotic experience, relationship.

8 JUSTICE: *a woman holding a pair of scales. Judge.* Balance, law, self-examination, conscience; submission, fairness, punishment.

10 WHEEL OF FORTUNE: *turning wheel with animals and humans. Change of Fortune.* Chance, fate, karma; irony; vision of the whole; changes.

12 HANGED MAN: *man hanging upside down by one foot. Spiritual Independence.* Isolation, surrender, initiation, sacrifice, transition.

7 CHARIOT: *man riding a chariot, a triumph. Victory.* Mastery, will, focus, strength; progress; persona, social face.

9 HERMIT: *a man carrying a lantern and staff. Seeker.* Interiority, withdrawal, independent values, inner search.

11 STRENGTH: *a woman and a lion. Inner Strength.* Courage, force, openness, endurance; reconciling the passions; serpent power, goodness.

13 DEATH: *a skeleton, the grim reaper. Profound Change.* Destruction and renewal; change of being and thought; mortality, endings.

THE MAJOR ARCANA

14 TEMPERANCE: *woman pouring water from one vessel to another. Balance and Art.* Moderation, caution, equilibrium; reconciling the opposites; care, balance.

16 TOWER: *stone tower struck by lightning, falling figures. Upheaval.* Catastrophe, divine intervention, stroke of fate; reversal, destruction of old structures.

18 MOON: *creatures emerging from dark pool, baying at the moon. Dream world.* Deep instincts, irrational fears; imagination, psychic powers and dreams, strange passions.

20 JUDGMENT: *figures rising from the tomb world. Awakening.* Enlightenment, rebirth, revelation, reward; rise up and change, resurrection.

15 DEVIL: *horned demon with chained figures. Bondage.* Repression, illusion; lust; materiality, material success; temptation, compulsion.

17 STAR: *woman kneeling by waters. Hope and Return.* Aspiration, optimism, beauty, healing, peace, promise; return to life.

19 SUN: *androgynous dancing figure. Culmination and Joy.* Synthesis, wholeness, achievement; perfection, acceptance, happiness.

21 WORLD: *garden, couple or children. Day world.* Growth, success, conjunction, coupling; splendor, freedom; simplicity, clarity.

Questioning the Tarot

ivining with the Tarot involves "reading" the cards in a specific situation. For most modern readers this involves a combination of learning the acquired meanings, feeling the deep processes behind the movement of the symbols, "seeing" into the situation in terms of the images presented, and integrating all these things with the inquirer's spontaneous sense of the images.

There have been many rituals, invocations, and magical procedures developed to work with the cards, but the basic procedure is simple. The inquirer, the person who has the question, mixes the cards, usually ending by bringing the deck together and cutting it into three piles, which the diviner takes up. Some people simply take a card at random and see how it "speaks" to the situation. The more usual procedure is to lay the cards out in a "spread," a predetermined pattern in which each place has a particular meaning.

The Fall of the Cards

There are many spreads, traditional and modern, of varying degrees of complexity. The spontaneous intersection of a symbol with this kind of *ad hoc* structure seems to be a particularly fertile way to generate information about how the imagination is moving. Some spreads are focused on particular problems, some have a particular shape. The reading of the cards is a combination of the meaning of the position and the card's symbolic field.

Spreads are used both individually and in readings. The power of the reading comes from the reader's ability to "see" and communicate the message in the fall of the cards and the inquirer's openness to the movement of the images. Most people expect a Tarot reading to reveal the hidden and predict the future – which it often does. The focus of most modern readers, however, is on understanding the forces at work in the present situation in order to take creative and positive action. They will involve the inquirer as much as possible, soliciting associations and creating an atmosphere in which the hidden can reveal itself. Such a reading may end by picking a particular card as a symbol of the transformative possibilities in the situation and focusing on it to mobilize the imagination.

Any interpretation is a combination of what the card can mean, its position, and the reactions it calls up in you. The best way to get to know the cards is to see how they act and react in readings. If any card occurs upside down in a reading, its meaning is thought to be reversed or delayed. This reversal can also mean liberation. Remember that any card, major or minor, is the key to an open-ended set of associations that includes your personal feelings about the images.

THE CIRCLE SPREAD

This is a circle spread using another famous deck, the *Tarot de Marseilles*. Codified by about 1600, the *Tarot de Marseilles* first appeared as hand-colored woodcuts. It became the standard European deck and was the foundation of the "occult" or "esoteric" school of Tarot interpretation. This deck was seen by Court de Gébelin in *Le Monde Primitif* (1781) as "key to the mysteries," the repository of "ancient Egyptian wisdom." The *Tarot de Marseilles* was also used by 19th-century occultists to connect with the letters of the Hebrew alphabet, Cabalistic magia, and astrological imagery. This 12-card spread can be seen as the 12 months of the year, the signs of the zodiac, or the 12 phases of any process. The center card is the significator, representing the person asking the question as the center of the circling images.

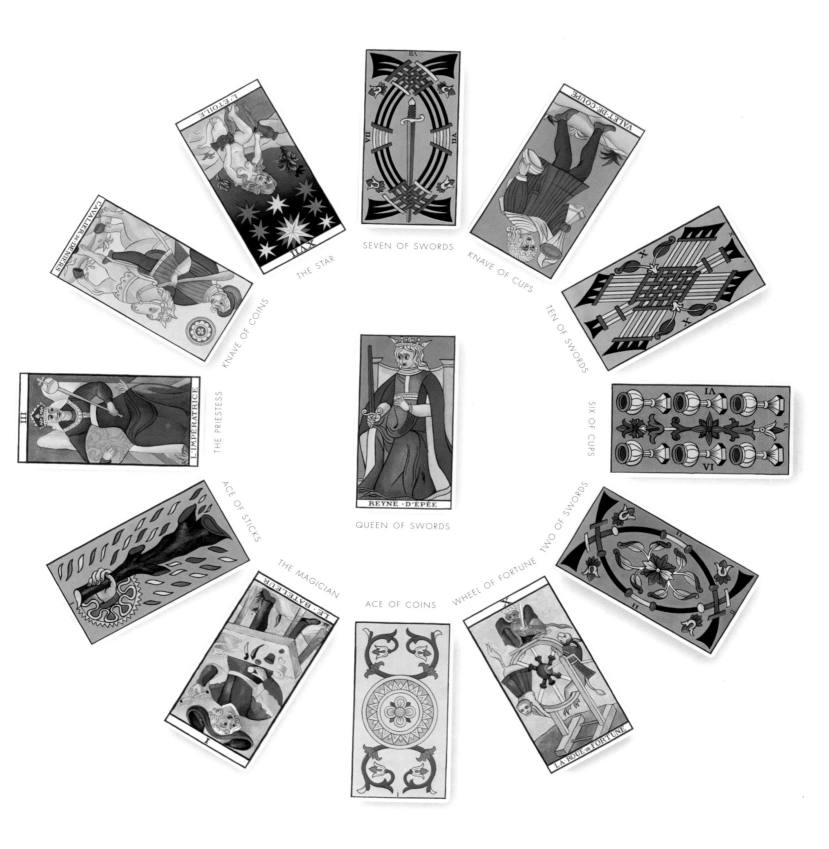

SEVEN OF SWORDS

THE STAR

KNAVE OF CUPS

VALET·DE·COUPE

L'ETOILE

TEN OF SWORDS

CAVALIER·DE·DENIERS

KNAVE OF COINS

SIX OF CUPS

THE PRIESTESS

L'IMPERATRICE

Queen of Swords

REYNE·D'EPÉE

QUEEN OF SWORDS

TWO OF SWORDS

ACE OF STICKS

ACE OF COINS

WHEEL OF FORTUNE

LE·BATELEUR

THE MAGICIAN

LA·ROUE·DE·FORTUNE

THREE-CARD SPREADS

THE QUESTION AND THE ALTERNATIVES

2. THE WORLD

1. THE TWO OF SWORDS

3. THE FIVE OF CUPS

THE CHALLENGE AND THE TOOL

1. THE TWO OF CUPS

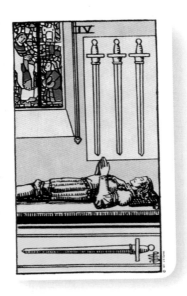

3. THE FOUR OF SWORDS

2. THE EIGHT OF PENTACLES

INTERPRETING THE THREE-CARD SPREADS

The three-card spread focuses on what you are confronting in a given situation. After you have mixed the cards, lay out three from left to right. The first card represents the past or what has brought you here, the second represents the present situation, the third, the potential of the future.

THE QUESTION AND THE ALTERNATIVES

Question: The inquirer, a man, feels his major relationship is in a crisis. Where is the relationship going, what does it need?

※

1. THE CENTRAL QUESTION: Two of Swords. *This relationship is bound and constrained. Emotions are not expressed. This is a precarious balance based on tension and constriction.*

※

2. ALTERNATIVE: World: *Joy, achievement, success, but, more importantly, opening up the relationship both emotionally and socially.*

※

3. ALTERNATIVE: Five of Cups: *Loss, the pain of separation, regret. If the relationship is not opened to the world, it will end.*

THE CHALLENGE AND THE TOOL

Question: The inquirer, a man, feels very uncertain in his major relationship. What is happening, what is his place in it?

※

1. WHAT BROUGHT YOU HERE: Two of Cups. *This is the beginning of a relationship, a pledge of love and support.*

※

2. THE CHALLENGE YOU ARE FACING: Eight of Pentacles. *Work, training, skill, involvement with one's work for its own sake, relation to your community through work.*

※

3. THE TOOL AVAILABLE TO YOU: Four of Swords. *This indicates a withdrawal, pulling back or holding back to gather strength. The problem in the relationship seems to involve work. This advises the inquirer to pull back and define his own area of activity.*

By changing the order, you can change the emphasis. Lay a card in the center, then one to either side. This can represent the challenge of the moment and the alternatives you face in the present situation. Another variation is to lay a card on the left to represent what has brought you into this situation, a card on the right to represent the challenge you are facing, and a card in the center as the tool or resource you have to work with.

These examples use the Rider-Waite deck. This is probably the most popular Tarot deck in existence. It grew out of the tradition of the Order of the Golden Dawn and its synthesis of magical systems. The deck was created by A. E. Waite and published by Rider & Company in 1910. It was illustrated by Pamela Coleman Smith, whose images play a very central part in its popularity. Waite saw the Tarot as a symbolic presentation of universal ideas containing all the implicitness of the human mind. Its symbols were the truths embedded in the consciousness of all, which were recorded in secret literature and esoteric traditions.

SEVEN-CARD SPREAD

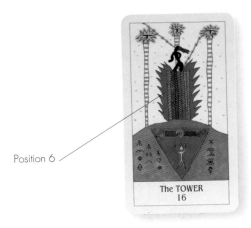

Position 6

The TOWER
16

THE TOWER

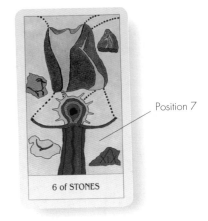

Position 7

6 of STONES

THE SIX OF STONES

Position 1

KNOWER of STONES

THE KNOWER OF STONES

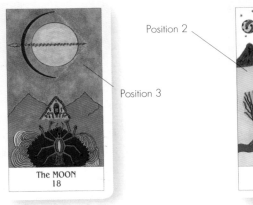

Position 3

The MOON
18

THE MOON

Position 2

The EMPRESS
3

THE EMPRESS

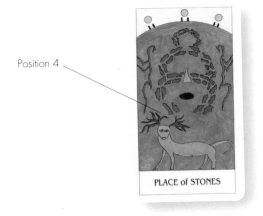

Position 4

PLACE of STONES

THE PLACE OF STONES

Position 5

The LOVERS
6

THE LOVERS

SEVEN-CARD SPREAD

The seven-card spread expands on the current situation to show what lies underneath it and what its goals might be. Lay the cards out in a central row of three to represent the dynamic of the present moment, with two cards beneath them to indicate the unconscious forces driving the situation and two cards above that may be seen as its goals.

This example uses a contemporary deck, the Shining Woman Tarot by Rachel Pollack. Shining Woman redefines the suits as Trees, Rivers, Birds, and Stones and the Court cards as Place, Knower, Gift, and Speaker. It uses an eclectic mix of shamanistic, tribal, and prehistoric art to address feminist and goddess concerns without being simplistic or dogmatic. It is an example of how modern decks are creating new worlds for Tarot.

Question: The inquirer, a man, wishes to start an independent business. Will he fulfill himself through this independent work?

※

1. WHAT BROUGHT YOU HERE: Knower of Stones. *He has been led to this work through his ability to find meaning in concrete, everyday things.*

※

2. THE CHALLENGE: Empress. *In this context, separation from the Mother and fear of falling back into her womb.*

※

3. TOOL: Moon. *Deep creative impulses, dreams, the nonrational, the inner woman as opposed to "thinking it all out."*

※

4. UNCONSCIOUS DRIVES: Place of Stones. *This shows a desire for a safe yet flexible and responsive place in the world.*

※

5. UNCONSCIOUS DRIVES: Lovers reversed. *Withdrawal from existing sexual and romantic relationships; need to be alone.*

※

6. GOALS: Tower. *This destroys existing structures, mental and literal. It points at a dramatic break from the past and the seeds of an entirely new way of life.*

※

7. GOALS: Six of Stones reversed. *The project will be achieved through cooperation with others, helping them fulfill their visions and needs.*

THE CELTIC CROSS

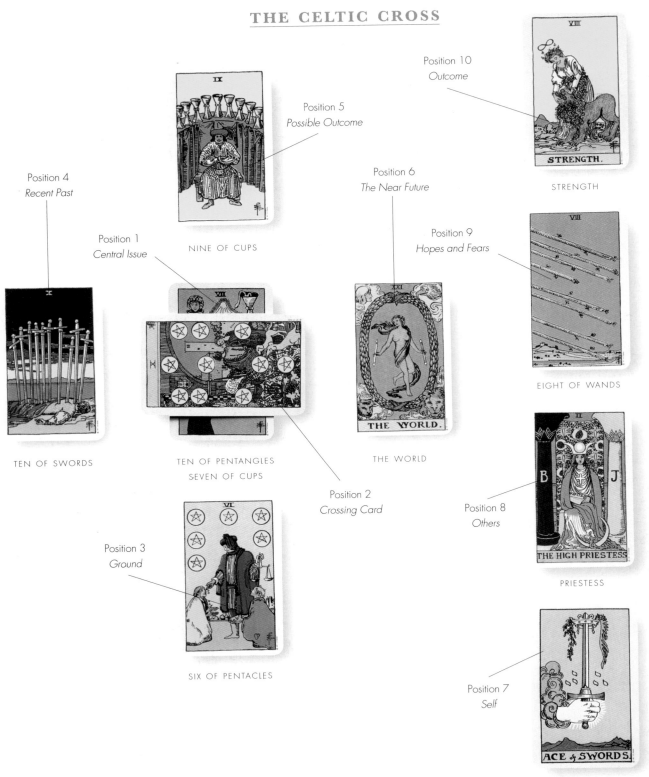

Position 10
Outcome

STRENGTH

Position 5
Possible Outcome

Position 4
Recent Past

Position 6
The Near Future

Position 1
Central Issue

Position 9
Hopes and Fears

NINE OF CUPS

EIGHT OF WANDS

TEN OF SWORDS

TEN OF PENTANGLES
SEVEN OF CUPS

THE WORLD

Position 2
Crossing Card

Position 8
Others

PRIESTESS

Position 3
Ground

SIX OF PENTACLES

Position 7
Self

ACE OF SWORDS

CELTIC CROSS

The Celtic Cross is probably the best-known spread, for it is directly associated with the Rider-Waite deck. The Celtic Cross has ten positions, each of which has a particular meaning.

POSITION 1: Central Issue: *the essential situation examined in the reading, the core of the complex of cards.*

※

POSITION 2: Crossing Card: *a counter influence or development from the central issue.*

※

POSITION 3: Ground: *influence of the past, roots, and causes.*

※

POSITION 4: Recent Past: *most recent developments; an influence that is leaving the situation.*

※

POSITION 5: Possible Outcome: *the potential of the situation; an alternative development; contrast with the final outcome; can represent a goal or something to be avoided.*

※

POSITION 6: The Near Future: *an influence that will soon affect you, a transitory aspect.*

※

POSITION 7: Self: *an attitude, activity, or character trait that affects the situation.*

※

POSITION 8: Others: *environment; can refer to specific people or the general situation.*

※

POSITION 9: Hopes and Fears: *what you expect from the situation, good or bad.*

※

POSITION 10: Outcome: *the likely result of this combination of forces; the direction things are heading; an image to work with, it represents the most probable potential of the situation unless things are changed.*

Question: The inquirer, a woman, is thinking about ending a major love relationship. Is this the right thing to do and the right time to do it?

※

1. CENTRAL ISSUE: Seven of Cups. *This indicates her desire is at this point only a fantasy. It is not connected to reality around her.*

※

2. CROSSING INFLUENCE: Ten of Pentacles. *The wish is thwarted by a desire for security and an inability to really look outside the fixed situation.*

※

3. GROUND (THE PAST): Six of Pentacles. *She and her friend may give to one another, but only from a position of power.*

※

4. RECENT PAST: Ten of Swords. *Heavy, melancholic atmosphere, strife and wounding, exaggerated feelings of pain and anguish.*

※

5. POSSIBLE DEVELOPMENTS: Nine of Cups. *Material well-being, a time to enjoy yourself after a crisis; also, danger of being cut off from the spiritual aspect of things.*

※

6. APPROACHING INFLUENCE: World. *Success, achievement, joy, insight; more importantly, the ability to open all the aspects of the situation and deal with them joyfully and fully.*

※

7. ASPECT OF SELF INVOLVED: Ace of Swords reversed. *She is unclear about her motives and how she contributes to the situation. She must develop her ability to discriminate between old experiences and actuality.*

※

8. OTHERS (ATMOSPHERE): High Priestess. *The relationship is in an atmosphere of silence, secret, and keeping things hidden. This also indicates a deep intuitive bond that cannot find its way to expression.*

※

9. HOPES AND FEARS: Eight of Wands reversed. *She is afraid the current situation will simply go on forever.*

※

10. OUTCOME: Strength reversed. *She does not have the strength or clarity to make a separation at this time. She should look more deeply at her motives and the influence of her own past experiences on the present.*

Carved in Wood and Stone

 unes are the magical alphabet of the North, of central and northern Europe. Though they were used as a form of writing, particularly for short magical inscriptions, their primary use was divination and decision making. The word "rune" means "whisper" or "secret." They are a system of secret talking and sacred signs, symbols that connect you with ancestors, spirits, and the living world.

Runes as a system of divination and communication actually arose from a collision between cultures from two ends of Europe. They combine very old signs and symbols, seen on pottery, standing stones, ritual objects, and cave paintings throughout the North as early as Paleolithic times, with a variant of what is probably an old Etruscan or North Italic alphabet.

One myth of origins has to do with the *Völsungr*, an ancestral northern tribe that wandered into Europe ahead of the great Ice Age. They were seen as semidivine beings who cared for the world, guardians of the primordial forests and the "dragon-paths," the ancient lines of connection between things. They "sowed the world" with the signs and the wisdom of the Ur-runes, which offer help to anyone suffering need or oppression.

At some point this Ur-horde of signs encountered one of the early Mediterranean alphabets. Through this collision it became a divination system, a magical writing. The act of putting these two things together, of seeing that magic, system, and insight are simultaneously possible, is described in a myth of Odin. This god of wisdom, divining, and the Horde of the Dead, hung upside down on the World Tree for nine days, "dedicated to himself." At the end of this shamanistic journey he "saw" how the magical and the systematic power of signs – and of the mind – could be put together. He "took up the runes."

Isa

Othila

Wunjo

Berkana

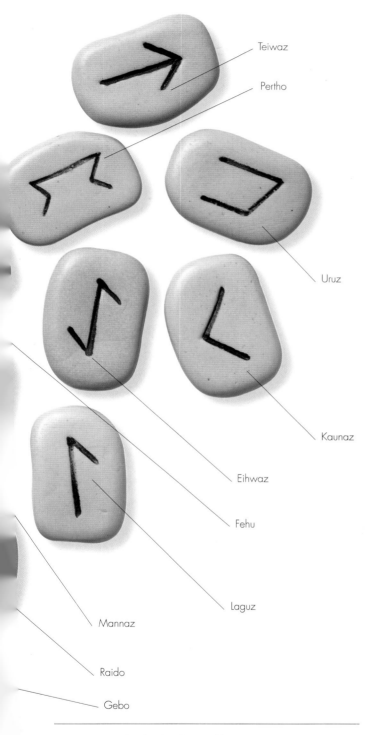

Teiwaz

Pertho

Uruz

Kaunaz

Eihwaz

Fehu

Laguz

Mannaz

Raido

Gebo

OPPOSITE: Odin's birds, a brace of fierce eagles associated with the Northern god of wisdom and divination.

ABOVE: Fourteen of the runes of the Elder Futhark.

The oldest and most often used form of the runes is the collection of 24 Germanic rune-staves that is called the *Elder Futhark*. This collection of signs defines an imaginative world inhabited from Paleolithic times until well into the 17th century. As late as 1700, people were burned for using them.

The 24 signs are arranged in three families, or *aett* (plural *aettir*), of eight signs each. The sequence of signs in each *aett* is significant, and each is ruled over by a particular spirit: *Freya* and *Frey*, goddess and god of fertility, love and increase; *Heimdall*, the Watcher and keeper of the Rainbow Bridge to the Heavens; and *Tyr*, war-leader and spirit of the Just. Each rune is a symbolic storehouse and a magical talisman with a field of meanings that connects objects, creatures, feelings, experiences, spirits, and archetypal processes. They are seen as a description of the inner structure of reality. Their movement in a particular situation articulates the way *Wyrd*, fate, is weaving our lives.

Because the runes did not go through the fixation of meaning associated with imperial culture and the development of a universal compass (see pages 60–5), their fields of meaning remain fluid and individual. Old texts and traditions, written much later than the signs themselves, give sets of associations, but the intuition still has free play. This is one of the reasons for their modern rediscovery.

For the runes are more than a way of sending secret messages. They exist in the middle of a group of "pagan" practices that includes weaving spells, speaking with the dead, and traveling in the spirit. They were inscribed on objects to give them power and potency, used to curse enemies, and seen as doorways to identification with a pagan god. They would be used to examine the life-path of a newborn child or to determine the path a tribe would follow. The cultures that used the runes put a high value on women and the power of the goddesses. Wise women and runemasters used these signs to understand what the gods wanted; to see and change the shape of coming events.

Casting the Runes

There has been quite a bit of modern interest in rune divination. Collections of runes are now commercially available, along with various sets of instructions on how to use them. Some rune workers advise you to make your own from strips of wood you have cut or stones you have gathered during a sea-storm.

Runes are kept in a leather bag or box from which they can either be cast or drawn. The oldest description we have of casting or divining with runes comes from the Roman historian Tacitus, about 98 C.E. He was describing Germanic tribes encountered as the Roman legions attempted to subdue northern Europe. He observed that when a tribe or a family needed information about what was to come or faced an important decision, they would cast the runes. They would cut a branch from a "nut-bearing" tree, cut it into small strips, and mark the strips with the divinatory signs. A priest or the head of a family would cast these strips or "staves" onto a white cloth. After an invocation to Odin, All-father and god of divination and poets, he would pick up three staves, one after another, and "read" their meanings. If the answer was negative, the action would be abandoned. If positive, it would be confirmed through bird-signs or omens taken from the sacred white horses.

Ceremonially, casting the runes is called "Riding the Wagon," suggesting that for a moment you sit in the riderless wagon drawn by the sacred white horses and see what is past, passing, and to come. You lay a white cloth down to define the *shoat*, or direction, of casting. Ideally, this will be on the east–west axis or facing the sun. You focus on the question, then take a handful of the runes at random from the bag and cast them in front of you. The ones that fall right-side up are read. The reading is influenced by whether the rune is reversed or not.

LEFT: Odin, the Zeus of the Northern world; he brought the runes to humanity as a way of communication and divination.

THE THREE SISTERS

You can also take runes from the bag and lay them in a spread, a predetermined pattern like those used in reading Tarot cards. A basic spread is the group of three that represents the three sisters who weave fate. Pick three runes at random and lay them out from left to right. The first signifies past influences on your question; the second, the quality of the present moment; the third, the potential future.

1. Teiwaz   2. Fehu   3. Isa

THE FOUR DIRECTIONS

Another basic spread, used to see into the factors behind a given situation, is modeled on the Four Directions. It uses five runes and, ideally, is laid out on the actual north–south axis. Lay the runes out in a circle, clockwise, starting with the north above and ending with the center.

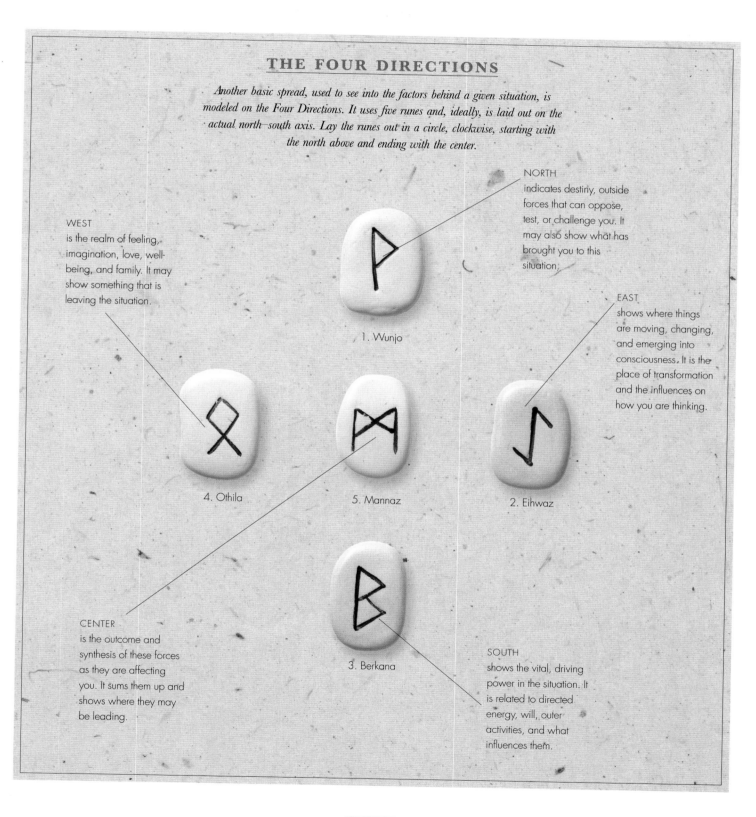

NORTH
indicates destiny, outside forces that can oppose, test, or challenge you. It may also show what has brought you to this situation.

WEST
is the realm of feeling, imagination, love, well-being, and family. It may show something that is leaving the situation.

EAST
shows where things are moving, changing, and emerging into consciousness. It is the place of transformation and the influences on how you are thinking.

1. Wunjo

4. Othila

5. Mannaz

2. Eihwaz

CENTER
is the outcome and synthesis of these forces as they are affecting you. It sums them up and shows where they may be leading.

3. Berkana

SOUTH
shows the vital, driving power in the situation. It is related to directed energy, will, outer activities, and what influences them.

The Elder Futhark

ere are the 24 signs of the Elder Futhark, with a brief description of the field of meaning that surrounds them. As with all divination methods, the more you know about the signs, the more they have become a part of your imagination, the more information you will obtain.

Some rune workers have built elaborate tables of correspondences linking the signs to directions, times of day, colors and moon phases. But here lies the danger of over-interpretation, of feeling that the fields of meaning are fixed and static. Let the symbols surprise you. Don't be afraid of meanings that pop up, suggested by the situation at hand.

MAKING YOUR OWN RUNES

Now that they are regaining popularity, it is easy to buy sets of runes from a store. However, it is much more satisfying to make your own, because they are then truly attuned to you. Make stone runes by collecting ocean pebbles (preferably during stormy weather), then painting or scratching the signs on them. You can also make wooden runes, although this may be more difficult. You need fresh wood, newly cut from a nut or fruit tree. The rune signs are marked on the pale inner part of the wood. When you cast your own runes, throw them onto a white linen or cotton cloth.

ABOVE: Large rune staffs being wielded by magicians. This 17th-century illustration comes from a translation of *A Compendious History of Goths, Swedes and Vandals.*

RIGHT: A runestone made in the 9th century C.E. It is a commemoration to a dead son, and contains an ode to Theodoric, King of the Goths.

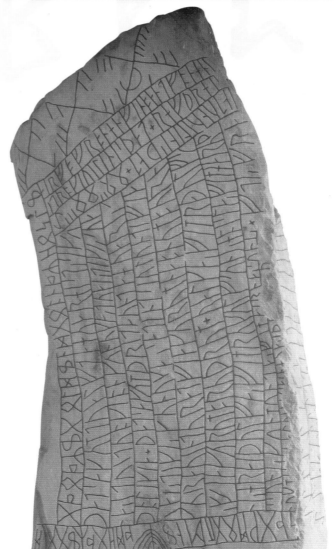

THE FIRST AETT

Fertility, increase, love, basic life forces

 FEHU: cattle, wealth; financial strength and security; something won or earned; the Primal Cow, the Sow, the fertile originating animals; starting point, our common beginning; power, success, control of riches; the imperative to give and share. Sacred to Freya, goddess of fecundity and love.

 URUZ: wild ox, raw creative power; a huge, fierce animal, impossible to domesticate; sexual energy, strength, and speed; unpredictable power; collective strength, the common good; test, adventure; greed. Sacred to Thor, god of thunder and strength.

 THURISAZ: thorn bush, conflicts; troll, demon, giant; defense, protection, "a sharp and evil thing, grim for those who fall among them"; the hammer of Thor, the crusher; male power, penis, the "prick"; unstable, change for the worse. Sacred to Loki, trickster and shape-changer.

 ANSUZ: god's blessing; source of blessing and joy; language; the divine breath; the sacred ash, the world tree; hold fast, protect, guarantee of order. Sacred to Odin, god of wind and spirit.

 RAIDO: wheel, travel, the right move to make; road, ride, journey; directed activity, the vehicle and the way; channel energy, conscious effort; personal transformation. Sacred to Thor and thunder.

 KAUNAZ: burning, danger to health; torch, fever, ulcer, abscess; mental or physical discomfort; illumination, light in the darkness, regeneration through death; a ship, a skiff. Sacred to Heimdall, the underworld watcher.

 GEBO: gift; sacrifice and generosity; a sacred mark, dedicated to the gods; giving and receiving; talent and ability as the gods' gift; to help someone, join together; love relation, the lover's kiss; the Bountiful Goddess, abundance.

 WUNJO: joy, pleasure, comfort, ecstasy; the wind-vane, ability to stay in harmony with the flow of things; those who live without sorrow; prosperous, content; the happy balance; fulfilled wishes; fellowship, shared well-being; the "better life." Sacred to Odin, who knows the directions.

SECOND AETT

Openings to the other worlds; Heimdall, the Watcher, who keeps the Rainbow Bridge
to the Heavens; the icy bridge to the Underworld; limitation, fate, the inner journey.

 HAGALAZ: hail, the sudden destroyer; uncontrolled forces, inner and outer; hail of weapons; winter, delay; influence of the past, destruction of past structures; the oldest Norn, Urd, voice of the past; disruption, accident, unavoidable bad luck; challenge to change, upheaval in personal unconscious. Sacred to Heimdall the Watcher and Mordgud, keeper of the icy bridge to the Underworld.

 NAUTHIZ: necessity, need, constraint; misery, exhaustion, scarcity, absence; caution; the helper, hard work to overcome need; work on oneself, the opus; the firebow and block, mother of firelight. Sacred to the Norns, weavers of fate, and Nott, goddess of night who gives birth to day.

 ISA: ice; obstacles; psychological blocks to thought and action; stasis, coldness, loss of energy; end, termination, death; powerful inexorable forces; intensifies meaning of any other rune it is associated with.

 JERA: year, harvest, realization, plenty; promise of success; the abundant year, thriving crops, summer; the generosity of kings; fertile, vital; peace, the sacred marriage between heaven and earth; good timing, right order, culmination, prosperity. Sacred to Freya and Frey, the bountiful couple.

 EIHWAZ: the yew tree, force, motivation, purpose; need to acquire; long-living, "stands hard and fast"; a joy, the guardian of flame, green throughout the winter; the hunter's yew-wood bow, the hunt; the "bleeding tree," death, regeneration and rebirth; gate to the underworld.

 PERTHO: hearth, womb, dice cup; the game played between desire and destiny, the dance of life; vagina, female fertility; brings things to fruition; sexual intercourse; joy, laughter, music; makes fertile and reveals what is hidden. Sacred to Frigg, the All-mother.

 ALGIZ: protection, shelter yourself and others; hold on to what has been earned; the elk, who protects himself from enemies; the hand sign to ward off evil; temple sanctuary; elk-sedge, a plant that wounds whoever touches it; aspiration toward the divine; a very strong sign of protection against enemies or conflicting forces. Sacred to Heimdall, the Watcher.

 SOWULO: sun, life force, day, hope, attainment; good health, harmony, contact with higher self; guide of sailors, light of the world; beneficent magic, spiritual power to resist disintegration; guidance, healing, victory. Sacred to Balder, the beautiful god, and the Solar Wheel.

THIRD AETT

*Tyr, sky god and war-leader of the heavenly pantheon;
synthesis, connection to the spirit and to others; integration.*

 TEIWAZ: victory and justice; success in war and law; honor, leadership, authority; "a sign that never fails the noble one in the darkness of night"; victory and protection, widely-used amulet; the Shining One, the vault of heavens, the Pole Star; knowing your strength; steady, reliable; optimism, courage, faith; self-sacrifice; the spear-sign, a brave and noble death. Sacred to Tyr, lord of the heavens and war-leader.

 BERKANA: the birch tree, birth and growing; mental and physical fertility, personal growth, prosperity in an enterprise; the green and shining tree; youth, vigor, beauty; purification, new beginnings; the Breasts of the Earth Goddess; spring.

 EHWAZ: horse; a message from the gods; status, pride, joy; clear confirmation of signs around it; a comfort to the restless. Sacred to Frey, summer sun and erect penis.

 MANNAZ: human; culture, memory, intelligence; connection to others; what we share in happiness; awareness of our shadow; adornment, augmentation. Sacred to Odin, the All-father, and Heimdall, the Watcher.

 LAGUZ: water; imagination, intuition, mystery, flow; all that flows and changes; lake, sea, wave, waterfall; the medium of passage, risk, success in travel and acquisition, but with possibility of loss; ebb and flow of tides; the leek, power of irresistible green growth pushing up through the earth. Sacred to Njord, god of the wealth of the sea.

 INGUZ: male potency, the erect phallus; peace, prosperity, protection of the hearth and home; beacon, light, fire-sign; potential energy accumulating for burst of fertilizing power. Sacred to Frey, summer sun and consort of Freya.

 DAGAZ: day, daylight, security, certainty; clarity; midday, midsummer; light, health, prosperity, strength, joy; right time to plan and embark on an enterprise; divine light; balance between light and darkness; the "door" of the year; the light that brings hope and happiness. Sacred to Heimdall, the Watcher.

 OTHILA: inheritance; guarding and passing on sacred values; patrimony, material and spiritual heritage; ancestral lands, estates, property; spiritual values, fundamental ideas; belonging, togetherness; liberty of individual and clan; duty to resist oppression; integrity, wise use of resources.

In some divinatory collections, there will be a 25th Rune left blank and called Wyrd, or "the part of fate." It indicates that something you cannot know or control will decide the matter at hand.

Rolling the Dice

ivining with dice is another way to open the Book of Fate. The "throw of the dice" is an old and deep metaphor for the way individual desire and the forces of destiny intersect. Several African divination methods use a set of marked bones or wooden dice to key collections of stories, praise poems, and predictions. Romans divined with *astragals*, the knuckle bones of sheep. Greek dice divination, associated with the gods Hermes and Athena, was much older and, in the end, more popular than the great oracle centers. In late Mediterranean antiquity a series of street oracles flourished using number and alphabet dice to key phrases in an oracle book.

The dice are also a hidden mirror of the cosmos. Their random fall shows the interaction between the order of the universe and the individual event. The Chinese game of mah-jong, which uses 144 different image tiles portraying Guardians, Directions, Elements, Colors, and Numbers, is today used mainly for gambling. It reproduces an old divinatory method that involves the placing or "fall" of elements on a cosmic grid. Similarly, European fortunetellers used a simplified and formulaic dice divination system descended from the late antique astrological practice called "The Part of Fortune." Dice representing the planets would be thrown onto an astrological diagram of the Houses. The result was read as the part that luck would play in the different areas of a person's life.

LEFT: Sheep knuckle bones, or *astragals*, used in Roman divinatory techniques. They were cast like dice.

ABOVE LEFT: Mah-jong tiles, from the Chinese game now played for fun and profit. It echoes ancient divinatory methods based on the Five Transformative Elements and the Four Directions.

ABOVE: Babylonian astrologers scanned the skies tracking the movement of the planets against the fixed stars, like dice on a black baize cloth.

HOW TO DIVINE WITH DICE

In the fortuneteller's method, three dice are used, producing the numbers 3 to 18. Each number has a meaning. They are thrown onto a circular layout of the Houses, where each division represents an area of the person's life.

THE NUMBERS

The meanings of the numbers thrown are

3 Unexpected favorable developments

4 Disappointment, discontent

5 Something unknown brings happiness

6 Loss in business, gain in spirit

7 Delays and obstacles through scandal

8 An unwise course; strong outside influences

9 Success in love, reconciliation

10 Birth, new beginnings, promotions

11 Illness, parting, anxiety

12 Good news through a message; seek advice

13 Sorrow, unhappy long-term developments

14 A new friend; substantial assistance from others

15 Beware! You are tempted into injustice or vice. Don't do it!

16 Good for voyages, set out now!

17 Changes of plan; let yourself be guided by advice from outside

18 Great good luck, happiness, and gain in the near future

THE DICE

The individual numbers on each die have meanings:

1 Favorable, but be careful

2 Cultivate your relationships

3 Success

4 Disappointments, sorrows

5 Favorable trend

6 Uncertain situation

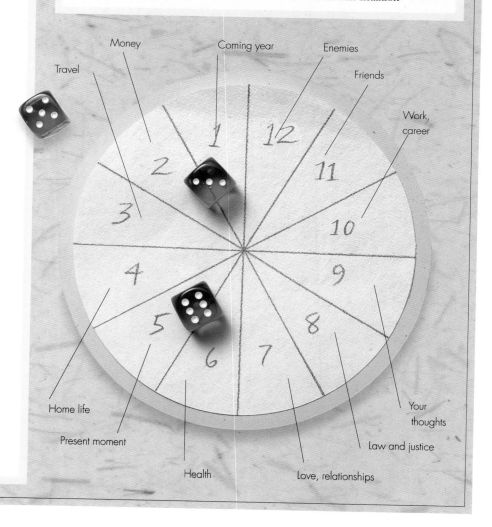

Money

Coming year

Enemies

Friends

Travel

Work, career

Home life

Present moment

Health

Love, relationships

Law and justice

Your thoughts

Mo and Sho Mo

In most cultures, dice are now used almost exclusively for gambling and games. The old divination books have been lost. Traditional Tibet, however, developed extremely sophisticated methods of dice divination to indicate the actions of karma, the influence of particular deities, and efficacious spiritual practices, as well as pointing out the favorable or unfavorable quality of the time in specific areas of the inquirer's life.

These practices are called *Mo*. There were a great variety of *Mo* cards and books that gave images and predictions attached to the numbers the dice would produce. Dice and seeds were also thrown onto boards divided into squares. They could represent possible methods of medical prognosis and treatment, or the 21 forms of the Great Compassionate Goddess, Tara. In such a system you might receive these responses:

2 THE TURQUOISE SPRING: *The dried valley will yield springs, plants will become verdant, timely rain will fall. The absent will return. Do the worship of the enemy god and your own deity. This is good for marriage.*

or:

9 THE INVALID: *Sickness due to grandparent demons. Agriculture is bad, cattle suffer. Offer the black cake of three heads and do "calling for luck." Bad outlook for desires, credit, business. Perform "obtaining long life": Mend the road and repair the* Mani *stones. Home life is bad. Read the* do mang *spells. The ancestral demon is to be suppressed. Avoid conflicts, new plans, and long voyages.*

ABOVE: A traditional Tibetan *tanka* showing the wheel of life in the demonic grasp of Mara the Tempter. *Tankas* are sacred painted scrolls or banners, which hang in Buddhist temples where they are used as meditation aids.

ABOVE RIGHT: Manjushri, the Buddhist Bodhisattva of wisdom and insight. Bodhisattvas are beings who have reached enlightenment themselves but remain in the world to help others reach the same state.

Such a system could also indicate possible states of rebirth. Lamas would use a grid of 56 images, each graphically representing a phase of existence in one of the Six Realms. Each image had a name and the names of six other related states of being, each preceded by a letter of the alphabet or "seed-syllable." The same six letters were inscribed on a die. Starting from the human realm, the die would be thrown the requisite number of times to trace the possible path of future incarnations.

The best-preserved and most penetrating forms of Tibetan dice divination are called *Sho Mo* and rely on divination books associated with a specific protective deity. These systems were very popular and were relied on by monks and laypeople alike. The divinations were often performed by monks for laypeople and keyed a set of rituals that the monks would perform. They also indicated which particular mediations and spiritual sutras would be efficacious. This form of dice divination helps you see an event or situation clearly in its interconnection with all other events. It shows you what spirit energies are working behind the scenes and gives a prediction about how this energy will develop in various parts of your life. If it is done selflessly, it becomes an important part of the "Bodhisattva's path," the practice of continual giving for the "happiness of all sentient beings."

There are two major ways to practice *Sho Mo*. One, sponsored by the Protectress *Palden Lhamo*, uses three dice engraved with the numbers 1–6. The other, of which there is now a complete English translation, is sponsored by the Wisdom-God *Manjushri*, and uses one die engraved with six root-syllables. Both key texts that consist of an overall image and a series of specific interpretations.

LEFT: A Tibetan *Mo* die showing three of its facets.

ABOVE: The Wheel of Life, the Tibetan symbol for the cosmos and the cycle of rebirth and karma (fate). The segments of the wheel (there may be five or six) show the realms in which people can be reborn: heaven; the abode of jealous gods; the animal kingdom; hell; and the human realm. The rooster, snake, and pig in the hub of the wheel symbolize arrogance, hate, and greed – considered to be the roots of human misery.

MANJUSHRI'S ORACLE

To use this oracle you must visualize Manjushri, invoke him, and recite his mantra,
OM AH RA PA TSA NA DHI. You then throw the die twice, which produces one of 36
possible combinations of the six seed-syllables of his mantra:

AH AH	The Stainless Sky		TSA AH	The White Umbrella of Good Fortune
AH RA	The Flaming Rays of the Sun		TSA RA	The Great Fiery Weapon
AH PA	The Nectar Rays of the Moon		TSA PA	Empty of Intelligence
AH TSA	The Bright Star		TSA TSA	The Streamer of Fame
AH NA	The Ground of Gold		TSA NA	The Mara Demon of Aggregates
AH DHI	The Tone of Vajras		TSA DHI	The House of Good Tidings
RA AH	The Bright Lamp		NA AH	The Golden Mountain
RA RA	Adding Butter to the Burning Flames		NA RA	The Demon of the Heavenly Son
RA PA	The Demon of Death		NA PA	The Overflowing Jeweled Vessel
RA TSA	The King of Power		NA TSA	The Scattered Mountain of Sand
RA NA	The Dried-up Tree		NA NA	The Mansion of Gold
RA DHI	The Door of Auspicious Visions		NA DHI	The Treasury of Jewels
PA AH	The Vase of Nectar		DHI AH	Manjushri Appears
PA RA	The Pool without a Source of Water		DHI RA	The Endless, Auspicious Knot
PA PA	The Ocean of Nectar		DHI PA	The Golden Female Fish
PA TSA	The Demon of Afflictions		DHI TSA	The White Conch
PA NA	The Golden Lotus		DHI NA	The Golden Wheel
PA DHI	The Nectar-like Medicine		DHI DHI	The Jeweled Banner of Wisdom

MANJUSHRI'S ANSWER

Here is an example. It is the answer to the question posed to Manjushri asking what these pages on divination can offer.

If NA AH, the Golden Mountain, appears, then firmness and stability are seen, just as the golden mountain reaches to the heavens. The sign of this divining is "the unchanging auspicious symbol."

FAMILY AND PROPERTY: These are steady and firm.

INTENTIONS AND AIMS: These are excellent and will bring stability to your life in the future.

FRIENDS AND WEALTH: Possessions and friends are stable, and will remain so because of the power of this steadiness.

ENEMIES: There are none; your power is stable.

GUESTS: Neither lost nor harmed, they will take a while to arrive.

ILLNESS: None.

EVIL SPIRITS: There are none bothering you at present.

SPIRITUAL PRACTICE: Firm and good, strong and steady.

LOST ARTICLE: It has not been found by someone else.

WILL THEY COME? WILL THE TASK BE ACCOMPLISHED? There will be a delay of your present project in favor of another,

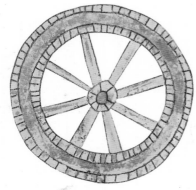

but what has been started will have a successful outcome.

ALL REMAINING MATTERS: Successful; but traveling will involve delay. Read *Avatamsaka Sutra* (on interrelatedness). Rely on *Vajra*-deities and mother-deities of the Destroyer family (skillful means that destroy illusions). *Kishitigarbha* is your special deity. Good fortune will increase if you rely on mantras of *Locani, Vaishravana,* and *Jambhala* (wealth and female enlightenment).

This prediction is "holding your place and not moving." It represents the excellence of all activities performed on a stable foundation.

OPPOSITE AND ABOVE: Each of the six syllables of Manjushri's mantra are marked on the Mo die, one on each face. In combination they form specific images such as the NA AH, the Golden Mountain (below right), DHI PA, the Golden Female Fish (top left), DHI NA, the Golden Wheel (top right), RA PA, the Demon of Death (above left), or NA NA, the Mansion of Gold (above right).

Mala- or rosary-divination is related to these dice and number practices. It uses the string of prayer beads that every monk and most laypeople carried. The diviner poses a question, then takes hold of the string of beads, each hand grasping a bead chosen at random. He counts the beads between his hands by threes from both sides to the middle, until there is a remainder of three, two, or one. One remaining bead is a *falcon*; two beads are a *raven*; three beads are a *snow lion*. This procedure is repeated three times.

The first answer announces whether or not the spirits support the project in question: a *falcon* indicates support; a *raven* indicates hostility, and a *snow lion*, slow but stable progress. The second answer describes the environment: good luck, obstacles, or smooth progression. The third answer describes the arrival of travelers: imminent arrival and good news, obstacles and bad news, or a delay with good results in the end.

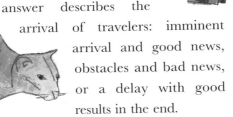

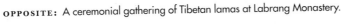

OPPOSITE: A ceremonial gathering of Tibetan lamas at Labrang Monastery.

CENTER: Tibetan rosary beads, carried by monks and laypeople.

ABOVE TOP: A raven, indicating hostility, is symbolized by two beads remaining.

ABOVE CENTER: A falcon, indicating support, is symbolized by one bead remaining in the process of *mala*-divination.

ABOVE: A snow lion, indicating stable progress, is symbolized by three beads remaining.

BEAD COUNTING

Another method counts the beads twice, and predicts from the order of the two results:

IF ONE COMES AFTER ONE:
Everything is favorable.

IF TWO COMES AFTER TWO:
The cloudless sky will be darkened, there will be loss of wealth.

IF THREE COMES AFTER THREE:
Prosperity is at hand in all things.

IF THREE COMES AFTER ONE:
Rice plants grow on sandy hills, widows obtain husbands, poor men get rich.

IF ONE COMES AFTER TWO:
Every wish will be fulfilled; you will escape from danger.

IF ONE COMES AFTER THREE:
God's help is at hand. Worship the gods.

IF TWO COMES AFTER THREE:
Mediocre results, legal problems.

IF THREE COMES AFTER TWO:
Turquoise fountains spring forth and fertilize the ground; unexpected food, escape from any danger.

IF TWO COMES AFTER ONE:
Bad omen, contagious disease will come. If you worship the gods and propitiate the demons, it can be prevented.

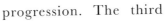

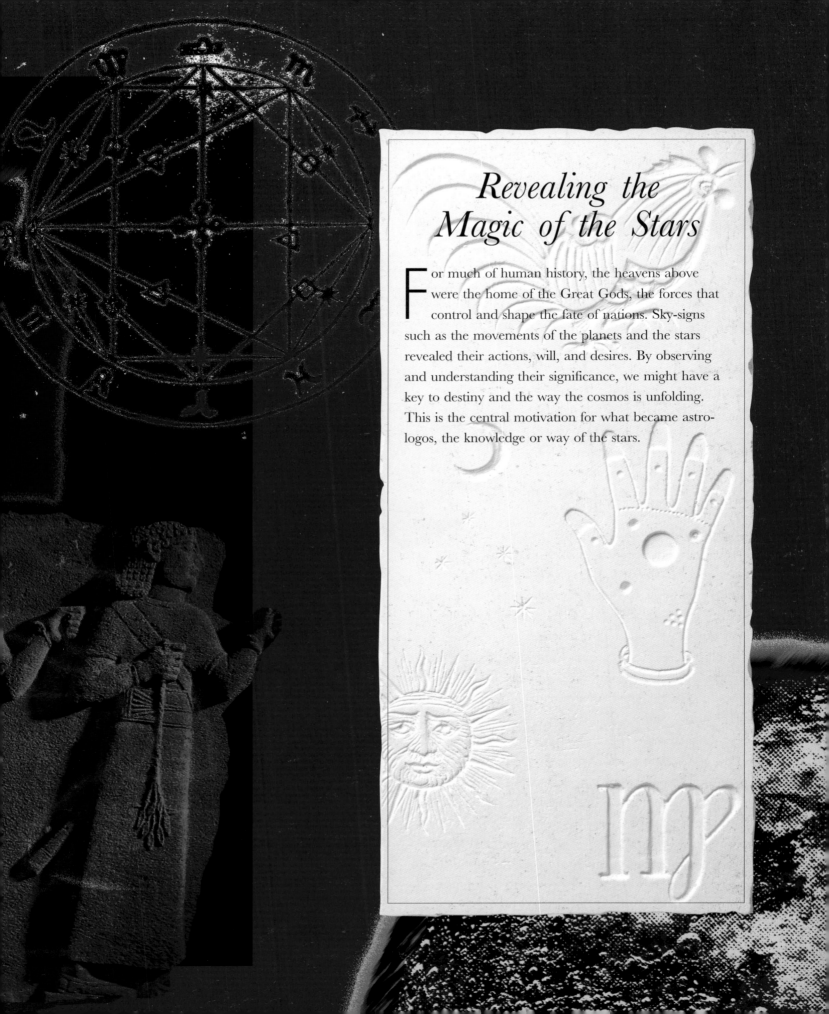

Revealing the Magic of the Stars

For much of human history, the heavens above were the home of the Great Gods, the forces that control and shape the fate of nations. Sky-signs such as the movements of the planets and the stars revealed their actions, will, and desires. By observing and understanding their significance, we might have a key to destiny and the way the cosmos is unfolding. This is the central motivation for what became astro-logos, the knowledge or way of the stars.

Building Mansions in the Sky

Astrology as we know it today is a product of Hellenistic or late antique civilization. It combines Chaldean and Egyptian astral religions with Greek astronomy, mathematics, and myths. When the system appeared at the end of the third century B.C.E., its origins were ascribed to the Egyptian god Thoth or Hermes. The practitioners of this divinatory system, however, were called "Chaldeans," a term that had very little reference to the actual history of Mesopotamia. The system developed in *Magna Graecia*, as the Mediterranean area was called after the conquests of Alexander the Great. It spread to India and the Islamic world, becoming the basis for their astrological sciences.

However complex the system of interpretation became, the mythic base of astrology is the attraction of the sky. We tend to ignore this, for we are cut off from the heavens by a layer of ambient light, the light from our cities and electrical power sources, and by a mythological shift away from "transcendence," the desire to "rise above" the mundane. For the people of the ancient world, the alternation of day and night, the "great lights" of sun and moon, the appearance and disappearance of the "wandering stars," played out the drama of the high gods. Watching the sky-signs was not only a way to know what may happen. It opened a divine realm, where you could dwell in contemplation, free of the compulsions of this world below.

The height and expanse of the sky point at transcendence, its light, heat, and moisture suggest the fertile source of life. The sky has been imagined as an overarching vault, a celestial tent, a black-glazed bucket or gourd, a bowl or egg, or a goddess arching over her reclining husband, the Earth. The stars have been seen as holes in the vault, or as pieces of the sun and moon broken off and conscientiously tended by spirits. The Milky Way has been seen as a river of milk, semen, or souls flowing on into eternity; as the trunk of the World Tree; as the footprints left by the founding heroes; or as the intertwining of two great snakes that produce the world. In many myths, the souls of the dead must climb up to the sky along mountain paths or on a tree, rope, ladder, vine, spider's web, or rainbow. For the home of the soul was in the heavens. It was a "world above," with its own inhabitants and its own realities.

There is a central paradox in many myths of the sky. The sky and the earth were once in close communion. Separating them was necessary to begin human life, but, at the same time, the withdrawal of the heavenly gods left the world a barren place. Shamans, prophets, diviners, and other "technicians of the sacred" continually seek to reestablish communication with this creative source of the spirit, to connect us once again to our "heavenly home."

Sky-signs and Omens

The transcendent nature of the sky gave "sky-signs" a great importance. They were a means of understanding the actions and desires of the departed gods. Weather patterns, particularly thunder and lightning, were direct "atmospheric" comments on human actions. The regular appearance of stars and planets, and irregular variations on those patterns, provided others. In many Northern myths, the Pole Star was the "Nail of the Firmament," with other star-groups circling around it in a dance that defined the year. The appearance of certain star groups, such as the Pleiades, Orion the Hunter, or the Dog-star Sirius, marked off an agricultural calendar for the old Greeks. Hesiod's *Works and Days* is an example of this sort of an omen-book, offering agricultural signs interspersed with moral and philosophical observations. This originated a style that idealized the farmer's life as exemplifying fundamental virtues in harmony with the heavens.

The Mesopotamians kept long lists of celestial omens and their meanings, seeing them as communications from the gods to the king. Egyptians defined certain star groups as marking the eternal "round of the year." Eclipses of sun and moon were of particular importance, marking significant conflicts or changes among the celestial hierarchy. Many cultures developed ways to predict when they would occur, then observed in which parts of the heavens they happened in order to find their meaning. The meteorite or "stone

from the sky" was another important symbol, a direct communication of the power and fertility of the heavens. In some cultures, all crystals were considered sky-stones that could transform the shaman's body or reflect what was going on in someone's soul.

OPPOSITE BOTTOM: A treatise on astrology, *Flores Astrologici*, written in Latin, shows the Sun (Sol) driving his chariot around the heavens. Leo, the sign ruled by the Sun, appears on the chariot wheel. He is followed by Venus in her chariot, drawn by her emblematic doves and guided by her son Cupid. Glyphs for Taurus and Libra, the two signs that Venus rules, are shown on the chariot wheels.

OPPOSITE TOP: A Babylonian view of the cosmos from c. 500 B.C.E., carved in stone.

ABOVE: Detail from a 19th-century Sanskrit manuscript entitled *Jewel of Essence of All Science* shows the constellations of the western and eastern sky in their imagined pictorial forms.

LEFT: A 16th-century treatise on astrology from Turkey, featuring the sun sign Capricorn the Goat and its attributes.

The Ritual Calendar

In many cultures, the observation of particular omens was complemented by sophisticated astronomical measurements. These observations were primarily used to provide the frame for a ritual calendar; a procession of festivals, rituals, myths, and images that kept human culture linked with the gods above. In particular, Mesopotamia, China, India, and the Mayan cultures of Central America used very sophisticated observations to track the paths of the gods.

There are two basic types of calendars in the world, the *solar* calendar based on the yearly movement of the sun around the "circle of the horizon," and the *lunar* calendar based on the continually repeating phases of the moon. The solar cycle, with its equinoxes and solstices, became the way to organize time in the West and is used today as an "international standard." The lunar cycle and the phases of the moon were the basis for most Eastern calendars, in particular, those of China and Tibet.

The evolution of the calendar was not just a way to record events. The cycles of sun and moon supported a round of festivals and ritual occasions through which humans participated in the creative quality of time. The solar calendar defines the seasonal round through the myth of the solar hero, the yearly death and rebirth of the Light. It is marked by the summer and winter solstices, the points when the sun "stands still" in the sky and changes direction, and by the spring and fall equinoxes, when the sun crosses the celestial equator and day and night are equal.

LEFT AND OPPOSITE RIGHT: The moon and the sun, the bases of all the world's calendars.

ABOVE: August, from *Les Tres Riches Heures du Duc de Berry,* a 15th-century book of hours. This is one of the most exquisite representations of the Western calendar, with an image for each month showing the activities of the Duke's court and estate and giving precise zodiacal information.

OPPOSITE LEFT: A Tibetan *tanka,* or banner, depicting the Paradise of Shambhala. It is supposed to be a mythical, mountain-girt country to the north of Tibet. A city containing a royal palace and a garden is in the center.

These mark the annual death and rebirth of the sun and inspired most Western ritual activities. They were observed with great subtlety in many ancient cultures and provided the orientation for many ancient monoliths and religious monuments. Stonehenge in England is said to be one such edifice.

The lunar calendar supports several different ritual systems. In contrast to the sun calendar, where the division into months is fairly arbitrary, each month of the lunar calendar begins with the new moon, reaches a high point with the full moon and ends in the dark of the moon. Each day has a particular quality that is auspicious for some activities and inauspicious for others. This calendar still governs the imaginative life of many Eastern people. It reached a ritual high point in the Tibetan vision of time, based on the life of the historical Buddha.

In traditional Tibet, time was seen as a mother goddess that nurtured the process of enlightenment. Just as the land provided lakes that were oracle mirrors and mountains that were the abodes of protective Buddhas guiding the old savage gods, the endless moon cycles opened the path of enlightenment symbolized by the Buddha's life. His birth, enlightenment, and death all occurred at the full moon of the fourth month. His first teaching was celebrated on the fourth day of the sixth lunar month. On lunar New Year, the entire nation devoted itself to two weeks of dance, ritual, and celebration in honor of the miracles that marked the transformation of time.

In the *Kalachakra* "time machine," a ceremony, vision, and ritual, the Buddha manifests as the fabric of time itself, turning the cycles of the calendar into a machine for compassion that assists in the evolution of all beings born and unborn. This vision of time, which has analogies in Western ideas of the return of the golden age, leads to the flowering of *Shambhala*, a paradisical state in which all will be devoted to the quest for enlightenment. It is enacted through the construction of a complex sand-particle *mandala* over six feet in diameter, containing palaces that represent the Body, Mind, and Speech of all possible Buddhas. Mantra syllables represent 712 different archetypal deities. After several days of initiations, rituals, and blessings, this palace of virtual reality is destroyed. The sand particles, each a "fractal" that contains the entire vision, are swept into a vase, taken to a body of water and consigned to the underworld dragons who spread them through the worlds below.

Making the Map of the Heavens

In its origins, Western astrology was a "science of kings." It began in the omen-lore and observation of the heavens that kept the king connected to the divine powers, revealing what the Chinese called the "mandate of heaven." In Hellenistic Greece, this science of kings became a map of the interlocking cycles of the heavens that could be used to describe the fate of any person or event. Each person became a microcosm that duplicated the endless play of the heavens. The Greeks did not invent divination by the stars. The basis of *astro-logos* came from the Egyptians and the "Chaldeans." The Greeks took over ideas and practices from these cultures and fused them with their own myths and their mathematics.

The Chaldeans were traveling astrologers from Mesopotamia, a product of the first extensive contact between Greeks and Persians in the wake of the conquests of Alexander the Great. These Chaldean priests spread a new form of ancient Babylonian star-lore throughout the Mediterranean. One of the landmarks in the development of this new kind of star-divination was the establishment of a school of "Babylonian science" on the island of Cos about 280 B.C.E. The Chaldeans brought the "cult of the stars," or astral gods, and the idea of astrology as fate in the religious sense, for they saw "heavenly omens" as keys to the fate of all beings on earth.

Other fundamental ideas such as the circle of the year, medical astrology, and the precise calculation of eclipses came from Egypt, a culture the Greeks revered as a "mother of secrets." Out of this mixture the Greeks created an immense apparatus to describe the way human destiny was created. This system centered on a few basic principles that still hold good:

- *The "stars" are the fundamental creative agents in the organization of the cosmos. They express the equilibrium and harmony of the world and the fate of each individual being within it.*
- *Each "star" has special qualities, positive and negative, which "act at a distance" to produce effects on living beings.*
- *The influence of the stars on living beings is different according to where they are in the heavens at any particular time.*
- *The influence of a star cannot be understood alone. It can only be understood through its relations to all other stars. These relations are both positive and negative.*

THE CIRCLE OF THE ANIMALS

The word "star" actually means two different things. What we now call signs of the zodiac were "fixed stars" and what we now call planets were "wandering stars." The basic idea of the heavens as a circle of "fixed stars" originated in Egypt. Sky-watchers separated out 12 star-groups or constellations and gave them particular names and qualities. These 12 star-groups were set off as having a special quality that described the journey of the sun throughout the year. They were the 12 stages of that journey, each stage corresponding to a month, and were described as animal-gods, gods having animal qualities. So the circle of the year was a circle of these animal-images or *zodiac*.

In the hands of later mathematicians, the literal star-groups were turned into names for 12 equal segments of an ideal celestial circle. When the solstices and the equinoxes were precisely identified, this circle became independent of any particular location on the earth. It was the celestial circle of signs, the circle of fixed stars that, when viewed from earth, makes a complete revolution each day. The signs have many mythical associations. They each act as a *quality* or style of being that defines and intensifies the things it influences. The 12 signs or fixed stars in their modern version, with dates and elemental associations, are shown on the following pages.

THE SUN SIGNS OF THE ZODIAC

Together these signs produce the circle of fixed stars that defines the limits of the universe. They were associated with character types, animals, plants, metals and stones, winds, colors, and flavors. According to the principles of sympathetic magic, they could be invoked, intensified, or warded off through charms made from these materials or by smelling, eating, or wearing the things associated with them.

ARIES OR THE RAM *(cardinal fire)* acts aggressively, impulsively, and with initiative. It gives force, virility, and a desire for combat. It indicates an explosion of energy, tending to excess, unstable, mobile, and fertile. It represents youth, renewal, progress, and contradiction.

March 21 – April 19.

TAURUS OR THE BULL *(fixed earth)* acts steadily, thoroughly, and with conviction. It gives weight, endurance, and earthly strength and is a sign of unconscious processes at work. It indicates mothers, basic affections and desires and is a sign for the earthly paradise. It represents hopes to come.

April 20 – May 20.

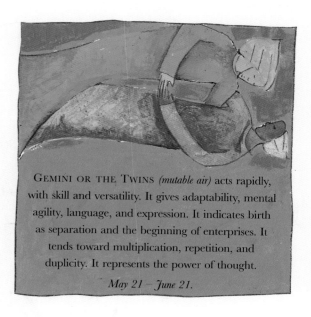

GEMINI OR THE TWINS *(mutable air)* acts rapidly, with skill and versatility. It gives adaptability, mental agility, language, and expression. It indicates birth as separation and the beginning of enterprises. It tends toward multiplication, repetition, and duplicity. It represents the power of thought.

May 21 – June 21.

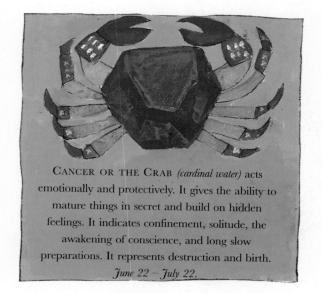

CANCER OR THE CRAB *(cardinal water)* acts emotionally and protectively. It gives the ability to mature things in secret and build on hidden feelings. It indicates confinement, solitude, the awakening of conscience, and long slow preparations. It represents destruction and birth.

June 22 – July 22.

THE SUN SIGNS OF THE ZODIAC

LEO OR THE LION *(fixed fire)* acts powerfully, gloriously, and seeks to dominate. It gives pride, force, and royal power, and the ability to bring things to light. It indicates kings, the father, fortune, and triumph, as well as vanity, oppression, and megalomania. It represents authority in the world.

July 23 – August 22.

VIRGO OR THE VIRGIN *(mutable earth)* acts carefully and prudently, seeking for justice. It gives a cold intelligence, a need for purity, and a sense of order in practical things. It indicates the sacred virgin, waiting, promises, and potentials. It represents material ready for transformation.

August 23 – September 22.

LIBRA OR THE BALANCE *(cardinal air)* acts rationally and fairly through weighing alternatives. It gives measure, elegance, and a love of beauty, as well as hesitation, indecision, and the need to control. It indicates tribunals, judgment, and process. It represents a marriage of the opposites.

September 23 – October 22.

SCORPIO OR THE SCORPION *(fixed water)* acts intensely, passionately, and secretly. It is poison and its cure, bitter emotions and passionate intensities, treason, death, and resurrection. It indicates what is hidden and the end of things, as well as the mystery of illumination. It is the sign of transformation.

October 23 – November 21.

THE SUN SIGNS OF THE ZODIAC

SAGITTARIUS OR THE CENTAUR *(mutable fire)* acts magnanimously, idealistically, and enthusiastically. It gives a quick spirit, rectitude, and penetration. It indicates riches, optimism, and the power to convince. It represents evolutionary change.

November 22 – December 21.

CAPRICORN OR THE GOAT *(cardinal earth)* acts methodically and authoritatively. It gives caution, determination, and patience, as well as fear and avarice. It indicates what is cold, slow, and contracted, a sign for both the devil's lies and the hidden fertility of the horned god.

December 22 – January 19.

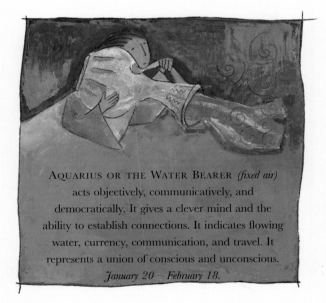

AQUARIUS OR THE WATER BEARER *(fixed air)* acts objectively, communicatively, and democratically. It gives a clever mind and the ability to establish connections. It indicates flowing water, currency, communication, and travel. It represents a union of conscious and unconscious.

January 20 – February 18.

PISCES OR THE FISHES *(mutable water)* acts sensitively, passively, with the quality of dreams. It gives a diffuse, deep, introverted quality that links with deep unconscious processes along with confusion and emotional sensitivity. It indicates fertility, achievement, peace, and the eternal return.

February 19 – March 20.

Aspects and Angles

ach sign has individual tastes, manners, affinities, ideas, rivalries, and hatreds. These are expressed through the "rays" the stars emit, enabling them to exert an influence on things and people and interact with each other. The circle of stars is like a group of people who are constantly looking at each other. Their rays continually cross and recross the interior of the circle. Certain geometrical relations make these contacts concrete. They also express the kind of relations between the stars that give significance to a particular moment. There are five basic geometrical angles through which the "rays" connect and solidify into specific relations. In modern astrology these are called *aspects*. These aspects were first used to help define the loves and hatreds of the 12 fixed signs. They were also used to express the relation between the "wandering stars" or planets, which is their major use today.

The 12 signs are combined with the four elements – fire, earth, air, water – to produce four sets of three signs or *trines* that harmonize with one another. They are identified as *cardinal*, or initiating, *fixed* or stabilizing, and *mutable* or dissolving to produce three sets of four signs or *squares* that are hostile to one another.

Modern astrologers tend to play down the antagonisms between the stars and see predictions as expressing potentials for growth and possibilities of development. The ancient world also recognized the shadow of these forces and their eternal antagonism. Manulius, a late antique astrologer, remarked in a dark moment that it is not concord but discord that reigns in the skies above. "Is it any wonder," he asked, "that human history is a tissue of crimes when the example comes from the powers that rule our destiny? It is the signs themselves that sow discord at our birth. It is because of the sky that the earth is divided against itself and a fatal enmity pushes the nations on to hate one another."

ABOVE: Planet trajectories as perceived on earth shown as imaginary projections on the night sky.

OPPOSITE IN PANEL: The four major aspects are Conjunction, Opposition, Square, and Trine. The positions shown on the horoscope grid of Venus in relation to Mars show how aspects are calculated.

MAJOR ASPECTS

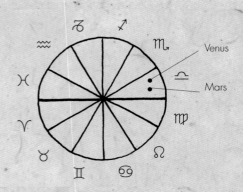

Aries

Taurus

Gemini

Cancer

Leo

Virgo

Libra

Scorpio

Sagittarius

Capricorn

Aquarius

Pisces

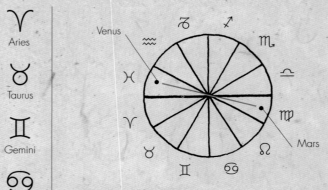

A CONJUNCTION (0°–8°) can only happen to planets. It came to occupy a very important place in the astrological interpretation of history. When two planets are within 8° of each other their forces are said to merge. The nearer they are, the stronger the influence, positive or negative. The "Grand Conjunction" of Jupiter and Saturn, for example, indicates major cultural upheavals.

AN OPPOSITION (180°) indicates that two qualities are placed in the relation of polar opposites that seek a way to co-operate while keeping their separate identity. The major characteristic is a kind of seesaw motion or alternation of the qualities involved, expressed as enmity or partnership. Though they are intimately connected, the qualities cannot both appear at the same time.

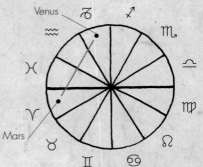

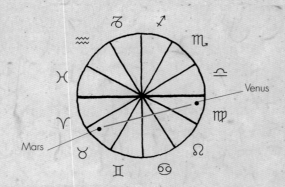

A SQUARE (90°) in ancient times was thought to express hatred. The qualities involved are attempting to frustrate each other. It is difficult and laden with tension, and can cause great problems, particularly when the stars involved are by nature hostile to each other. Modern astrologers regard this as a "life problem" that can be solved through time, patience, and understanding.

A TRINE (120°) is the most harmonious of relations, indicating that the qualities involved are working together smoothly and harmoniously to amplify each other. It can indicate great talents or potentials and can modify the relation of natural enemies. A Sextile (60°) is related to the Trine, indicating a weaker kind of harmonious connection, but one that can lead to optimism and opportunity.

The Wandering Stars

The signs of the zodiac or fixed stars furnish only one part of astrology's description of the heavens. They are like a fixed playing field, an eternal cycle. Onto this field are thrown the moving pieces of the game, the "wandering stars" or planets that are the instruments of destiny *par excellence*. They represent the singularity, the unique configuration of an individual life.

The theory of the planets and the divinatory practices associated with them were the specialty of the Chaldeans. When observed from earth, the planets take an erratic course through the sky, moving from sign to sign. Thus they were called the wanderers or messengers. For the Chaldeans, they were not just the messengers of the gods, but the gods themselves, much more important than the "circle of signs." They had names, myths, and stories, and were offered cult worship. To read their movement against the background of the skies was to read the heavenly story of the fates of all.

Chaldeans recognized seven planets. The Greeks united these planets with their own mythology, identifying gods and stars. This put the range of their mythology at the service of the planetary spirits. The "meanings" we now attribute to these planets come primarily from Greek myth. They are named according to the Roman version of the Greek gods. When the last of the planets, Neptune, Uranus, and Pluto, were discovered in the last 150 years, they, too, were given Greek names and took on qualities from Greek myths.

The planets act like a set of dice thrown onto the gaming board of the heavens. Some forms of astrological analysis literally used dice to determine planetary positions in a special kind of procedure called the *Part of Fortune*. Once in place, the planets are related to each other through the *aspects* and through the particular place on the board where they fell – one of the 12 *signs*.

PLANETARY INFLUENCES

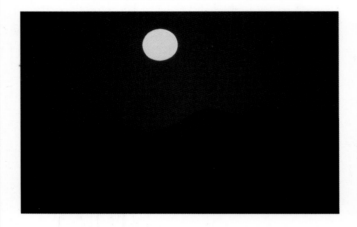

Here are the ten motive forces of life, as they occur in modern astrology. They are given in the old order, dependent on their perceived distance from earth as the center, along with the fixed star that they are said to "rule."

MOON *(rules Cancer):* emotions, feelings, needs, habits; the Mothers, emotional mirroring and reflection, personal unconscious, feminine responses and rhythms, dreams, and memories; water sources, the ocean. Associated with the goddess Artemis, the virgin huntress who presides over wild forests and childbirth. Traditionally the gate to entering life on earth.

MERCURY *(rules Gemini and Virgo):* communication of all kinds, learning, writing, mental skill and facility; how we put ideas and memories together; eloquence and fraud; connections, psychic transformation. Associated with Hermes, psychopomp and god of thieves, friendliest of gods to humans.

Mars

VENUS *(rules Taurus and Libra):* love, attraction, beauty, desire, attainment, and fortune; what we personally value and how we value it, art, voluptuous elegance, imagination, and the capacity to rearrange and renew the forms of the inner world. Associated with Aphrodite, foam-born goddess of beauty, and the images of desire.

SUN *(rules Leo):* ego, individuality, essential quality of life force; organizing image of identity, power, authenticity, authority, justice, display, pride, principle of organization. Associated with Apollo, god of light, poetry, and prophecy and Sol Invictus, the conquering sun.

MARS *(rules Aries):* aggressive energy, vigor, initiative, courage; what we hate and seek to destroy; the enemy, competition, weapons, soldiers, surgeons, butchers, young men. Associated with Ares, the "man-slaughterer" who loves combat and the clash of arms.

JUPITER *(rules Sagittarius):* expansion, generosity, aspiration, success, idealism; sovereignty, victory; religious and philosophical belief; teachers, travelers, beneficent authority; education and enlightened opinion; riches and honor. Associated with Zeus, ruler of the gods who understands the workings of destiny and controls the power of lightning.

SATURN *(rules Capricorn):* limits, restriction, inflexibility, contraction; deserts, bones, lead, melancholy; old men and strict controls; fixation on an earlier life; introversion, fear, anguish, pain, and hard labor; avarice and poverty; deep learning, long study, underground developments. Associated with Kronos, deposed god of a lost golden age who sends dreams and eats his own children.

URANUS *(rules Aquarius):* disruption, sudden change, revolution, genius, inventiveness, technology; untamed psychic energy, breakthrough, breakdown of established order. Associated with Ouranos, the oldest of the sky gods, whose severed genitals gave birth to the goddess Aphrodite Venus.

Saturn

NEPTUNE *(rules Pisces):* mystery, idealism, illusions; merging and dissolution, escapism and spirituality; the collective unconscious, the distant past, the return of the repressed; ocean, mists, fogs, and rivers; musicians, dancers, visionaries, alcoholics, and drug addicts, dependent and helpless people. Associated with Poseidon, god of the seas, deep passions, horses, and enveloping mists.

PLUTO *(rules Scorpio):* hidden power and transformation; eruptions, death, and rebirth, deep transformations; regressions, complexes, and reappearances; power of the underworld, effect on personal unconscious; miners, sewage workers, big businessmen. Associated with Hades, god of the world below, whose marriage to Persephone represents a creative relation between the living and the dead.

Jupiter

ABOVE AND LEFT: Jupiter, Mars, and Saturn, three of the traditional planets recognized by the Ptolemaic system and deemed to have great influence on the lives of people on earth.

Ptolemy's World

The complete expression of this astrological world was put together by the astronomer and mathematician Ptolemy (Claudius Ptolemeus, c. 100–178 C.E). It interconnected the earth, the planets and the stars as a series of interlocking "spheres," explaining their relations both mythically and mathematically. This produced a model of the universe that could account for and synthesize all heavenly observations made at the time. The Ptolemaic

universe was the model Western people used until the 16th and 17th centuries. It remains the magical model of the astrological world. It focuses all phenomena on earth as the center and sees heavenly bodies as living energies that, through their rays and powers, influence our existence.

Our world is at the center of this universe. It is made out of four fundamental elements: earth, water, air, and fire or ether. At the creation of the cosmos, the heaviest of these elements, *earth*, fell to the center to form a solid, immovable ball. *Water*

spread out over the surface of earth, forming rivers, seas, and the Great Ocean that surrounds the inhabited world, the *oikumenê*. It diffuses into the *air* that envelops the terrestrial globe, rolling and surging in clouds and fogs. This air is constantly in motion, agitated by the winds. It is dark and somber by nature unless it is illuminated by the rays of the stars. Air becomes clearer and purer as it rises toward the first of the planetary spheres. It is bounded by *fire* or *ether*, the fourth element. Ardent and light, with a natural tendency to rise, fire occupies the superior part of the cosmos, glowing with the light of the stars. The elemental world is densely peopled with souls. There is a huge cavern in the earth, where infernal gods rule over a people of shadows. The air is full of discarnate souls transformed into benevolent and malevolent *daimones*. Outside the circle of Ocean that surrounds the *oikumenê*, the souls of heroes dwell in bliss on the Fortunate Islands.

The orbit or *sphere* of the Moon, the first star, marks the boundary between the elemental or terrestrial world, given over to birth, death, corruption, and change, and the world of the celestial beings, who never die and never change. The orbit of each celestial body is a crystalline sphere that vibrates at a certain frequency, producing a music and a "ray" permeated with the quality of the star. The literal heavenly body can appear anywhere within its sphere.

Above the Moon there are six more spheres, each of which imparts a particular energy and a sinuous movement to the planets they empower. First is "quick" Mercury, the "shining one"; then Venus, the morning and evening star whose rays kindle

elemental world. They also imprint each soul at birth with a specific arrangement of their qualities. Souls who enter human life descend through the spheres of the planets, acquiring from each an "envelope" of their qualities and passions. The moment of entrance into the sub-lunary world fixes these qualities in a specific arrangement. This imprint can be described through the astrological diagram that shows the configuration of the stars at the moment of birth. The key to the configuration is the sign that is rising above the eastern horizon at the time of birth. It correlates or interlocks all the various cycles. Modern astrologers

beauty and desire; then the sun at the center point, the Fourth Circle, where he proudly regulates the revolutions of the heavens. Above this "heart of the world" come the boiling red fire of Mars, the luminous generosity of Jupiter, and the cold gleaming of Saturn that marks the limit of the planetary world. Above Saturn is the sphere of the Fixed Stars. Their immense orbit embraces all others and acts as the "motor of worlds." This is the limit of creation, a celestial region peopled by the Signs of the Stars, transcendent powers, and pure intelligences. Beyond them is the unthinkable void.

Each of the planets has a "procession" of qualities connected to it, a long chain reaching deep into the

call this sign the "ascendant," the sign that is ascending into the sky at the moment of birth. Old astrologers called it the "horoscope," the "observation of the hour" of birth.

OPPOSITE RIGHT: Arab and European astrolabes, dating from the 14th to the 16th century. Astrolabes were navigational instruments that used the fixed stars and the sun as their measuring points.

OPPOSITE LEFT: A 16th-century German engraving showing the universe according to Ptolemy, a system that had worked comfortably for almost a thousand years. Ptolemy's worldview persisted until Copernicus dropped his astronomical bombshell in 1543 and proved that the sun stood still and that all the planets, including earth, revolved around it.

ABOVE: An 11th-century horoscope chart with zodiac signs and planets.

The Moment of Birth

The *horoscope* or astrological diagram describes a set of interlocking spheres. The sphere of fixed stars or signs of the zodiac is the outer limit of this world. It modifies and conditions the impact of the spheres or orbits of the planets. Since late antiquity it has also been focused by another kind of cycle, the "sphere of the houses." This is divided into 12 parts, like the zodiac, that represent parts of an individual life. Each house is "ruled" by and partakes of the nature of one of the signs and one of the planets. The sign in the circle of the zodiac that is rising above the eastern horizon at the time of birth fixes a certain order and inter-relation of the signs and planets. The circle of the houses defines their influences in the drama of a specific life.

The revolution of the fixed stars and the orbits of the planets are thought of as "objective." The sphere of the houses is "subjective." It expresses the impact of the heavenly bodies on the course of a human life, showing where an intersection of planets and stars will take effect. The final expression of an astrological "complex" is thus a *planet* or motive force, modified by the quality of a given sign, exerting its influence in a certain area of life or *house.*

The sphere of the houses is fixed in place. The sphere of the stars revolves around it, locked into a particular relation by the ascendant that focuses the quality of the signs into particular houses. The orbits of the planets intersect within this sphere. The "inner planets" (Moon, Mercury, Venus, Mars) move very quickly, changing position from day to day. The "middle planets" (Jupiter and Saturn) move slowly. They will be in the same position for a group of people born at about the

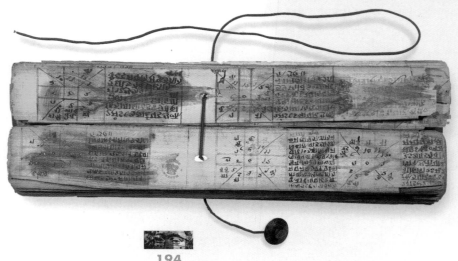

same time. The "outer planets" (Uranus, Neptune, and Pluto) move very slowly. They affect entire generations. The sphere of the houses tells where this generational influence is likely to be felt. When the movement and position of a planet in present time is plotted on the birth chart, another relation called a *transit* is established. The "objective" planet in present time is *transiting* or temporarily exerting an influence on the natal chart, forming aspects to the birth positions.

LEFT: A Nepalese horoscope for the years 1362–66. It is written on a book made from palm leaves.

OPPOSITE ABOVE: Scene from *The Deeds of Akbar*, a 16th-century book of miniatures depicting the life and times of Akbar, the Mogul emperor of north India. This scene shows astrologers casting a horoscope at the moment of birth of Akbar's son Timur.

ABOVE: The ancient observatory Jantar Mantar at Delhi in India.

THE 12 HOUSES

Here are the 12 houses in their modern interpretations, along with their associations to particular planets and signs.

FIRST HOUSE OR ASCENDANT *(Aries and Mars)*: outer personality, presentation, appearance, beginnings, how you project yourself to others.

SECOND HOUSE *(Taurus and Venus)*: possessions, resources, values, earning and prosperity, desires and appetites.

THIRD HOUSE *(Gemini and Mercury)*: relations (other than parents), communication, local travels, learning and teaching, mundane activities.

FOURTH HOUSE *(Cancer and Moon)*: father, home, origins, heredity, inheritance, inner emotions, hidden resources.

FIFTH HOUSE *(Leo and Sun)*: children, creativity, pleasures, love relations, play, the arts.

SIXTH HOUSE *(Virgo and Mercury)*: health and illness, work environment, service and care.

SEVENTH HOUSE *(Libra and Venus)*: marriage, major relationships, business and war, the "other," partners and enemies.

EIGHTH HOUSE *(Scorpio and Mars)*: death, wounds, hidden inheritance, shared resources, psychic and spiritual interests, going beyond self-interest.

NINTH HOUSE *(Sagittarius and Jupiter)*: long-distance travel, philosophies, dreams and visions, higher learning.

TENTH HOUSE *(Capricorn and Saturn)*: power, ambition, aims, prestige, authority, responsibility, career, the mother.

ELEVENTH HOUSE *(Aquarius, Saturn, and Uranus)*: friends, ideals, groups, social activities, legislative assemblies.

TWELFTH HOUSE *(Pisces, Jupiter, and Neptune)*: unconscious impulses, hidden enemies, hospitals, prisons, charities, secrets, sorrows, self-destruction, deep insights.

The Science of the Stars

Astrology or divination by the stars originated in late antiquity. The atmosphere of Hellenistic magic and Greek individualism transformed the science of kings into a way to imagine individual lives and destinies. It is a unique blend of science, symbolism, magic, and fate, the last formulation of the pagan cosmos. The "science of the stars" became a grand synthesis of late antique occult wisdom. It was the root of the magical doctrine of the macrocosm and the microcosm, that each individual is a model in small of the entire cosmos.

Because of its foreign origin and the predictive power it gave to "read" the heavens in a potentially subversive way, the science of the stars was periodically forbidden by Roman emperors, and astrologers were driven out of Rome. Rationalist writers like Cicero ridiculed it, while more serious philosophers used it to debate the subject of "fate." Did the stars reveal what *will* happen, or what *may* happen? From the first century onward, it was generally accepted at a popular level that fate could be predicted. This led to another great "magical" discussion about using astrological symbols to *escape* the compulsion of fate, or *heimarmenê*, and rise to the contemplation of a higher world.

ABOVE: Before its decline in the face of the scientific method of the 17th and 18th centuries, astrology was considered to be a respectable science, inseparable from astronomy, alchemy, and healing. Here astrology is personified in female form in a fresco on the ceiling of the Escorial Palace in Madrid, Spain.

The Work of the Devil

With the beginning of the Christian empire and the writings of Augustine that defined all pagan divination as the work of the Devil, astrological practices and books were formally banned. Examining a birth chart, like all other forms of divination, became a capital crime. Astrology then went east. With the closing of the philosophical school of Athens in 529, Greek scholars emigrated to Persia where they were granted asylum. The Greek texts they translated into Pahlavi formed the ground for a flowering of Arabic astrology. These practices also reached India, where they combined with native myths to produce a variant that gives great importance to lunar mansions and the calculation of the effects of past and future lives.

The influence of Arabic astrology survives in Madagascar as *Vintana* and *Sidiky*. This kind of divination produces astrological signs that are projected onto the field of a house. The borders of the house represent the 28 lunar days and their auspicious and inauspicious moments. Symbols in the center of the rectangular field signify spirits of the stars and the day-signs. The work of the astrologer is to "witness fate" by locating an ominous event in its appropriate position and relations. The symbol systems combine medical and ritual indications. The method of deriving the signs uses both astronomical and geomantic calculations.

Along with many other elements of pagan culture, astrology reentered European history through translations from Arabic. This occurred in two waves, one during the

9th to 12th centuries, the other in the Renaissance. The Church evolved an ambivalent attitude to the science of the stars throughout this period, attempting to separate the "wisdom" or "scientific" part, which described the way God's creation worked, from the "predictive" part that was heresy and the work of pagan devils.

Astrology Reborn

The great flowering of astrological literature occurred in the Renaissance. The science of the stars became part of the Hermetic Tradition of transcendental magic, and a subject of argument for all scholars. Violent controversies arose, ostensibly centering on the debate between "fate" and "free will", but actually focused on magic and the return of the pagan cosmos.

Philosophers such as Marsilio Ficino defined a whole set of practices based on astrological images of the gods to help "make your life agree with the heavens." Rooms and palaces were decorated with these images to make a model of the pagan cosmos, a "virtual reality" into which the philosopher could project himself. This kind of imagining was the basis of the huge "memory theaters" or systems of categorizing and visualizing all possible knowledge that formed another part of Renaissance magic. Astro-medicine and astrological types also became very important. One of the great controversies of the Renaissance, perhaps its defining feature, was a complete revisioning of the "Saturnian type." It turned the traditional image of a melancholy, bitter, evil outcast into a scholar and prophet.

The Reformation and the "Enlightenment" brought two other kinds of polarization. The struggle between Northern Reformers and Southern Priests to "renew" the Church was also fought in terms of astrological divination and the personality of the Saturnian type.

Italian cardinals and scholars of the Church had fully adopted astrological imagery. They used it and the theory of the "Grand Conjunction" of Saturn and Jupiter to predict the rise of an evil Antichrist prophet in the North, Martin Luther. This analysis included an examination of the reputedly very negative position of Saturn in Luther's birth chart. Luther and the circle around him repudiated astrological imagery and took a stance as "omen-priests" interpreting the "wonder-signs" that showed the rise of a great power of renewal. In this polemic, astrology was repudiated not only as pagan but as elitist.

Superstition and Revival

In the 17th century, with the development of the scientific method and modern philology, the underpinning of the tradition of Hermetic Magic was destroyed. The prestige of this sort of magic, and thus of astrology, came from a belief that its texts represented a *prisca theologia*, a pure knowledge of God that went back to the very origins of the world. Scholars using new linguistic techniques demonstrated that all these texts were late antique "forgeries" at the same time that the first scientists were showing that myths were really "only your imagination." Astrology fell completely into the shadows, becoming popular superstition. It flourished there, completely cut off from respectable culture, producing a long series of popular almanacs, textbooks, and magazines.

With the Occult Revival of the late 19th and early 20th centuries, astrology took on yet another face. It became the organizing system for the creation of a new esoteric tradition. The Theosophical Movement of the 1880s and the Order of the Golden Dawn were the major agents of this revival. Astrology became a part of what one religious scholar called a "return of the repressed" cosmos of the goddesses, a vision of the world as interconnected and magically available. Today it flourishes as a subculture, providing many people with an insight into how their lives connect with the world of myths and symbols.

What Does Astrology Do?

odern astrologers tend to be "scientific" about what they do. They use precise astronomical observations and incorporate new astronomical discoveries. When a group of planetary fragments named Chiron was discovered in orbit around the sun, astrologers immediately searched for both its precise mathematical place in the chart and its divinatory meaning as a representative of the old Greek healing god for which it was named. Contemporary astrology uses a wide range of computer programs to make the "erection" of a horoscope, gathering data, and the computation of transits available to all.

Yet it is obvious that astrological symbolism has nothing whatsoever to do with the *content* of science. The system is earth-centered and relies on a kind of influence or "ray" completely foreign to scientific thought. So what does astrology do? Perhaps the best explanation would be to see it as a divinatory system relying on "chance," as do the Books of Fate. Its symbols express a psychology in the deepest sense of the word, where individual meaning connects with outer events. For whatever we might scientifically construct, there is a profound sense in which we each experience things as a center. The use of a system of astrological analogies to express the connection between the world and human fate reflects a deep insight into the transience, the singularity, and the importance of human lives. The astronomical positions of the stars and planets move this system of symbols and analogies, just as the fall of the dice, or the laying out of the cards, or the distribution of sticks or stones move the symbols in other ways of divining.

What this does is to locate "complexes," centers of energy, emotion, and associations that interact in each of us to create the way we perceive things. It is difficult to overestimate the part these complexes play in shaping what we experience. By becoming acquainted with these hidden forces, we can creatively engage the way our imagination is shaping the world each day. Astrology, like other major divination systems, affords an opportunity to do this. It is a way to imagine things that can connect you to deep structures of the soul.

The Varieties of Astrological Experience

Erecting or "casting" a model of the heavens and reading its interconnections is a complicated procedure. You can ask a professional astrologer, get a computer-generated chart, or take on the mathematical and geometrical task yourself. The information you obtain through making this chart can be used in many different ways.

The fundamental way to use the chart is to imagine yourself through the complex of symbols it portrays. This locates where and how basic drives and possibilities take effect, and describes the "styles" you use to imagine yourself. This is reflected in the *Natal Horoscope* or birth chart. In ancient times this was your fate. Modern astrologers look at it as a display of talents, liabilities, life problems and goals, characteristic relationships, and imaginative styles. By calculating and comparing the movement of the planets as they leave the natal chart, you may predict crises and crossroads, challenges, changes of attitude, and points of spiritual evolution. Another variation is the *Relationship Horoscope*, which superimposes two natal charts on each other to produce a composite that describes the potential of the relationship between the two people involved.

Mundane Chart

The *Horary Chart* is an old form that has been revived in the last few years. It is made to answer a specific question.

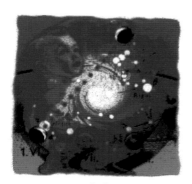

Natal Chart

You pose the question and construct the chart for the moment the question is asked. The associations to the symbols provide the answer. The horary chart is where the expression "casting a horoscope" came from. In ancient and medieval times it was made by throwing dice or casting stones to determine the position of the signs and planets. This practice also connects with geomancy (see pages 118–23), which came to be regarded as a form of astrology in the 15th and 16th centuries.

Mundane Astrology is the study of the great conjunctions that influence events and collective movements in the *mundus*, or world. From this point of view,

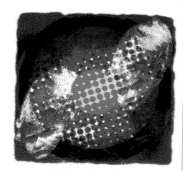

Relationship Chart

groups, institutions, nations, organizations, and empires all have a "soul" that can be described by a chart erected at their birth or at a critical moment in their growth. Horoscopes erected at the solstices or the equinoxes can give insight into the psychological climate for an institution or for the world as a whole.

The *Local Space Chart* shows where the orbits of your natal planets intersect the local horizon at a given place on earth. It is derived from the natal horoscope and projected onto the plan of a building or a

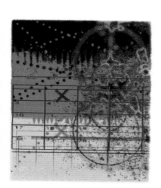

Horary Chart

location. This shows how your drives and motivations intersect with a particular structure. It can show you what to expect, for example, when you move into a new house, or demonstrate how to use the potential of your present dwelling to the fullest.

The *Electional Chart* is another revival of an old type of prediction that shows the quality and potential of a given moment of time. Astrologers were often asked to predict

Local Space Chart

the most favorable time to begin something. This is a major concern of Eastern or Lunar astrology and produces a chart of auspicious and inauspicious moments for a wide range of activities. An Electional Chart reveals the possibilities in a given moment of time, showing whether it is open or closed to a certain kind of activity. Modern computer techniques allow electional astrologers to run through a wide range of possibilities. The Electional Chart is connected with old ideas of the *kairos*, or opening in time, that allows an action to succeed.

OPPOSITE AND ABOVE: Astrology can be viewed as a divinatory system that focuses on an individual's psychology (opposite). Areas it can be used for include birth (top left), relationships (center left), to ask a specific question (bottom left), institutions or businesses (top right), housing (center right), and finding an auspicious date for special activities (bottom right).

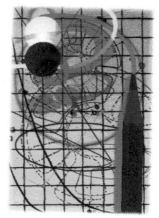

Electional Chart

Other Traditions

The remains of a very old Meso-American astrological system still exist in remote Mexican and Guatemalan villages. This oral tradition is the last trace of a 260-day calendar used by the builders of the great sacrificial pyramids of Mayan and Aztec cultures.

The astrology of the "day-keeper" depends on two interlocking cycles. There is a 20-day cycle of signs that depicts the stages of life, beginning as the Alligator and ending as the Flower. Every human birth is under the auspices of one of these signs. Another circle of 13 days intersects the basic cycle, so that each of the 13 greater days becomes a 20-day cycle. This intersection produced a Book of Fate composed of 260 complex symbols that was used by priests, diviners, and "day-keepers" throughout Meso-America. The complex of day-signs was both a calendar and a divination system. To find which day-sign was influencing a given event, diviners

would draw handfuls of crystals and beans from their hidden sacks. By counting them out in sets of four they could produce the heavens' answer to an inquirer's question.

Chinese astrology is the other major system still active in the modern world. It is an extremely complicated system that provides the basis for almost all Eastern calendars and divination systems. The traditional starting date for the Chinese calendar is 2637 B.C.E. when, according to legend, the First August Emperor worked out the cycle of 60 years that lies at its heart.

The Chinese calendar balances lunar and solar systems of time-reckoning. The lunar year consists of 12 irregular moon-months, while the solar year consists of 24 two-week periods known as the Twenty-four Joints and Breaths. To coordinate the systems, the length and starting point of the lunar months are varied from year to year, with an extra month being added about every three years. The moon cycles give an auspicious or inauspicious quality to each day, while the cycle of solar Joints and Breaths forecasts weather conditions, such as Constant Rain, Awakening of Insects, Small Harvest, White Dew, Minor Snow, or Great Cold.

The most important divinatory element is a 60-year cycle made up of the Ten Heavenly Stems

STEMS AND BRANCHES

The Cycle of Heavenly Stems and Earthly Branches is called a sexagenary cycle because it has a sequence of 60 combinations. The Heavenly Stems make up a cycle of 10 years (different to the 12-year animal cycle), and the Earthly Branches, a cycle of 12 months. To gather information for a proper Chinese natal chart, you need to know the animal name of the year of birth and its Heavenly Stem, and the Earthly Branch character for your month of birth. The Stem and Branch system also applies to days and hours. The ancient Chinese week had 10 days, and the 24 hours in each of them was divided into 12 Earthly Branches, each corresponding with 2 Western hours. This system is still used to figure out the other factors necessary for a proper natal chart, your day and hour of birth.

As in Western astrology, specially calculated charts exist to help you figure out these combinations. The names of the Heavenly Branches and Earthly Stems are shown below.

TEN HEAVENLY STEMS

These names apply to years and days:

Chia • Yi • Ping
Ting • Wu • Chi
Keng • Hsin • Jen • Kuei

TWELVE EARTHLY BRANCHES

These names apply to months and hours:

Tzu • Ch'ou • Yin
Mao • Ch'en • Ssu
Wu • Wei • Shen
Yu • Shu • Hai

and the Twelve Earthly Branches. The cycle of Heavenly Stems repeats six times while the cycle of Earthly Branches repeats five times to produce the complete cycle of 60 years. These interacting cycles also describe the 12 months, the 7 days and the 12 double hours. Using the tables of Stems and Branches, an astrologer will generate the most important formula in Chinese divination, the "Eight Characters." These are the Stem and Branch names associated with the hour, day, month, and year of a person's birth. They open the lists of predictions and symbols used to examine virtually all questions. One primary use is in the Marriage Horoscope, where the sets of characters are compared in order to see if the two candidates for a marriage are compatible, or if a given date will be auspicious for their union. There are also 28 constellations or star groups that indicate whether a given day is auspicious or inauspicious for particular activities. These constellations can also be determined through a very prestigious form of dice-divination. In contrast to Western astrology, the constellations have nothing to do with an individual's birth, but are attached to particular days of the year.

OPPOSITE BOTTOM: The Caracol observatory at the Mayan city of Chichen Itza. It was designed specifically to study the movements of Venus.

OPPOSITE CENTER AND TOP: Beans and crystals used in the divination systems of Meso-America.

LEFT: The table of Stems and Branches is used to divine whether partners planning marriage will be compatible or not.

The Cycle of Animals

 ike Western astrology, the Chinese system orbits within its own system of symbols. It connects with actual astronomical observation at a few key points: the phases of the moon and the solar solstices and equinoxes. The most accessible and best-known part of this symbol system is the circle of 12 emblematic animals that correspond to the Twelve Earthly Branches. In this system, each lunar year is connected to an animal. People born in that year have the attributes of the year-animal. The hour of birth provides another animal that is your "secret partner," a hidden influence that helps you.

The 12-year cycle of animals repeats continually. It is meshed with a five-year cycle of the "Elements" or Transformative Processes: Water, Fire, Wood, Metal, Earth. The combination of an animal and an element gives the character of a year and of all the people born in that year, while the birth-hour animal makes the characterization more subtle. For example, the year 2000 will be a Metal Dragon year. This is a time for caution. The power and self-assertion of the Dragon is made more inflexible and ferocious by the solidifying quality of Metal. This could be a time of argument and conflict between major powers.

The primary popular use of the animals is to determine compatibility in emotional relationships.

THE CHINESE ZODIAC

Here are brief characterizations of the animals in cyclic order, with their hour, their years, and their most positive and negative relations to other animals. The Chinese year usually begins within a few days either way of the beginning of February.

RAT: smart, quick-witted, intelligent, sociable, full of charisma and charm; devious, secretive, greedy, acquisitive. *Loves* Dragons and Monkeys, *hates* Horses.

Hour: 23.00–00:59. *Year:* 1900, 1912, 1924, 1936, 1948, 1960, 1972, 1984, 1996, 2008.

 OX: industrious, long-suffering, honest, sincere, reliable, hard-working; stubborn, sulky, narrow-minded, impatient. *Loves* Snakes and Roosters, *hates* Goats.

Hour: 01:00–02:59. *Year:* 1901, 1913, 1925, 1937, 1949, 1961, 1973, 1985, 1997.

 TIGER: courageous, enthusiastic, bold, dynamic, optimistic, lucky, keeps promises; impulsive, vain, disobedient, hot-headed. *Loves* Horses and Dogs, *hates* Monkeys.

Hour: 03:00–04:59. *Year:* 1902, 1914, 1926, 1938, 1950, 1962, 1974, 1986, 1998.

 RABBIT OR CAT: quiet, wise, docile, astute, thoughtful, refined, conservative; cunning, possessive, fussy, obsessive, snobbish. *Loves* Goats and Pigs, *hates* Roosters.

Hour: 05:00–06:59. *Year:* 1903, 1915, 1927, 1939, 1951, 1963, 1975, 1987, 1999.

DRAGON: original, energetic, resourceful, brave, direct, enthusiastic, adaptable, creative; arrogant, tactless, critical, quick-tempered, unpredictable. *Loves* Rats and Monkeys, *hates* Dogs.

Hour: 07:00–08:59. *Year:* 1904, 1916, 1928, 1940, 1952, 1964, 1976, 1988, 2000.

SNAKE: shrewd, subtle, discreet, insightful, compassionate; proud, manipulative, indolent, malicious, possessive, cold. *Loves* Roosters and Oxen, *hates* Pigs.

Hour: 09:00–10:59. *Year:* 1905, 1917, 1929, 1941, 1953, 1965, 1977, 1989, 2001.

HORSE: vivacious, hardworking, popular, independent, friendly, sociable, enthusiastic, enduring; selfish, vain, restless, reckless. *Loves* Tigers and Dogs, *hates* Rats.

Hour: 11:00–12:59. *Year:* 1906, 1918, 1930, 1942, 1954, 1966, 1978, 1990, 2002.

GOAT OR SHEEP: artistic, cultured, gentle, intelligent, sensitive; fussy, self-centered, dependent, insecure, indulgent. *Loves* Rabbits and Pigs, *hates* Oxen and Dogs.

Hour: 13:00–14:59. *Year:* 1907, 1919, 1931, 1943, 1955, 1967, 1979, 1991, 2003.

MONKEY: energetic, versatile, resourceful, clever, persuasive, funny; sly, superficial, lying, impudent, sneaky. *Loves* Dragons and Rats, *hates* Tigers.

Hour: 15:00–16:59. *Year:* 1908, 1920, 1932, 1944, 1956, 1968, 1980, 1992, 2004.

ROOSTER: colorful, flamboyant, resilient, courageous, passionate, protective, punctual, industrious; conceited, rude, boasting, aggressive, bossy. *Loves* Oxen and Snakes, *hates* Rabbits.

Hour: 17:00–18:59. *Year:* 1909, 1921, 1933, 1945, 1957, 1969, 1981, 1993, 2005.

DOG: caring, unselfish, devoted, persevering, resourceful, honest, deep; anxious, pessimistic, nervous, cynical, withdrawn. *Loves* Tigers and Horses, *hates* Dragons and Goats.

Hour: 19:00–20:59. *Year:* 1910, 1922, 1934, 1946, 1958, 1970, 1982, 1994, 2006.

PIG OR BOAR: cheerful, sincere, home-loving, esthetic, diligent, obliging, unpretentious; materialistic, superficial, naive, lazy, stubborn, greedy. *Loves* Rabbits and Sheep, *hates* Snakes.

Hour: 21:00–22:59. *Year:* 1911, 1923, 1935, 1947, 1959, 1971, 1983, 1995, 2007.

OPPOSITE AND ABOVE: The 12 animals of the Chinese zodiac in their accepted order: Rat, Ox, Tiger, Rabbit (or Cat), Dragon, Snake, Horse, Goat (or Sheep), Monkey, Rooster, Dog, and Pig (or Boar). The Ox presides over the year from 8 February 1997 to 27 January 1998.

THE FIVE ELEMENTS

*The Elements or Transformative Processes that
modify the animal signs repeat every five years.
They add qualities that reinforce or alter the
year-animal's characteristics:*

METAL
Makes things solid and clear. It gives form.
Metal will make something more dependable
or, conversely, exaggerate its fixed or
conservative qualities.

WATER
Makes things flow, dissolving fixities. It makes
a stubborn sign adaptable, but may make an
adaptable sign overly diffuse.

WOOD
Marks beginnings. It makes things open, firm, and
able to carry a load. Wood will fix a mercurial
quality but may intensify the tendency
to materialism.

FIRE
Makes things adventurous and charismatic.
It displays essential qualities but may exhaust
resources and intensify impulsiveness.

EARTH
Stabilizes and realizes things. It gives a methodical,
reliable, and compassionate quality but can
become very dull and plodding.

Ritual Misfortunes

Tibet used both Greek or Indian and Chinese astrological systems. The Indian form, called "white" because Indians wore white clothes, never became popular. Chinese astrology, called "black" because Chinese astrologers wore black clothes, became the major system used by laypeople and monks alike.

In this system the heavens were seen as the 12 Chinese animals and the Five Elements or Processes interacting to form an ideal 60-year cycle. The calendar and the compass followed the Chinese system, using the Elements and the Eight Trigrams of the *I Ching* to describe interlocking cycles of existence. These elemental images became *Dakinis*, or purified psychic beings, that personified both directions of the heavens and levels of existence. No birth, marriage, or funeral would take place without an astrological reading to indicate if it was in accord with the movement of these celestial powers. Readings for a particularly important event would be undertaken by a *tulku*, a reincarnate lama who had conquered death to assume consciously a new corporeal existence.

The most common form of reading was a year chart, indicating what the coming year would bring for a person's life force, physical body, power, luck, and intelligence. The year chart provided a readout of the activities of the elemental spirits. It relied on the Chinese cycle of animals and elements to predict which rituals and ceremonies were necessary to counteract the negative activity of the demons of metal, water, earth, wood, and fire. These Five Elements or Transformative Processes were analyzed according to four degrees of relationship: *mother*, or affection; *son*, or neutrality; *friend*, or weak affection; and *enemy*, or antagonism. Each hour and day could also be related to an auspicious or inauspicious moment.

This analysis was furthered through consulting a geomantic or "magic square" arrangement of the Eight Trigrams of the *I Ching* that indicated the migrations of benevolent and malignant spirits. The year chart compared the present configuration of elemental forces with the natal arrangement in order to point out areas of conflict, opportunity, and danger. It looked at the year of birth, the relevant trigrams, the symbolic age of the inquirer, the connection to earth elements, and the *Mewa*, or psychic power configuration. It showed what could be expected in the year to come and which conflicts required ritual exorcism and ceremonial expiation. The particular Tibetan element in such an analysis lies in the idea that all of these elemental conflicts are products of past-life actions and experiences and that they may be resolved through ritual and spiritual practices.

OPPOSITE: The Five Elements indicate what kind of energy is expressed; in the 60-year cycle, each zodiac animal goes through each form of elemental energy.

ABOVE: Nepalese *tanka* showing the zodiacal oracle with the 12 Chinese astrological animals arranged around the edge. Buddhist symbols decorate the inner wheel.

Opening the Gates
of the Dreamworld

Most traditional cultures have seen dreaming
as communicating with other kinds of
realities. Dreams show us what forces are
shaping our imagination, for what were called ghosts
and spirits are also forces and memories beyond our
immediate control that are at work within us. Dreams
act as a hidden stage on which they can communicate
with us, as do the various parts of our bodies. The
dream-maker, a deep center in each of us, uses dreams
to foreshadow coming events, both inner and outer,
and create strategies to deal with them.

Dream Divination

 reams may be clear and vivid, or strange and labyrinthine. Though they use our thoughts, experiences, feelings, and memories, they do not speak our normal language. Dream images contradict themselves, relate seemingly unrelated things, and create impossible events. This constant taking apart and putting together generates symbolic energy. It moves us and can act as a system of internal guidance. By interacting with dream images we can play a part in creating our own future.

Many modern forms of psychotherapy use dreams as a way to get at things that are usually hidden from normal awareness or to analyze how key symbols are acting in the imagination. Modern "dream workers" are continually coming up with ways to "put you in touch with your dreams" through dream groups, art, dance, poetry, and creating rituals. Sleep researchers are using the physiological changes that they see occurring in dreaming to posit a connection between how the brain works and how the quantum world of subatomic particles works – a "dreaming universe." Dream-divination has another emphasis. It presumes that dreams have a message for the dreamer. Its goal is to make this message clear.

Accounts of dreaming from the ancient world show how important this process was. Dreaming was a place where you could enjoy the company and the guidance of the gods. The quality of modern dreaming reflects our desire for this dreamworld. It shows our imagination constantly at work "symbolizing" the events and things we encounter in order to build a language of dream.

Most people in a tribal or a traditional society knew something of the language of dreams and had a personal contact with the dreamworld. Clear dreams that foretold coming events and required little or no explanation were a part of their lives. This "Big Dream" was a particular style of dreaming that impressed by its clarity and impact. "Inspirational" dreams might reveal the plan for a temple,

a work of art, a business venture, or the resolution of a problem. Other kinds of dreaming relied on dialogue with the dream interpreters to find the message. These dream-diviners were familiar with the symbols of their culture and how these symbols might be moving in an individual situation. They were adept at creating the kind of meaning that connected people and let the dream flow into their lives.

ABOVE: *The Nightmare* by Henry Fuseli (1741–1825) suggests that what we find on the other side of the door between sleep and waking may not always be what we like. However, nightmares can sometimes have positive messages, and learning to examine and interpret dreams, pleasant or unpleasant, can help guide behavior in daily life.

goddess in the dreams of the initiate and the priest. Taoist practices that used drugs to destroy inner "corpse-worms" or "corpse-demons" that plot our destruction were judged effective when the initiate dreamed that his father and mother had died, that a grave had been destroyed, that his house was burning down, or that he was undergoing the five types of mutilating punishments.

Thresholds

In most cultures there is a threshold or barrier between the dayworld and the nightworld, just as there is a transition zone between other opposites that interact but do not directly touch each other like night and day, sun and moon, light and shadow, inside and outside, life and death. Partially this barrier is fear, our fear of death. The figures in the dreamworld have long been thought of as the souls of the dead. This points at a primary characteristic of the dreamworld. It breaks things down and takes them apart, sometimes violently, sometimes subtly. Dream-divination is ultimately concerned with reassembling a meaning from this breakdown. The first step, however, is to fall apart. This opens you to one of the guiding spirits of the underworld of dreams: Eros, the god of love and desire who is constantly taking us apart and putting us back together again.

Images of the Threshold of Dreams or the entrance to the nightworld reflect this deconstruction. The boundary between waking and sleeping is portrayed as a Dark Door, a hole in the ground, a shadowy crossroads, the entrance to a tomb. It is a dimming, a lowering or wounding of the light, and often it first leads into the shadows, to what has been refused or repressed, and a host of angry or vengeful figures. To enter the dreamworld we go down – into the underworld, the unconscious, the unacknowledged, and the unknown. The entrance is often through ruins, slums, and shadows that take apart what we thought we were.

The Shaman Interpreter

This sort of dream work was part of the shaman's role. It was expected of all sorts of priests, wise people, and religious figures, from the Babylonian *barû* priest to the street diviners of China, Japan, or the Hellenistic Mediterranean. People would take troubling dreams to lamas in Tibet, to medicine people or the circle of elders in Africa, or to wise women in Old Europe. Doctors and healers used dreams to analyze the course of a disease or the progress of a treatment. Specific events in a dream would also indicate if a religious aspirant was ready for an initiation or how a spiritual process was working. Initiation into the cult of Isis, for example, depended on the simultaneous appearance of the

Remembering Dreams

e all dream, usually three or more times each night. Though some dreams will not let us forget them, more often we cannot remember what went on at night. If you want to remember your dreams, you must pay some attention to the night world. Keep a notepad by your bed, so you can write things down when you wake up. But don't wake up too quickly. The chances are that just as you are waking up, you are moving out of a dream. Stay there in the zone between sleeping and waking, and gently bring back the last image, feeling, or thought that was slipping away. As you let it come into focus, you will discover that it is connected to other images, and that you can follow their trail back into the dreamworld. Feel your way back until you reach a cutoff point, then move forward again and establish the main images. Let the dream as a whole slowly come into focus, like a photographic image in a developing tank. Make a little keyword or phrase for each image cluster. Don't be too concerned if you can't remember everything. Nobody can. And putting the story together is also a part of the process.

KEEPING NOTE

When you feel the dream is assembled in your mind, write it down quickly, without thinking too much about it. Use the keywords you made for each scene to help call it back. With some practice, you will be able to recall three or more separate dreams each morning, like islands in the sea of night. Later in the day go back to the images and refresh your memory. This will gradually open your memory for images.

The Place and the Language of Dreaming

The process we call dreaming probably goes on all the time. Poets, artists, and seers have all attested that there is a constant flow or river of images beneath our normal kind of thinking. It breaks through into our awareness as visions, hunches, close encounters, and the sudden realization that something is "symbolic," weighted with a hidden significance. Some people have seen this flow of images as infantile, primitive, meaningless, or dangerous, something we must, at best, tame and control. Others see it as a source of spirit, creativity, and guidance.

Descriptions of dreaming in traditional cultures see it as both a *place* and a *language*. It is a place of encounter, a kind of stage where dream-events unfold and various kinds of beings interact. What were called gods, souls, ghosts, spirits of the body, previous lives, and important thoughts become real. They become the players on the dream stage, acting out their roles for our interpretation.

Perhaps the best description of this place is the *Imaginal Realm*, a place at once real and imaginary. It is peopled by the potential structures of experience, which have been imaged as heavens and hells, gods and demons, archetypal landscapes and figures.

nets of associations that are pregnant with meaning. We experience dreams as *happening* to us. They feel as if they come from somewhere outside, and they show attitudes, standards, and actions that are often quite different from what our ego, this thing we call "I," believes to be true. This can challenge or compensate, help or correct. It takes part in a kind of ongoing balancing act in the psyche as a whole. Dreams do this by being dramatic. They are images that also tell stories, present characters, suggest plots. They ask for dialogue by presenting you with a challenge and an invitation to interact with the imaginal situation they have portrayed for your benefit.

The Ball Is in Your Court

Dreams, at least as we remember them, have a structure. They take up a stance or an attitude toward what is going on in the dayworld. There is an enormous amount going on in a dream, but the most important part may be the very last scene. This is traditionally the clearest time to dream, at the very end of the night. It may also point at what is just about to happen. Some dreamworkers call this the *lysis*. It is like the last scene in a play that is a summing up of the night's dream-events, a connection, and a challenge. The ball is in your court now. This is your homework. It is what you should think about to continue the dream-dialogue. Pay attention to this last scene in the dream you have remembered. Carry it around with you during the day. Think about it, feel into it, let it come in contact with what you are doing. Speak with it like a friend who has had a strange but very interesting experience that you want to understand. As you do this, you will feel the connections open between the dream images and what you "normally" do. At some point the "message" will pop out. Then you are ready to dream again. Do this for a while and you will notice that your dreams begin to connect with one another.

As a language, dreams seem to represent a special kind of thought process, an interaction of images that mirrors and comments on our normal ways of thinking. Dreams are mysterious. They put things together in impossible ways that "mystify" logic yet feel as if they have direction,

---

OPPOSITE: Dreams of flight and falling are universally experienced. Flight is an important dream symbol.

ABOVE: The state of sleep allows us to access images and encounter messengers that we miss in daily waking life.

The Dream God

Dream images can take many forms and support many meanings at the same time. One of the problems is to focus this field of meaning in order to enter into a direct relation with its transformative power. One of the ways to do this in the ancient world was *incubation*, a word that literally means "sleeping in the sanctuary." You would take a specific problem, something from which you suffered, to a dream shrine that was under the auspices of one of the healing gods or earth powers. At the shrine you would go through purification and meditative ceremonies and then sleep in the central room dedicated to the god. The god would appear to you in sleep and give you specific instructions about your disease or problem. Often, you were then asked to record the dream-appearance and make a votive offering demonstrating your cure.

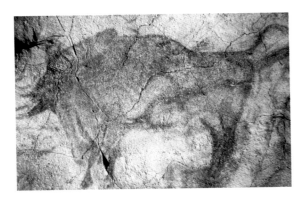

The cult of Asklepios, and the related dream cults of Serapis, Isis, Trophonius, and Calchas, probably provided the model for the dream-shrines in the Celtic world, with their sleep-chambers, votive offerings, and Dark Doors to the chthonic powers. A related form is called "Bull Sleep." A shaman or priest would sleep in one of the special sites wrapped in the hide of a bull. This would produce a dream answer to the question he was asking. Chinese magistrates, upon taking their position in a new city, would often sleep and dream in the temple of the City God, soliciting advice from the spirit of the city they would govern.

The Vision Quest

The Vision Quest was a kind of incubation used throughout North America to acquire a spirit-protector, a cure to disease, promote success in hunting, find power to recover from mourning, name a child, enter a secret society, or enact revenge. It was always carried out under a strong emotional impulse and might involve literal or ritual self-mortification. The normal procedure was to go into solitude, fast, and supplicate the spirits to take pity on the sufferer. Among the Crow nation, the quest lasted four days, and the vision usually occurred on the fourth night. Most often, a specific figure, in some way related to the tribe's collection of myths, appeared as an answer to the dreamer's supplication. The dreamer entered into a special relation with this figure, who would recite the formula of adoption: "I will have you for child." The dreamer would collect certain objects and behave in certain ways given by the spirit in order to keep the connection during the time after the vision.

TOP: Cave painting of a bison at Altamira, Spain. Such paintings may have helped to inspire hunters to dream of the location of their prey.

ABOVE: The Dwarfie Stone on the volcanic island of Hoy off the Orkneys in Scotland. This was probably a cell for dream incubation and rituals.

THE CULT OF ASKLEPIOS

One of the most famous of these dream incubation cults was the cult of Asklepios in the antique Mediterranean. Asklepios was a mythical healer, a son of Apollo, the god of prophecy, who himself had been turned into a god. Asklepios united a whole set of opposites in his person, the most prominent being night and day, the earth and the sky. He was particularly associated with the healing combination of water, snakes, trees, art, music, theater, and the power of the underworld. Asklepios had an extremely strong aura of kindness and healing. Through him illness, which was thought of as *penia* (lack or poverty), was converted to *ploutos* (wealth, plenitude, fullness).

The cult of Asklepios and its dream-shrines were spread throughout the Mediterranean, but the major shrine was at Epidauris. All other shrines were established by a translation of the cult from Epidauris and the ritual transportation of one of its holy snakes. The shrine at Epidauris is a cluster of buildings: temple, theater, hotel, and the *abatons*, or dream centers, set in a beautiful open landscape. A five-mile-long sacred road connects it to the port. The buildings, which are still standing, were noted for their beauty in the ancient world. The site abounds with snakes, wide spreading plane trees, and pure springs. The entrance is formed by six stone pillars that record famous cures effected by the god.

Any person could be admitted to the sacred precinct, except the dying and those about to give birth. You performed rites and cleansings, then made a preliminary sacrifice that was used to determine if this was the decisive moment to dream. Prayers were offered "at the hour of the sacred lamps" for the god's presence in dream. Then you would go to sleep in the central shrine, the *abaton*, lying on the skin of your sacrifice. If the moment was right, the god would appear in a dream or in a vision. He might come as the bearded man of his statues, as a boy, or accompanied by his wife and daughter. He could also appear in his animal form as a snake or dog. He would touch the part of the body that was ill, then disappear. The patient would wake up cured.

Asklepios might also enter into dialogue with the dreamer, giving specific injunctions. Often people would dwell at the shrine over a period of time, beginning a dialogue with the god and experiencing his power and kindness. The dreams were not interpreted, for they were clear injunctions. The dreamer was required to write them down, often turning them into art, and make a votive offering to the god.

ABOVE: The dream incubation center at Cos, one of the many shrines where the god Asklepios was invoked.

The Dream Goddess

In Japan, dream incubation was associated with both Shinto and Buddhist deities. The most famous of these shrines were those connected to the Bodhisattva *Kannon*, in Chinese *Kwan Yin*, the Compassionate One.

Here again dream incubation focuses the power of dreams on a specific problem. If you were the pilgrim, harassed by some insoluble problem, you would journey to the shrine, observing ritual purity and furnished with a gift for the deity. You made a vow to stay at the shrine for a specified time, often 7, 21, or 100 days. During that time, through prayer, meditation, abstinence, and offerings, you sought the intervention of the god. You would sleep each night in the main hall of the temple, as near to the inner sanctuary as possible. The divinity would come in a dream, often on the last night of the vigil.

People came to these shrines with three sorts of problems, and were offered different kinds of cures. Each came in the same kind of dream, in which the deity appears from the inner shrine and speaks directly to the dreamer, or acts through

ABOVE AND LEFT: The goddess *Tara* (above) and the god *Avalokiteshvara*, both Tibetan Bodhisattvas of active compassion. They are the equivalent of the Japanese *Kannon* and the Chinese *Kwan Yin*.

a miraculous boy or an old Buddhist priest. Dreamers might be cured of sickness. A man suffering from incurable leprosy spent seven days in the shrine of Kannon, whereupon a boy appeared from the inner sanctuary at the goddess's instructions and licked the leper's entire body. When he woke, the man was cured.

Dreamers may be cured of their sorrow. A noblewoman, divorced from her husband and deeply miserable, came to the temple for a seven-day sleep and was given a numinous vision of Kannon who handed her a jewel. The dream-jewel was in her hand as she woke. She took it home and, soon after, her husband returned and she bore a child. The family lived happily ever after.

Dreamers might also be given a symbolic glimpse into their fate. Here the dream goddess will hand them a symbol. A young noblewoman received a two-sided mirror. One side showed her mourning and weeping, but when the mirror was turned it revealed a rich robe, a curtain, and the glimpse of a beautiful garden. The goddess said: "This will make her happy."

In Tibet, the practice of dream-divination is particularly associated with the goddess Tara, the "savioress" and Bodhisattva of Active Compassion. Here a person will go into a meditation retreat to acquire her blessing. This involves visualizing her form and reciting her mantra. At some point during this retreat, she will give a sign that her gift of divination has been conferred. With this blessing, the dream-diviner can, whenever necessary, pose a question or problem, meditate on the goddess before sleeping, and receive a dream vision in answer to the question. This capacity can be and is used to help others.

INCUBATING A DREAM

If you are able to remember dreams and "entertain" their images, you can ask your dreams to help you with a specific problem on a particular night. Choose a night when you are not tired or overstressed and you have time in the morning to remember dreams. Don't overeat and don't drink.

First, in the evening, go over what has happened to you during the day. Look at what you did and felt, whatever stirred your feelings. Write down the main points. These may act as triggers or help you understand what you dream.

Then think about your problem. Look at it from all angles. Stir up your feelings. Note down what is involved, what you want, what you may have to give up, why it is a problem. Then make a one-line phrase that clearly states what information you need.

Repeat this phrase as you are going to sleep, like a lullaby or a mantra. If your mind wanders into worry or anxiety, gently pull it back. Affirm your real desire to learn something new about the situation, but don't think or worry about it.

Whenever you wake up, in the night or in the morning, write down whatever is going through your mind, be it a thought, a feeling, a memory, an idea. Don't limit it to dreams. The answer can come as a clear idea, a sudden perspective, or even a song playing through you. If you dream, write down the dream. It may be immediately clear. If not, let a few hours go by, then go back and work with the images. Try to understand the dream itself. See if it connects with any of your feelings from yesterday, or the field of associations to your problem. As you enter the dream images, the connections will probably emerge. If there are none, the message may be pointing you in a completely different direction.

ABOVE: You can use your own dreams as a personal oracle, asking a question or guidance and noting down the answers they give.

The Gates of Horn and Ivory

reams also lie. Impossible things happen, false scenarios are enacted. In fact, lying or changing the meaning of things is one of their central characteristics. If dreams have a message, how do we know if it is true or false? To put the problem in a subtler way, *how* do dreams mean things?

For many traditional diviners, one criterion was the time of day or night in which the dream occurred. Dreams that occurred at the break of day, when light returned and the soul was considered to be free of the confines of the body, were considered to be a more accurate reflection of the spirit world. Dreams earlier in the night would tend to reflect concerns and desires of the previous day or bodily preoccupations. The dream before dawn or the last dream of the night was the most likely to be a direct communication.

The old Greeks had a system of sorting dreams that seems to reflect something of their ambivalent nature and connects that ambivalence to divination. According to this myth, dreams arise from the depths of night and earth by means of Morpheus, a shape-changing god who remains forever in the world of sleep. Even a god, to appear in a dream, will take a shape from Morpheus. These forms enter the world of our dreaming, however, through one of two gates, the Gate of Horn or the Gate of Ivory. It is very important for the dreamer to understand through which gate the dream has come.

These two qualities inspired a great deal of later dream commentary, being simplified into "true" and "false," or "important" and "junk," or "God" and the "Devil." The two gates are much subtler than that. Horn is a fertilizing power, the "mind-fluid" sprouting forth into the world. It is the "force that through the green fuse drives the flower," exuberance, and power, as in the Horn of Plenty.

The Greek word used for ivory, on the other hand, links it directly to the tusks of a wild boar, and the savage sideways slashing movement he makes that rips, tears, and wounds whatever he encounters. This is the deconstructive, wounding or pathologizing power of dream, the *advocatus diaboli*. It is not simply death and disaster. It represents a wounding or "blackening" process that checks, redirects, and limits us. Thus it is not the "size" or clarity of the dream that determines how we should act on it, for some very clear dreams have come from the Gate of Ivory, but the gate through which it enters our dreaming mind.

These two gates are the source of the basic signs seen in divinatory systems around the world meaning "good fortune" or "misfortune." They have both a literal and a metaphorical meaning that helps you understand *where* a desire is coming from and *how* to enact it, as well as what will happen. If "misfortune" is the spirit's way to wound us, to open awareness in another way, we can enact this desire imaginatively rather than experience it literally. This seems to be a maxim of the dream world: anything you cannot entertain imaginatively you may have to experience literally as fate.

Iroquois Dreaming

The Iroquois of North America, had a particularly vivid appreciation of this paradox of dream. Much to the horror of the French Jesuits who first encountered them, the Iroquois had a "religion of dreaming." They felt that dreams represented "wishes of the soul" and that these wishes must be imaginatively played out or they would be literally encountered. A warrior, for example, who dreamed of being captured in battle and tortured, would implore his neighbors to turn this into theater and treat him, for a day, as a captive enemy. This turned away the literal enactment of the wish.

The practice has a parallel in the statues and talismans used by shamans to "eat" negative dreams, or the elaborate exorcism ceremonies listed in Babylonian books of dream omens. This is more than superstition. It recognizes the ambivalent reality of a dream as a motivating power and seeks to move or enact it in a safe way. The Iroquois had "festival times" in which deep fantasy wishes and sexual desires could be "acted out," a "time out of time" like the old Roman practice of *Saturnalia* when, for a day, masters became slaves and slaves became masters. Balinese communities enact a ceremony called "Taming the Winds of Desire" when a person has sickened because of an unacted "wish of the soul." Directed by shamans, these ceremonies give people a chance to act the desire out in trance, with the support and understanding of the community around them.

OPPOSITE LEFT: Fruitful, empowering dreams enter the sleeping mind through the Gate of Horn.

ABOVE: Wounding, destructive dreams come through the Gate of Ivory.

LEFT: Many dreams come to us when we are in the state of reverie, the space between sleep and wakefulness, when we are neither in the world nor out of it.

Dreams in Ancient China

long with the division into "fertilizing" and "deconstructing" dreams, most cultures involved with dream-divination moved toward defining types of dreams in terms of interlocking spheres of symbols or categories of interpretation. These exist something like the various possible energy levels of an electron circling the atomic nucleus. Depending on the context, a dream might make a quantum leap from one sphere of symbolizing to another. Chinese dream categories are a good example of this.

Chinese diviners regarded dreams as one among many forms of divining, important but not exclusive. Any big dreams or important questions would be confirmed through other forms. Dreams themselves may be "true" in various ways.

DREAM CATEGORIES

The earliest recorded examples of Chinese dreams come from the *Classic of Songs* (*Shi Ching*), about 600 B.C.E. Here, nobles dream of bears, snakes, and flying banners covered with symbols that diviners interpret as assuring potency, good harvest, and many offspring. A dream book from about 200 C.E. lists several other categories:

DIRECT DREAMS are immediately understood, clear messages from the gods.

SYMBOLIC DREAMS are to be interpreted through the cultural and mythological symbols they contain.

CONCENTRATED OR INCUBATED DREAMS are the answer to a question posed by the dreamer in which he "earnestly seeks" a solution through "concentrated sincerity."

THOUGHT DREAMS reproduce the way someone is thinking.

SOCIAL DREAMS are dependent on the social status and position of the dreamer for their meaning.

SEASONAL AND ENVIRONMENTAL DREAMS are produced by the change of the seasons or the direct effect of the environment.

ANTITHETICAL DREAMS oppose what the dreamer normally values.

MEDICAL DREAMS show disorders and imbalances in the body, keying a complex system of organ and element symbols.

TEMPERAMENTAL DREAMS are dependent for their meaning on the character, likes, and dislikes of the dreamer.

By determining what kind of dream he was dealing with, the dream-diviner could offer a more precise connection to a particular set of symbols.

Chou's Book

The best-known Chinese dream book is "Old Mister Chou's Book of Auspicious and Inauspicious Dreams." This is a part of the *T'ung Shu*, an almanac that has been published in China for about 2,000 years. The core of the *T'ung Shu*, or "Book of Myriad Things," is a lunar calendar that was constructed annually by imperial astrologers to show auspicious and inauspicious

days. Assembled around it is an extraordinary collection of divination methods, medical practices, advice on living, legends, charms, number charts, and geomantic calculations that continues to grow and change. Some of the material is used only by professional diviners. Other parts provide a day-to-day survey of what is auspicious and inauspicious that is used by everyone. It is also a powerful charm.

Families will buy the book before the New Year begins in February. It will be wrapped and carefully placed on a high shelf. On New Year's Eve, when all the family has gathered, the old year's almanac will be respectfully taken down from its hook by the door and the new one put up in its place to serve as talisman, calendar, dictionary, advisor, and life planner. The old almanac will be taken to a temple to be burned, so its power can return to heaven.

"Old Mister Chou's Book of Auspicious and Inauspicious Dreams" is attributed to one of the legendary creators of the *I Ching*, the Duke of Chou. It has seven categories of dream themes, with a list of simple symbolic occurrences in each, given with auspicious and also inauspicious variations. This illustrates an early formulaic approach to dream-divination, in which key elements are singled out of the narrative as significant. The occurrence of one of these symbols in a dream is significant but not decisive, for it will always be confirmed through other kinds of divination. The symbols are grouped under the headings:

Heaven and Weather Signs • Houses, Gardens, and Forests • Gods, Fairies, and Spirits • The Body • Music and the Harmony of Relationships • Creatures, Birds, and Beasts • Clothes, Jewels, and Other Things.

OPPOSITE: Even sleeping giants have dreams that need to be interpreted.

ABOVE: Modern Chinese people still use Chou's "Book of Dreams" to work out their lucky or unlucky days.

LEFT: Traditional dream divination is still used even in hyper-modern cities such as Hong Kong.

Another distinct dream genre was the Imperial Dream, when the emperor dreamed not as a person but as the Son of Heaven. This sort of dreaming was a potential communication from the Lord on High. Only the emperor could communicate with the highest power in heaven. These were political dreams of the highest order and could have significant effects on the entire country. They too were carefully verified.

The most common form of verification for dreaming used either the yarrow stalk oracle (*I Ching*) or the *Ka-puei* (or *chiao pei*), or temple blocks. These were two pieces of a bamboo root split in half, each with a convex and a concave side. When ritually prepared and cast, they could produce a yes, no, or neutral answer that was considered very important. Another important verification method in the case of spirit visitation dreams was to carefully compare the details of the dream with the recognized attributes of the deity who had appeared and, conversely, to check the details of the options for action against the dream images to determine which had been recommended. A valuable tool here was the incredible flexibility and divinatory origin of the Chinese written language. A word or character used to describe a situation would have a visual shape and, at the same time, a phonetic pronunciation that linked it with ten other characters with which it could be interchanged. This opened the range of possible associations.

The *Mao Shan Revelations* (c. 370 C.E.) is another model for dreaming, a Taoist model that uses dreams as a communication between the adept and a series of celestial beings. These dream texts interconnect scriptures, personal encounters with spirits by a visionary teacher, charms, alchemical recipes, and an ongoing dream journal. The inspired teacher provides visions that illuminate the scriptures at the same time as he interprets the dreams of those he is teaching.

Other dream books such as *Interpretations from the Forest of Dreams* (1636) continued to develop lists of symbols and their relative meanings in a very sophisticated fashion. These symbols were a common property of the culture and could be used by specialist and laypeople alike.

The Yellow Emperor's Medical Classic, another of China's oldest books, organizes lists of dream symbols according to the vital organ or elemental process they represent. When alien, pathogenic elements invade the system, they cause the souls of the organs to flutter about and produce dreams. Too much *yin* produces dreams of crossing water; too much *yang* produces dreams of burning houses. An overabundance of both produces dreams of killing. Upper body excess brings dreams of flying; lower body excess, dreams of falling. The Five Transformative Processes or "Elements" – Wood, Fire, Earth, Metal, and Water – also play an important part. These processes are linked in different series through which they either engender or destroy one another. By analyzing the predominant process in a dream, you may predict the potential dangers and changes in the dreamer's organic makeup.

The dream was also literary. One basic motif illustrated the vanity and futility of social aspirations in a very hierarchical society. An ambitious young man falls asleep, sees all his ambitions realized and then destroyed, and wakes to find his entire life has passed in the time it takes

CHOU AND THE STRAW DOGS

There is a story about this protean dream text that comes from the Three Kingdoms period (220–264 C.E.). One day a man came to the dream-diviner Chou Hsuan and asked him: "Last night I dreamed of straw dogs. What does this mean?" The diviner told him that he would soon eat a very pleasant meal. This is what happened.

The man returned and said that once again he had dreamed of straw dogs. Chou said to him: "Be very careful or you will fall from a carriage and break your legs!" This too, unfortunately, soon happened. The man came a third time to tell Chou that he had dreamed of straw dogs. Chou replied: "Please be extremely careful or your house will burn down." And so it did.

Finally the man came to Chou and told him that he had not really dreamed at all. He had made up the dreams to test the interpreter. Chou replied: "But it was the spirits that moved you to say those things; it is no different than if you had dreamed them." But why then were the interpretations so different? Chou told him that straw dogs, a very important cultural symbol, were used as sacrificial offerings. First they were part of a very important ceremonial meal. When the ceremony was over, however, they were thrown beneath the wheels of a carriage and crushed. Finally they were taken away and burned. All of these things happened to the man who "dreamed" of straw dogs three times. The interpretation focused on one key image in the "dream," related it to its shared cultural symbols, and connected it to the specifics of the dreamer's situation.

to cook gruel or wash your hands. Another literary motif developed around spirit-possession. A man or woman will encounter a spirit, usually a fox or a ghost, and fall in love or be seduced. This can lead to a wasting death or, in later examples of the dream genre, to the opening of an alternative reality, a fantasy world more pleasant and potent than normal life. The literary masterpiece *Dream of the Red Chamber* shows the dream as an overall metaphor for the life of the passions. Within it, however, individual dreams continually challenge the dreamer to awake from his or her compulsive attachments. A pair of "lucid dreamers," a Buddhist monk and a Taoist priest, travel blithely through the many different levels of existence.

Dream-divination in all these forms deals with the interconnection between spirits, processes, symbols, and the multiplicity of possible meanings.

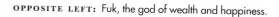

OPPOSITE LEFT: Fuk, the god of wealth and happiness.

OPPOSITE CENTER: Luk, the god of high rank and affluence.

CENTER TOP AND BOTTOM: Wood and Earth, two of the Five Transformative Elements.

ABOVE: A monk meditating. Meditation can lead to a state that hovers on the threshold of sleep and wakefulness; dreams that occur in this state are particularly powerful.

Dream Yoga

The Buddhist attitude toward dream is another important tradition. Dream is a metaphor for cyclic existence and the life of the passions – empty, vain, illusory, and full of suffering. Paradoxically, individual dreams can signify awakening from the life of illusion and compulsion. It was a dream that caused the Han emperor Ming-ti (100 C.E.) to send emissaries to central Asia to bring the sacred texts of Buddhism to China. Many Chinese and Japanese Buddhist monks kept dream journals to record visitations by spirits, precognitive dreams, and dreams that dramatized particular spiritual problems.

Like other Buddhist dream books, these journals sought to distinguish between "unreal dreams," produced by the imbalance of the elements in the body or the experiences of the previous day, and "divine" or prophetic dreams. Dream yoga, a very radical approach to dreaming, evolved out of this split. It reached its fullest development in Tibet.

Tibetan books of dream-omens such as the *Illuminating Mirror* are quite straightforward. The feeling tone of a dream event will reproduce itself literally in life. If you dream of a growing field of wheat, you will reap a harvest of blessings. If a horde of noxious insects attacks you, you are being overpowered by evil desires. Dream yoga, however, is much more complex. The goal of the enlightened being is to *stop* dreaming.

Dream yoga is a meditative practice developed between the 8th and 15th centuries to "Release Oneself from the Essential Delusion." It begins in the deliberately cultivated

experience of profound "disillusionment," the conviction that everything in normal existence involves dissatisfaction and suffering. Dream yoga instructs the practitioner in how to become aware of dreaming within the dream and thus "train in the illusory body of the dream state." Mantra, devotions, and meditation practices enable the adept to become fully aware that he is dreaming within the dream and to manipulate the images. This awareness is transferred into waking reality, which becomes equally empty of innate existence. When the yogi can fully realize the illusory nature of both waking and sleeping, he perceives the "fundamental clear light" that exists behind all mind-derived appearances. He literally stops dreaming.

Deity yoga, a form of tantra, frees awareness from compulsive identification with the dream of existence by generating the dream-body of a specific deity and merging with it. The yogi sees his body as a divine body and views everything that occurs as the activities of a god. This identification frees him from the conceptions of ordinary existence and acts as an antidote to the idea of a self. The ordinary ego disappears, to be replaced by a divine awareness.

An even more radical dream practice is called the *Dance of Chod*. The awakened dreamer produces the image of a *tolpa*, or demon, and allows it to tear him apart, symbolically enacting the destruction of the ego. These *tolpas* have been known to become visible to others and to take on an independent existence. They have sometimes literally murdered their creators.

Lucid Dreaming

Lucid dreaming is related to the first stages of dream yoga, when the dreamer becomes aware that he is dreaming inside the dream. This kind of dream had a special status in early Christianity, in medieval Islam, and in Buddhism because it indicated the dreamer was waking from the dream of the world and its attachments. The lucid dream emerged as a secular phenomenon in 19th-century Europe, in the era of spiritism and the occult revival. In the last 20 years it has become the object of study by sleep researchers and dream laboratories. It is now seen as a "peak experience" in the Dreamwork Movement.

In a lucid dream, you become aware that you are in the dreamworld. This can happen spontaneously or can be induced. There is usually a sudden intensification of the sensory quality of the dream and an ecstatic mood. The dreamer can consciously interact with other dream characters, or take on their identity. He may transform, though not control, the dream environment and travel where he wishes. The lucid dream seems to lead naturally toward light and transcendence. Lucid dreamers repeatedly ascend or fly toward the heavens, or say that they have experienced the fundamental source of light.

Another characteristic of the lucid dream is the emergence of the Inner Guide, Inner Self Helper, or Center who explains the dreamworld and tells the dreamer about him- or herself from a spiritual viewpoint. This figure can and does produce helping or healing dreams and a host of paranormal experiences. She or he is usually encountered in a high, light-filled place and takes on the guise of a guru, angel, monk, or helpful spirit.

OPPOSITE: The sage Bharadwaja from the Hindu epic *Adhyatma Ramayana,* in a classic yoga pose.

RIGHT: The Biblical Jacob dreamed of a ladder that he climbed to reach heaven, in a fine example of lucid dreaming.

The Dream Book

The way dreams are put together implies they can be "read." It has often reminded people of a language. The establishment of a dream book in which this language was explained or deciphered was a major project in many cultures. Greek empiricists, Chinese philosophers, Islamic mystics, Tibetan lamas, European psychologists, and American scientists have all offered versions of the dream book that unites a philosophy of dreaming with a specific interpretation of dream symbols.

The earliest Western dream books are the magnificent animal paintings in Paleolithic caves such as Lascaux. Hidden in virtually unreachable parts of deep caverns, they portray the interchange between humans and animals, on which life depended, as a kind of dreaming. Each image is a symbol-center, nucleus of a myriad stories, magical enactments, and possibilities.

Mesopotamia had a complex hierarchical culture based on labor-intensive agriculture, with great cities surrounding monumental ziggurats and palaces. Here we meet the *barû* priest and his library of omen-tablets, record of the interaction in dream between the gods, kings, and founding heroes. Dreams were seen as *direct*

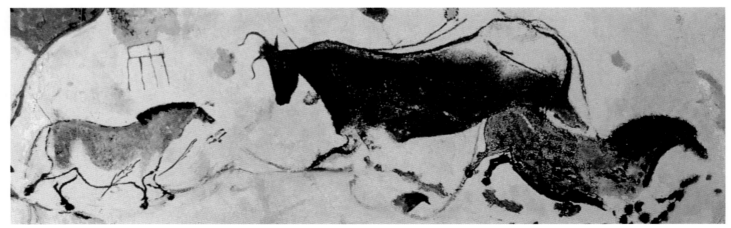

messages from the gods; as *omina* or the movement of known patterns; or as *symbola*, an unknown interaction that boded ill and demanded rituals or even exorcism. Thousands of dreams were recorded, along with interpretations and outcomes of the situations. These were not just simple formulas, but part of an on-going interaction with the protective and destructive powers these people felt around them.

Three sets of dream *omina* survive from Egypt, lists of favorable and unfavorable dream situations keyed by the words: "If a man see himself in a dream as ... " They include rituals to ward off or deliteralize the effects of an evil dream. These were probably associated with the temples of Serapis, the dream god, where "learned men of the magic library" had received the god's mandate to interpret dreams.

Hebrew scripture is full of the dreams of the prophets that connect heaven and earth. The Talmud has over 200 references to the various causes and meanings of dreams, ranging from angels, hairy goat demons, and night witches to overeating. The literature evidently supported a rich variety of dream interpreters. In one section Rabbi Binza reported that he once took a dream to 24 different dream interpreters in Jerusalem and received 24 different readings – all of which came true.

Dreams were a major source of inspiration for the Islamic religious practice. Medieval Islamic culture developed the dream book and dream reading into a high art. The science of dreams was considered "the prime science since the beginning of the world." A rich oral tradition developed around the legendary figure of Ibn Sirin. Through contact with Greek dream books, Arabic dream literature became extremely sophisticated. The dream book of *ad-Dinawari* is a vast compilation, assembling dream material that acts as a great screen on which the religious, emotional, and social life of tenth-century Baghdad is projected in all its richness and complexity.

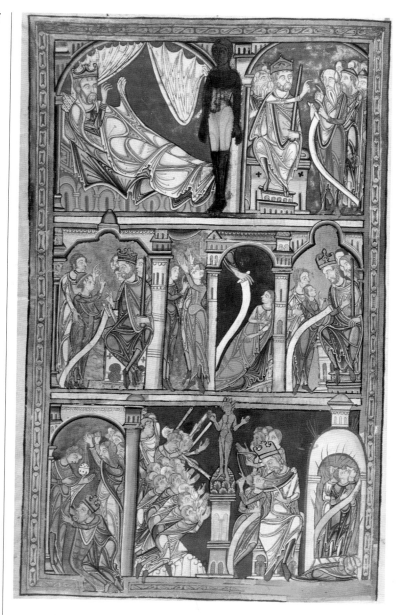

OPPOSITE BOTTOM: The cave paintings of Lascaux may have functioned as an inspirational book of dreams for a preliterate civilization.

OPPOSITE TOP: The Tower of Babel, the temple shrine or the City of Babylon.

ABOVE: The dreams of Nebuchadnezzar, the Babylonian king who conquered Israel in 586 B.C.E. His dreams were interpreted by the Jewish visionary Daniel.

The Great Divide

The history that most profoundly affects us, however, is the shift in divinatory practice and the interpretation of dreams that occurred in the late antique world from about 300 B.C.E. to about 400 C.E.

The old Greek world saw dreams as "visitations." Gods and the souls of the dead visited people or sent messages to them through their symbols and attributes. The *onieropolos*, or dream reader, was an integral part of this world, a combination of craftsman and magician who could help weave the fabric of meaning. The art of dream reading, it was said, was fundamental to civilization. It freed men from being paralyzed by the fear of death.

Enter the Philosophers

The age of the philosophers changed this. Hippocrates, called the father of medicine, defined dreams as diagnostic. While not denying the "prophetic dream," he elaborated a vocabulary of physical and psychological diagnosis. Aristotle, the father of analysis, said that *all* dreams were somatic, though they might quite subtly show what was going on in the body. Plato, the father of idealist philosophy, attributed dreams to the *daimones*, though when he said this he spoke through the "suspicious" female character of Diotima. He also defined a very influential model of the soul that was to play a great part in later thought. According to him, there are three souls, the lowest of which, a vicious animal lust, must be ruled by the highest power that can intuit the world of perfect forms. Most dreaming, he maintained, simply sets free this animal lust and should be severely restrained. Only a purified man, in touch with the highest parts of his soul, could hope to have a "true" dream.

Later neoplatonic philosophers such as Iamblichus developed detailed instructions on how to recognize the various kinds of gods, spirits, *daimones*, and heroes in

dreams. Dreams that came from the gods were clear, vivid, and luminous. Turgid or confused dreams came from demons. They were the body's way of discharging its imbalances. They might be of interest to doctors, but not to philosophers. In the enormously influential *Commentary on the Dream of Scipio*, Macrobius arranged a compendium of dream lore around a detailed description of a celestial ascent, a journey through the spheres of the planets toward the heavenly light. The lower spheres of dreaming were patrolled by a new kind of demon, the *incubus*, a male demon who copulated with women, and the *succubus*, a female demon who seduced men. Both the celestial ascent and the lore of the demons made this the most popular dream book in medieval Europe.

OPPOSITE: Zeus, Hera, Apollo, and Artemis; the classic Greek gods.

ABOVE: Aristotle and Plato. Both had theories about dreams.

Sent by the Gods

Just as psychotherapies flourish today, in ancient times the streets were full of diviners. Much of this dreamwork was evanescent, focused on individual problems like a particular reading with a divination system. Most of the texts are lost. One example does survive, however – the *Onierocritica* of Artemidorus. This book was meant for the professional diviner and analyzes over 3,000 dreams. Many of them are divine epiphanies, which are carefully examined to see if the god is true to his or her cult image and attributes. This was a very important criterion.

Traditional cultures have a pantheon of images to "hold" the activity of the soul, figures that inhabit their dreams to an extent we find unimaginable, and create an intense feeling of connection to the world. The lack of such figures is probably the single most distinctive feature that separates us from traditional societies. It is reflected in our dreams by our constant attempt to create a personal mythology.

Artemidorus saw dreams as a kind of text that must be translated into useful knowledge for the dreamer. He divided dreams into useless (*enupnion*) and meaningful (*onieros*). Useless dreams passively reflect the state of the body and its minor upsets. Real dreams "excite and awake the soul" to a knowledge of future events. Dreams are "sent by the gods" and are "the work of the dreamer" at the same time. For the gods must take on a shape to enter your dreams, and you are a participant in creating that shape. Being morally and physically calm in your normal life helps to make this kind of dream clearer. The real dream could foretell the future and assess the possibility of happiness, which was a gift of the gods. It was divided into the *theormatikon*, a clear vision that needed no interpretation, and the *allegorikon*, the puzzling dream that spoke through enigmas and involved the dreamer in a long process of dialogue and translation. The symbols in these allegorical dreams were divided into many categories, and each was given a wide range of different meanings. Artemidorus insists that all dreams must be seen in relation to the life, mood, situation, and character of the dreamer. It is the interpreter's responsibility to present something that the dreamer can use; a tool, a hope, a warning, an affirmation, a symbol.

Closing the Dream Book

The real divide, however, came with the rise of the Christian Church to political power. Christian leaders, with the power of the army behind them, wholeheartedly attacked pagan culture. Divination in all forms was made a capital crime. The temples were closed, the statues destroyed, the books were burned, and the groves cut down. This was also an attack on the dreamworld. *All* dreams were declared false, for they were sent by the pagan demons and gods. These gods and *daimones* were none other than the fallen angels who followed Lucifer in his rebellious fall from heaven. One possible kind of dream, the celestial journey, may be sent by the Lord or one of his angels. But such a dream must happen to a righteous person and be authenticated by a religious official. All other dreams were, literally, works of the devil. The Dream Book was closed in the West for the next 1,500 years.

A Return to Dreaming

An ethnologist and historian of religions once remarked that two of the 20th century's most characteristic developments – Marxism and psychology – were actually divination systems. The dream as an art motif and cultural icon returned to Western culture in the 19th century. It was only with the beginnings of psychology that some sense of divining through dreams reemerged.

There has been a great interest in dreams and dreamwork in the development of modern psychotherapy. Though divination and therapy are by no means the same thing, there is a divinatory element in most dreamwork and a therapeutic aspect to most divinatory practices. A modern dreamworker once asked if dreams know where we are going or stimulate us to change. The same could be asked of divinatory symbols. And the answer to both questions is yes.

There are a great number of dreamwork techniques being used today that are also divinatory styles, for they ask a question of the dream and seek out meaning to help the dreamer. They seem to center on five basic approaches or tactics, symbolized as an action taken toward the dream.

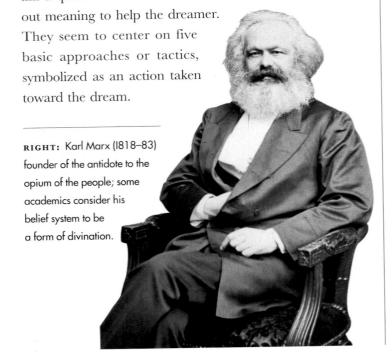

RIGHT: Karl Marx (1818–83) founder of the antidote to the opium of the people; some academics consider his belief system to be a form of divination.

MODERN INTERPRETERS

The significance of dreams, a preoccupation of the great classical thinkers, has also exercised some great minds in the 19th and 20th centuries. Below is a brief survey of the work done and the theories put forward from the various schools of dream therapy and interpretation.

Sigmund Freud

ATTACKING THE DREAM: Sigmund Freud, the self-proclaimed "father" of psychoanalysis, had much in common with Plato when he said that dreams showed the "wild beast" within us peeking out of his (well-deserved) chains. Freud envisioned the dreamworld as a swamp to be cleared. His motto was: Where *id* (the dream and the unconscious) was, there *ego* (rational consciousness) shall be. Freud's basic tenets were that dreams disguise forbidden desire and that, ultimately, there is only one desire, a trauma that haunts us from childhood: to have sexual intercourse with the parent of the opposite sex and kill the parent of the same sex. This gives us a picture of the ego being constantly shunted back and forth across the unconscious dream-field between Sex (*Eros*) and Death (*Thanatos*). A Freudian dream-divination looks at the images in terms of repressed desires to Have It or to Kill It. The dream takes us back to the primal mud and our goal is to clean up the swamp.

EMPOWERING THE DREAM: Carl Gustav or C.G. Jung, Freud's rebellious heir, saw the dream as an oracle. His idea of the dreamworld was a vast repository of myths and symbols that could come to our aid in times of distress. Jung's motto was: "Called or not called, the God will be there." Jung maintained that the dream compensated for the lacks of the conscious mind in a variety of ways. He connected and amplified dreams through a vast range of symbol systems, piling myth on top of myth. The center of Jung's system was the process of alchemy and transformation, and he spent quite a while working with "occult" images. Several of Jung's ideas – introversion and extroversion, personality types, the descent to the underworld, synchronicity – have become part of popular understanding. A Jungian dream-divination would look at the images as clusters of symbols and associate them with myths. It would connect them with archetypal figures of Jung's own mythology of the soul – the Shadow, the Persona, the Anima and Animus, the Great Mother, and the Wise Old Man. Jung once remarked that we feel isolated in our world because the things around us no longer have a symbolic value and the profound emotion this value brings. The symbols in dream compensate for this loss.

ENTERING THE DREAM: *Fritz Perls*, a renegade from psychiatry, saw the dream as a projection of the rejected and disowned parts of the dreamer's personality. He felt dreamwork could be better done in a group, so he replaced the analyst's couch with the "hot seat," the center of the group's attention. He developed Gestalt ("whole being") therapy to express the idea of getting all the parts back together. This approach doesn't worry about understanding. It concentrates on "experience." The dream is an existential message from yourself to yourself, and every part of it is you. You take on the identity of all these different parts, talking, acting, or dancing them out. This leads to a dialogue with an "empty chair" in which you play two parts of yourself confronting each other. Or to body work that intensifies the feeling of a rejected dream part so it can be deeply

Fritz Perls

Carl Gustav Jung

experienced. In a Gestalt dream-divination, forget myths and symbols. All you see is a part of yourself. The idea is to get it together.

SHARING THE DREAM: *Montague Ullman*, a psychoanalyst turned "democratic dreamworker," turned Perls' hot seat into a "sharing experience." Ullman wasn't as concerned with the dream itself as he was with the dynamics of "dream sharing." He thought that dreams were about connectedness to others and our survival as a species. He was very interested in telepathic dreams and communal dreams literally shared by several people. Ullman created the idea of the Dreamgroup, probably inspired by an ideal portrait of the dream life of a Malaysian tribe, the Senoi. In a Dreamgroup, you tell your dream, then hear it responded to by all the others as if it were their own. People can ask you to tell them more about an image, but they may not offer a comment, an opinion, or an interpretation. The responses set up a "projective field" that helps you come to your own insights. You take it all as information and express your thanks. A Dreamgroup-divination would ask several people what the images meant to them. The emphasis is on sharing an experience.

THINKING THE DREAM: *Calvin Hall*, chairman of a university psychology department and sleep researcher, pioneered the Content Analysis of dreams. His goal was to bring dreams into the realm of ego psychology by showing they were thinking in disguise. The "content" of dreams is ideas. To interpret a dream, you must translate it into the ideas it refers to. Hall's motto might be: "Let's think about it and establish a norm." He treated dreams as objective social phenomena, collected thousands of dream reports, and analyzed them according to the conceptual systems they present. These were crossreferenced according to the age, gender, social class, and education of the dreamer. A Content Analysis dream-divination would look at the images as the elements or themes that have specific ideas as their content. It would compare the dream with others of the dreamer's social group.

Dream-Divination Reappraised

The antique or traditional world regarded dreams as a language of signs we could use to deal with the events of our daily lives in an imaginative way. Dreams and dream-signs were an interface with the gods. Dream divination was the technique of using these signs, a way to interact creatively with the natural and the spiritual worlds.

Much of the old significance of dreaming is now returning in modern ways of talking about and working with dreams. Sleep researchers who study brain function during sleep compare it to the operation of quantum mechanics, a "fertile chaos." They have also found that depriving a person of dream sleep leads to psychosis. Psychologists see it as the "royal road" to the unconscious. On a popular working level, dreaming plays a major part in virtually all kinds of therapy. Working with dreams has become a part of many people's lives.

Most people today regard dreams as meaningful and see them as offering a connection to creative energies that can enrich their lives. Dreams give them access to ways of knowing that would otherwise be closed to them. There are many sorts of dreamwork to help you use the language of dreams to "see" the flow of events, both inner and outer. By using these or other techniques to enter the dreamworld, you can find the real treasure of meaning and beauty hidden there. Here is one technique that uses the oracles we saw earlier in this book.

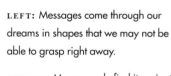

LEFT: Messages come through our dreams in shapes that we may not be able to grasp right away.

BELOW: Many people find it easier to work with a counselor to help them ask themselves the right questions and capture all the nuances of their dreams.

DREAMING WITH THE BOOKS OF FATE

Here is a way to do dream-divination that has a lot in common with old methods. It uses one of the major divinatory systems or "Books of Fate" as a dream book. It can give you connecting symbols, road signs, and a deeper look into what archetypal forces your dream may be moving around. True to the oldest methods, this technique also relies on "chance" as a way to tease out hidden meaning.

First, remember your dream. Write it down and separate it into units or elements that feel whole to you. Feel into these elements, let them call up associations and memories until you have a sense of the movement and structure of the dream. Then for each element, lay out a card from the Tarot deck and look at how the symbol resonates with the dream element and all the symbols connect with each other. This can be very surprising and deepening. It can give you a kind of road map of the potential of the images, indicating which way they are moving and how they interact.

Another variation is to go through the same remembering and analyzing procedure, then ask the *I Ching*, "What is the meaning of this dream (for me)?" You will immediately see the image connections. The divinatory symbols can point out "auspicious" and "inauspicious" directions and give you an overall grasp of the movement or "moment" of the dream.

Hexagram 14
Great Possessing

Justice

Death

The Tower

Afterword

Divination is not simply a way to predict the future. In all its many varieties it is a way of knowing and speaking with a living world, a world that is en-souled. Still a part of traditional cultures, it offers an age-old way to imagine yourself and your place in the world and connect with its hidden patterns. Divination was considered to be a *lumen* or light added to our normal intelligence. It was used to identify the hidden forces at work in a situation and to suggest strategies to deal with them. The many varieties of divination, from the most simple to the most complex, act as a helping spirit, enabling us to navigate the journey of our lives. They give a voice to the world of the imagination and the mythic beings who inhabit it.

Afterword

ivination works through myths and symbols, mysterious images with many possibilities of meaning. These myths and symbols portray the way things are moving in the soul. This is a common denominator of all systems, from tossing bones and reading bird-signs to erecting a horoscope, making a Tarot spread, or working with dreams. The fundamental idea is that there is a flow or dynamic quality to life that can be perceived through the "chance" or random production of a symbol, a method that lets the "other" do the choosing.

The same qualities that we see in divination practices and theories are found in the metaphors and theories of quantum physics – synchronicity or "meaningful coincidence," the relativity of time and space, the idea of fields of energy and probability rather than concrete objects. Both insist on the crucial importance of the observer in creating meaning, the idea that an experience is created by an interaction between the future and the present, that events can move forward and backward in time and occur simultaneously in different places without a known cause to connect them. All of these ideas find a parallel in the traditional or magical world with its ideas of correlative thinking, qualitative time, and the interaction of mythic forces that can break through the limits of normal time and space. The mythic or traditional world of the diviner has much in common with the mysterious subatomic realm of quantum physics.

Often divination methods are divided into "inductive" and "deductive" systems; that is, you either intuit or see something in a vision or trance, or you study an exterior sign and analyze it according to a set of fixed meanings. But, as we have seen, divinatory symbols must be both intuitively perceived *and* thought about. In fact, they join these qualities. Others say that different systems emphasize the different ways we know things: thinking, feeling, sensing, intuiting.

Divination methods range from the simple to the extremely complex. Because they generate symbols – images charged with the power to connect the visible and invisible worlds – they are often formed into elaborate models of the cosmos, linking microcosm and macrocosm, and have had considerable political and social impact. This seems to be one of the natural directions of divinatory practices. The innate tendency of a myth or symbol constantly to generate and acquire new meaning shows the opposite tendency. The interaction between these two energies is what keeps a divination system alive and creative.

The act and art of divining seeks to open a "sacred space" in the imagination, a place where images are charged with symbolic power and where we can interact with the different forces at work in our soul and our world. The traditional world had many ways and places where you could speak with the spirit or spirits: oracles, signs, and omens; journeys into the invisible worlds; people who became voices for the gods. The signs produced were empowered as myth, and elaborate cosmic models were constructed to relate them and gather their associations and correlations. The end product of this process was the assembling of the "Books of Fate," both oral and written, that carried the myths of a culture and related them to individual situations. They offered continual creative contact between the individual and the imaginal world.

It is just this quality that has made divination so popular and important to people today. Just as quantum physics is rediscovering the "magical" qualities of matter, time, and space, so individuals are discovering that traditional divination systems allow them to see themselves in a way that connects them with the deep structures of their imagination and the way the spirit is moving them. It offers an alternative to deadening and soulless ways of thought, and emphasizes the mythic importance of the individual and her or his journey through life. It does this in such a way that we feel a real dialogue with the powers of the invisible world. Through this dialogue we begin to generate our own myths.

The use of temple blocks and sticks, as well as spirit mediums, geomantic and astrological divination, is still widespread throughout the East. In South America and many parts of North America there is widespread use of *Ifa* divination and possession cults. Even in urban situations, many Africans still rely on body-diviners and seers to give them insight into their problems. Modern Westerners most often contact divination through the "Books of Fate," although

dowsing has become a kind of way to be spiritually connected with energy in the earth.

Though it originated in the Renaissance and was developed in the 17th century, Tarot really entered modern culture through the occult revival at the end of the 19th century. The Order of the Golden Dawn made a great synthesis of magical systems accessed through the Tarot and created the first modern decks. Since about 1950 there has been a tremendous interest in the cards with the development of new decks and approaches. The basic ideas and strategies of Tarot were further used to give people direct access to a wide range of other mythologies.

Another modern divinatory interest centers on the *I Ching* or *Classic of Change*. It entered our culture primarily through the Wilhelm/Baynes translation in 1954,

OPPOSITE: A modern Chinese fortune teller and feng shui master using the Lo-Pan, or geomancer's compass.

ABOVE: A modern shamanistic drum designed for ritual purposes. It combines the glyphs for the 12 zodiac signs and the symbols for the three ancient seasons.

LEFT: Dr. Michael Harner who has reintroduced shamanism to the modern world.

Only Connect

Why the interest? All of these phenomena lie well outside mainstream thought and culture. From the perspective of traditional science they are meaningless. But they fill a great need or lack in modern culture, a need for personal contact with the worlds of soul and spirit and a sense of the importance of the individual's journey through life. Divination speaks to *you* directly and connects *you* with the movements of the world of spirit and imagination.

Do oracles speak the truth? Is divination illusion? Or delusion? Do predictions really ever "come true"? Anyone who has ever worked with a divination system has asked these questions and can provide numerous examples of the uncanny accuracy of divinatory symbols, often on a quite literal level. But the purpose seems to be to move you out of a simple true/false dichotomy and engage you with the images that are moving your soul. The work with these images is what moves you; it is both the process and the goal, the wave and the particle.

Divination has been called the aboriginal human act. It has played an important part in virtually every human culture, and is a central part of our cultural and spiritual heritage. As divination emerges once more from its exile in the shadows, it is a sign that we are seeking to connect with an exiled part of ourselves, an integral part of our spirit and our soul.

connected to the fields of depth psychology and Eastern philosophy. The images and system of the *I Ching* provide a way of thinking about synchronicity and the continual way of the *tao* in an unfolding world, besides giving people very practical help in times of need.

We have also seen an enormous expansion of interest in astrological divination. The "sun signs" are now part of popular culture and, with computer assistance, astrologers are reviving and developing increasingly sophisticated ways of using the "magic of the stars." Dreamwork, which lies on the borderline between divination and psychology, is also proliferating in many different forms. And people are becoming more aware of the significance of "synchronous" happenings – what the old world called omens.

ABOVE: Geomancy practiced in the Arabic style. Shells and stones are cast onto a pre-defined grid to reveal geomantic patterns.

RIGHT: Chinese men playing mah-jong, which is both a game and a divinatory technique.

OPPOSITE: The Tree of Life, a modern image of the esoteric system known as the Cabala.

Glossary

ALECTRYOMANCY Part of an animal divination ceremony in the ancient world in which a rooster was placed on the earth in the center of an alphabet containing grain seeds.

ALEXANDRIAN ATMOSPHERE Ancient form of geomancy and origin of alchemy, astrological charts and the occult image of man. *See also* Geomancy, Hermeticism.

ANIMA In Jungian psychology, the feminine principle present in the male unconscious. *See also* Animus.

ANIMUS The masculine principle present in the female unconscious.

ARCHETYPE Typical specimen; one of the inherited mental images postulated by Jung as the content of the collective unconscious.

ASTROLOGY Study of the motions and relative positions of the planets, Sun and Moon interpreted as terms of human characteristics and activities.

AUGUSTUS, GAIUS OCTAVIANUS (63 B.C.E.–14 C.E.). Adopted by Julius Caesar in 44 B.C.E. Became first emperor of Rome after defeating Mark Antony. Outlawed private divination and guarded the Sibylline Prophecies as an imperial secret.

BESTIARIES Moralizing medieval collection of descriptions of animals, real and mythical.

BONES Considered to have oracular powers, skull, thigh, and shoulder bones were frequently used in ancient ritual divination ceremonies.

CABALA Mystical interpretation of the "Key to the universe" using the 22 letters of the Hebrew alphabet as the language of God, each with a mystical meaning and magical power of transformation.

CATALYST Person or happening that influences an event or situation.

CHALDEA Another name for Babylonia. Chaldeans were the ancient Semitic people of the seventh century B.C.E., famed as astrologers and soothsayers.

CHAOS THEORY Modern concept in physics relating to the formless void of primordial matter supposed to have existed before the ordered universe took shape.

CHARLATAN One who makes false claims to knowledge or expertise that he or she does not possess.

CHIEN TUNG Process of Chinese divination to give advice on dealing with crises and decisions to be made.

CLAIRVOYANCE Gift of insight or second sight, awareness of things beyond the natural range of the senses, and ability to foretell the future.

COLLEGE OF AUGURS Prophets and soothsayers of ancient Rome with the ability to observe and interpret omens or signs to help guide the making of public decisions.

CORNUCOPIA In Greek mythology the horn of Amalthea, the goat that suckled Zeus. In art, the horn of plenty overflowing with fruit and vegetables representing great abundance.

COURT DE GÉBELIN, ANTOINE French Protestant clergyman and student of mythologies who decided in 1781 that the card game of Trumps was the lost Egyptian *Book of Thoth*, key to the mysteries of a vanished civilization.

CROWLEY, ALEISTER (d. 1947). British-born declared Satanist, self-styled "Beast 666" (or the devil), his attempts at contacting Satan in 1898 failed, as did his association with the Order of the Golden Dawn when he published their secret rituals in his "*Confessions*". *See also* Order of the Golden Dawn; Thoth, Book of.

DALAI LAMA The chief lama (priest or Buddhist monk) ruler of Tibet. Head of religious and political life whose successor is decided by a series of prophetic visions.

DICE Throwing the dice has long enjoyed a worldwide tradition as a method of foretelling the future and decision making.

DOWSING Used since ancient times in the search for underground water, the use of a divining rod relying on the holder's interaction with hidden forces in the environment.

DRAGON HOLES Chinese definition of places where the creative energy enters the inquirer and manifests itself.

ELECTIONAL CHART Used by ancient astrologers to predict and advise on the quality and potential of a given moment in time, now greatly helped by the use of modern computer techniques.

ELEMENTAL Motivated by, or symbolic of, primitive and powerful natural forces relating to earth, air, water, and fire.

EPIPHANY Moment of great or sudden revelation, such as the manifestation of a supernatural or divine reality.

EQUINOX Vernal and autumnal; the two yearly occasions at six month intervals when day and night are of equal length and the compilation of horoscopes has particular significance.

EXORCISM Religious ritual performed to expel evil spirits from a person believed to be possessed or a place supposedly haunted.

EXTISCIPY Ancient divination method using entrails of sacrificed animals or humans.

FREUD, SIGMUND (1856–1939). Austrian psychiatrist and originator of psychoanalysis, based on the free association of ideas and the analysis of dreams, particularly their sexual significance.

GEMATRIA Ancient occult science based on Greek and Hebrew alphabets regarded as symbols of the sacred structure of the cosmos.

GEOMANCY Prophecy made from patterns of a handful of earth cast down or dots drawn at random and connected by lines.

GNOSTICISM Religious movement characterized by a belief in intuitive knowledge that the spiritual element in man could be released from its bondage in matter, (regarded as heresy by the Christian Church).

GYPSIES Nomadic people who migrated from northwest India in the 12th to 15th centuries, famed as fortunetellers using Tarot cards. Name comes from the idea that their origins were Egyptian.

HAN defines Chinese people as contrasted to Mongols, Manchus, etc.

HAN DYNASTY Imperial dynasty that ruled China c. 206 B.C.E. to 221 C.E. expanding its territory and developing its bureaucracy.

HERMAPHRODITE Living tissue, i.e. plants, animal, or humans, having both male and female characteristics and genital tissues.

HERMES TRISMEGISTUS Greek name for the Egyptian god Thoth, who is credited with various works on mysticism and magic.

HERMETICISM Ritual associated with the ancient arts of astrology, alchemy, and transcendental magic, relating to the writings and teachings of Hermes Trismegistus.

HIEROS In ancient Greece, a diviner who interpreted the omens in animal sacrifices.

HOLY GRAIL Legendary cup used by Jesus Christ at the Last Supper, allegedly brought to Britain by Joseph of Arimathea. It became the sacred quest of medieval knights.

HORARY CHART Relating to the hours; origin of the expression "casting a horoscope."

I CHING Ancient Chinese book of divination and source of Confucian and Taoist philosophy. Reference to the text accompanying 1 of 64 hexagrams selected at random answers questions and gives advice.

IFA DIVINATION Based on geomancy; it originated in Nigeria where it remains a vital part of life. Ifa has traveled to the United States to become part of new Creole religious practices.

JUNG, CARL GUSTAV (1875–1961). Swiss psychologist whose criticism of Freud's emphasis on the sexual instinct ended their early collaboration, but who maintained a strong belief in the dream as oracle.

KARMA In Hinduism and Buddhism the principle of retributive justice determining the effects of a person's past deeds and reincarnations on his present life.

LOCAL SPACE CHART Derived from a natal horoscope; projected onto the plan of a building or location, it can predict the inquirer's fortunes therein.

MANTIS A diviner in ancient Greece who read bird-signs and had prophetic visions, a gift that often ran in families.

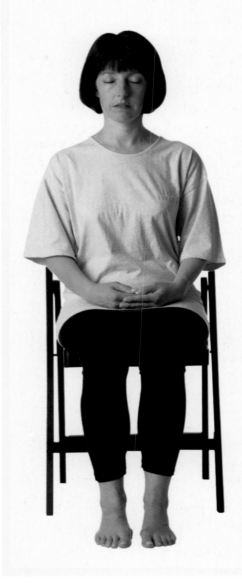

MANTRA In Hinduism and Buddhism, any sacred word or syllable used as an object of concentration and embodying some aspect of spiritual power.

MEDIUM Person accredited with powers to act as a spiritual intermediary between the dead and the living.

NECHUNG STATE ORACLE Plays an important role in Tibetan history and politics; it is consulted for all important decisions for the future and for warning omens.

NUMEROLOGY Study of numbers, such as figures in a birth date and their supposed influence in human affairs. Present-day numerologists use the system to give analyses of personality and compatability potential.

NUMINOUS EVENT Mysterious or awe-inspiring happening arousing spiritual or religious emotions.

ODU "Book" in the memory library of *Ifa* divination with 256 geomancy signs, the center of a circle of myths, stories, and ritual actions.

OINEROCRITICA OF ARTEMIDORUS Book that has survived, intended for the professional diviner, analyzing over 3,000 dreams based on their significance in relation to human desires and fears.

OINEROPOLOS The diviner or reader of omens in dreams in ancient Greece, where *Oinos* the lone eagle or hawk was associated with the destiny of kings.

ORACULAR GEOMANCY Sixteen signs originally produced by making and counting random marks made in earth or sand. *See also* Geomancy.

ORDER OF THE GOLDEN DAWN Described as the cornerstone of all modern occultism. Founded in 1887 by the Freemason William Wynn Westcott who claimed to have deciphered a coded alchemical manuscript (probably forged) containing initiation rituals of a secret German occult order, "Die Goldene Dämmerung." Although now allegedly extinct, its influence on literature, art, and music – particularly rock – has been immense. *See also* Crowley, Aleister.

OUIJA Board on which are marked the letters of the alphabet. Answers to questions are spelled out by a pointer or glass held by the fingertips of the participants and supposedly dictated by spirit-forces.

PALMISTRY Interpretation of character, telling fortunes, etc. by the configuration of lines, marks, and bumps on a person's hand.

PENDULUM A cord or light thread holding a balanced weight; held or mounted to swing freely under the influence of gravity, its movements will decide answers to any questions posed.

PHRENOLOGY Determination of the strength of human faculties by the shape and size of the skull overlying the parts of the brain thought to be responsible for them.

PHYSIOGNOMY Features or characteristic expression considered as an indication of human personality; the art or practice of judging character from facial features.

PONTO DE DESARREGAR Part of Brazilian Candoblé tradition. Ritual to replace serious misfortune by confidence, shared spirit, and benediction.

PRENESTINE FORTUNE Divination ritual in ancient Rome using dice and letters of the alphabet to foretell the future.

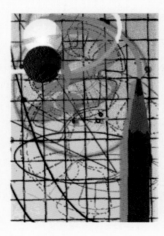

PSYCHIC Existing outside the possibilities defined as natural laws; mental telepathy. Person sensitive to paranormal forces.

PSYCHOPOMP Animal helper or guide in primitive cultures that helped to solve problems and foretell the future.

QUINTESSENTIAL In ancient philosophy, ether, the fifth and highest essence or element after earth, water, air, and fire. Thought to be the constituent matter of the heavenly bodies and latent in all things.

REICH, WILHELM (1897–1957). Austrian psychologist living in the United States. Ardent socialist and advocate of sexual freedom, he proclaimed a cosmic unity of all energy and built a machine (the orgone accumulator) to concentrate this energy on humans.

RIDING THE WAGON Ceremonial expression for casting the runes. The image is of sitting in a riderless wagon drawn by sacred white horses and seeing past, present, and future. *See also* Runes.

ROSE OF THE WINDS Divinatory practice based on the manipulation of yarrow stalks and associated with the *I Ching*.

ROSICRUCIANS Allegedly founded in the 15th century by German Christian Rosenkreutz (translated as "Rosae Crucis" – Rose of the Cross). Professing esoteric religious doctrines, venerating the emblems of the Rose and Cross as symbols of Christ's Resurrection and Redemption and claiming occult powers.

RUNES Characters of the Germanic alphabet of 24 signs derived from the Roman alphabet. In use in divination especially in Scandinavia from the third century to the end of the Middle Ages. Inscribed on stones or pieces of wood, each character thrown or cast, when read together is believed to have significant interpetation.

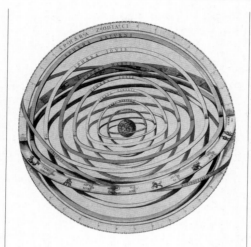

SCAPULOMANCY Bone-oracle divination mentioned in medieval Latin as one of the devil's instruments. Widely used by the Naskapi, a hunting tribe from Labrador, in search of new territories.

SCRYING BOWL Divining practice linking water and the mirror; the symbols produced are concerned with reflection, inspiration, and seeing the world of the dead.

SHAMAN Medicine man, especially among Native American tribes. Religion based on belief that the world is pervaded by good and evil spirits who can only be influenced by the shaman's control.

SIBYLLINE PROPHECIES Collection of sayings in ancient Rome regarded as sacred and jealously guided by Emperor Augustus. Bearing upon policy and religion supposedly brought from the sibyl, i.e. woman, oracle, or prophetess, who guided Aeneas through the underworld.

SNAKE WOMAN OR PYTHIA Medium or oracle in ancient Greece whose sacred divining was associated with the snake, the earth, and water sources.

SOLSTICES, WINTER AND SUMMER The shortest day of the year marks the beginning of winter, the longest day of the year marks the beginning of summer – events of great ritual significance in the solar calendar.

SUBLIMINAL Condition resulting from processes of which the individual is unaware.

SUNG DYNASTY (960–1279 C.E.). Imperial dynasty of China noted for its art, literature, and philosophy.

SWAMI Title of respect in India for a Hindu saint or religious teacher.

SYNCHRONISTIC Events that occur or recur at the same time or in unison and can be interpreted by omens.

TAOISM Chinese philosophy; according to Lao-tse the rational basis of human conduct, the course of life, and its relation to human truth. Advocates a simple honest life and noninterference with the course of natural events, a popular system of religion and philosophy that incorporates pantheism and sorcery.

TAROT Cards now used mainly for fortunetelling, consisting of 78 cards: 4 suits of 14 cards each (the Minor Arcana), and 22 other cards (the Major Arcana).

TEA LEAVES Domestic form of divining, popular in Europe since the introduction of tea in the 18th century; can also be practiced with coffee grounds. Popular with gypsies and amateur fortunetellers.

TEIRESIAS Seer in ancient Greece who was both man and woman, human and animal, alive and dead, blind and seeing – attributes that gave him access to the hidden significance of all things, more powerful than the gods themselves.

THEODOSIUS I (THE GREAT) (c. 346–395 C.E.). Christianized Roman Emperor who outlawed divination and dabbling with spirits as a capital crime since the Church had fixed the eternal meaning of all things.

THEOSOPHICAL SOCIETY Founded in 1875 and claiming to be derived from the sacred writings of Brahmanism and Buddhism. Claimed to have intuitive insight into the divine nature while denying the existence of any personal god.

THEURGICAL Descriptive of beneficent magic taught and performed by Egyptian neoplatonists who believed in the intervention of a divine or supernatural agency in the affairs of man and the working of miracles by such intervention.

THOTH In Egyptian mythology, a moon deity, scribe of the gods, and protector of learning and the arts.

THOTH, BOOK OF Created by Aleister Crowley and artist Lady Frieda Harris, it is a "modern" variant of the Tarot pack, claiming that the symbols present basic structures of the mind and imagination and in this sense lies their secret doctrine. *See also* Crowley, Aleister.

TOTEM Particularly among Native Americans, a species of animal or plant symbolizing clan or family and having ritual associations.

TRANCE Hypnotic state resembling sleep, in which a medium, having temporarily lost consciousness, claims to be controlled by a spirit guide as a means of communication with the dead.

TU'I-PEI T'U Book of Chinese prophecy regarding historical events and prodigies, a potentially subversive view of history officially prohibited on political grounds at the beginning of the 13th century.

UNIVERSAL COMPASS The hierarchical relation between the heavens, the surface of the earth, which is the center of human life, the underworld of the dead, and the future.

URIM AND THUMMIM Two mysterious Old Testament objects probably used as portable oracles and carried in the breastplate of the high priest. "And thou shalt put in the breastplate of judgment the Urim and the Thummim, and they shall be upon Aaron's heart, when he goeth before the Lord." (Exodus 28:30.)

VAUDOU (VOODOO) Haitian religious form of spirit possession with roots in old African cultures and modern American experience, which has enabled its supporters to survive long years of oppression.

VINTANA AND SIDIKY Form of Arabic astrology that survives in Madagascar with signs projected onto the field of a house to locate possible misfortune. Symbols combined medical and ritual indications using both astronomical and geomantic calculations.

VOLSUNGR Northern tribe of semidivine beings who wandered into Europe ahead of the great Ice Age. Caring for the world, they were guardians of the primordial forests and the "dragon-paths," the ancient connecting lines between all things.

WISE WOMAN Perhaps the earliest of diviners; seer, priestess, oracle, or witch. Her ability to "see" and watch over loved ones and children at great distances in bygone days when communication was extremely difficult was greatly sought after.

YAHWEH Old Testament name of God, revealed to Moses on Mount Horeb. Jehovah (from Hebrew YHVH, with conjectural vowels, perhaps related to "hawah" to be).

YARROW Common perennial herb (*Achillea millefolium*) with pungent smell and astringent taste, also known as *milfoil*. Yarrow stalks are used in *I Ching* divination rituals.

YEAR ANIMALS In Chinese astrology, each lunar year is connected to an emblematic animal, and people born in that year have the animal's attributes. The 12 are Rat, Ox, Tiger, Rabbit (or Cat), Dragon, Snake, Horse, Goat (or Sheep), Monkey, Rooster, Dog, and Pig.

YIN AND YANG The complementary principles of Chinese philosophy: Yin is negative, dark, and feminine; Yang positive, bright, and masculine. Their interaction is thought to maintain the harmony of the universe and to influence everything within it.

ZODIAC Imaginary belt extending 8 degrees on either side of the ecliptic. Contains in equal areas the 12 zodiacal constellations (signs of the zodiac) within which the sun, moon and planets appear to move. The astrological representation as a circle showing the symbols associated with the 12 signs is used as a divinatory device.

Further Reading

On Divination

GENERAL STUDIES

Alexandre Bouché-LeClercq, *Histoire de la divination dans l'antiquité* (4v), Paris, 1879–82, rpt. Scientia Verlag Aalen, 1978.

André Caquot and Marcel Leibovici (eds.), *La Divination* (2v), Paris, Presses Universitaires de France, 1968.

Toufic Fahd, *La divination arabe*, Leiden, 1966.

William A. Lessa and Evan Z. Vogt, *Reader in Comparative Religion*, 2nd edition, New York, 1965.

Michael Loewe and Carmen Blacker (eds.), *Divination and Oracles*, Boulder, Colorado, Shambhala, 1981.

John Matthews (ed.), *The World Atlas of Divination*, London, Headline, 1992.

J. Nougayrol (ed.), *La Divination en Mesopotemie et dans les régions voisines*, Paris, 1966.

Philip Peek (ed.), *African Divination Systems: Ways of Knowing*, Bloomington, Indiana, University Press, 1991.

Lynn Thorndike, *A History of Magic and Experimental Science* (8v), New York, 1923-58.

Jean-Paul Vernant (ed.), *Divination et rationalité*, Paris, 1974.

Marie-Louise von Franz, *Divination and Synchronicity: The Psychology of Meaningful Chance*, Toronto, Inner City Books, 1980.

"Divination," entry in *Encyclopedia of Religion*, ed. Mircea Eliade, University of Chicago Press.

"Divination," entry in *Hastings Encyclopedia of Religion and Ethics*, Edinburgh, 1908–26.

"Divination," entry in *Encyclopedia Judaica* (16v), Jerusalem, 1971.

For a brief look at the Golden Dawn tradition, see:

Chic and Sandra Tabatha Cicero (eds.), *The Golden Dawn Journal, Book I: Divination*, St. Paul, Llewellyn, 1994.

CHINA

Wolfgang Bauer, *China and the Search for Happiness*, New York, 1976.

Derk Bodde, "Types of Chinese Categorical Thinking," in his *Essays on Chinese Civilization*, Princeton University Press, 1981.

J. M. M. de Groot, *The Religious System of China* (6v), 1892-1910, rpt. Taipei, 1967; and "On Chinese Divination by Dissecting Written Characters", *T'oung Pao*, 1890.

David N. Keightley, *Sources of Shang History: The Oracle Bone Inscriptions of Bronze Age China*, Berkeley, University of California Press, 1978.

Joseph Needham, *Science and Civilization in China*, vol. 2, Cambridge University Press, 1956.

Ngo Van Xuyet, *Divination, magie et politique dans la Chine ancienne*, Paris, Presses Universitaires de France, 1976.

Chao Wei-Pang, "Origin and Growth of the Fu Chi", *Folklore Studies I*, 1942.

Ch'ing-k'un Yang, *Religion in Chinese Society*, Berkeley, University of California Press, 1961.

TIBET

Lama Chime Rinpoche, "Tibet," in *Oracles and Divination*.

René De Nebesky-Wojkowitz, *Oracles and Demons of Tibet*, The Hague, Mouton, 1956.

Berthold Laufer, "Bird Divination among the Tibetans," *T'oung Pao* xv, 1914.

"Looking into the Future," in *Chö Yang: The Voice of Tibetan Religion and Culture*, no. 6, 1994.

R. A. Stein, *Tibetan Civilization*, Stanford University Press, 1972.

Robert A.F. Thurman, *Inside Tibetan Buddhism*, San Francisco, Collins Publishers, 1995.

Austine Waddell, *Tibetan Buddhism*, New York, Dover Publications, rpt. 1972.

Bill Warren and Nancy Hoetzlein Rose, *Living Tibet: The Dalai Lama in Dharamsala*, Ithaca, New York, Snow Lion, 1995.

AFRICA

A. Adler and A. Zempleni, *Le Baton de l'aveugle. Divination, maladie et pouvoir chez les Mondang du Tchad*, Paris, 1972.

John Beattie and John Middleton (eds.), *Spirit Mediumship and Society in Africa*, New York, 1969.

Paul Gebauer, *Spider Divination in the Cameroons*, Milwaukee Public Museum Publications in Anthropology 10, 1964.

Marcel Griaule (trans. Robert Redfield), *Conversations with Ogotemmêli*, London, 1965.

E. J. and J. D. Kriege, *The Realm of the Rain Queen*, London, African International Institute, 1949.

Anne Retel-Laurentin, *Oracles et sorcellerie en Afrique noire*, Paris, Anthropos, 1973.

Robert Ferris Thompson, *Face of the Gods: Art and Altars of Africa and the African Americas*, New York Museum for African Art, Munich, Prestel Verlag, 1993; and *Flash of the Spirit*, New York, Vintage, 1984.

Victor Turner, *Revelation and Divination in Ndembu Ritual*, Ithaca and London, Cornell University Press, 1975.

Evan Zuesse, *Ritual Cosmos: The Sanctification of Life in African Religion*, Athens, Ohio, Ohio University Press, 1979.

NATIVE AMERICA

Bobby Grislybear Lake, *Native Healer*, Wheaton, Illinois, Theosophical Publishing House, 1991.

Kenneth Meadows, *Earth Medicine*, Shaftesbury, Element Books, 1995.

Jamie Sams, *Sacred Path Cards: The Discovery of Self through Native Teachings*, San Francisco, Harper Collins, 1990.

Sun Bear and Wabun, *The Medicine Wheel*, Englewood Cliffs, New Jersey, Prentice Hall, 1980.

Arthur Versluis, *Native American Traditions*, Shaftesbury, Element Books, 1995.

Shamans

Gary Doore (ed.), *The Shaman's Path*, Boston, Shambhala, 1988.

Nevill Drury, *Shamanism*, Shaftesbury, Element Books, 1996.

Mircea Eliade, *Shamanism: Archaic Techniques of Ecstasy*, Princeton, Princeton University Press, 1972.

Joan Halifax, *Shaman: The Wounded Healer*, New York, Crossroads, 1982.

Michael Harner, *The Way of the Shaman*, San Francisco, Harper and Row, 1980.

Holger Kalweit, *Shamans, Healers and Medicine Men*, Boston, Shambhala, 1992.

John Matthews, *The Celtic Shaman*, Shaftesbury, Element Books, 1991.

Shirley Nicolson (ed.), *Shamanism*, Illinois, Quest Books, 1987.

Oracles and Incubation

Hans Dieter Betz (ed.), *The Greek Magical Papyri in Translation*, Chicago University Press, 1985.

John J. Collins, *The Sybilline Oracles of Egyptian Judaism*, Missoula, Montana, University of Montana Press, 1974.

Joseph Fontenrose, *The Delphic Oracle: Its Responses and Operations*, Berkeley, University of California Press, 1978.

Robin Lane Fox, *Pagans and Christians*, New York, Alfred Knopf, 1987.

Mary Hamilton, *Incubation or The Cure of Disease in Pagan Temples and Christian Churches*, London, 1906.

C. A. Meier, *Healing Dream and Ritual: Ancient Incubation and Modern Psychotherapy*, Einsiedeln, Damon Verlag, 1989.

Martin P. Nilsson, *Cults, Myths, Oracles and Politics in Ancient Greece*, New York, 1972.

H. W. Parke, *The Oracles of Zeus: Dodona, Olympia, Ammon*, Oxford, 1967.

C. A. Patrides, "The Cessation of Oracles: The History of a Legend," *Modern Language Review* 60/4, October 1963.

Plutarch, *The E at Delphi, Obsolescence of Oracles*, in Loeb Classical Library, v. 306, London, Heinemann, 1936.

L. B. van der Meer, *The Bronze Liver of Piacenza*, Amsterdam, J. C. Gieben, 1987.

Seers, Prophets, and Prophecy Books

David Aune, *Prophecy in Early Christianity and the Ancient Mediterranean World*, Grand Rapids, 1983.

Edwyn Robert Bevan, *Sibyls and Seers: A Survey of Some Ancient Theories of Revelation and Inspiration*, London, 1928.

Wolfgang Bauer, *Das Bild in der Weissage-Literatur Chinas*, Munich, Moos Verlag, 1973.

H. E. Davidson, *The Seer in Celtic and Other Traditions*, Edinburgh, John Donald, 1990.

Alfred Guillaume, *Prophecy and Divination among the Hebrews and other Semites*, London, 1930.

John Hogue, *Nostradamus: The New Revelations*, Shaftesbury, Element Books, 1995.

Charles L. Lee, *The Great Prophecies of China*, New York, 1950.

Violet MacDermot, *The Cult of the Seer in the Ancient Middle East*, London, 1971.

A. T. Mann, *Millennium Prophecies*, Shaftesbury, Element Books, 1995.

Ottavia Niccoli, *Prophecy and People in Renaissance Italy* (trans. Lydia Cochrane), Princeton University Press, 1990.

R. J. Stewart, *The Prophetic Vision of Merlin*, Harmondsworth, Arkana, 1986; and *The Merlin Tarot*, Wellingborough, Aquarian Press, 1988.

E. Sutherland, *Ravens and Black Rain: The Story of the Highlands Second Sight*, London, Constable, 1985.

Robert Wilson, *Prophecy and Society in Ancient Israel*, Philadelphia, 1980.

Spirit Possession, Mediums, and Healing Cults

Roger Bastide, *The African Religions of Brazil*, Baltimore, 1978.

Jane Belo, *Trance in Bali*, New York, 1960.

Carmen Blacker, *The Catalpa Bow*, London, 1975.

Erika Bourguignon (ed.), *Religion, Altered States of Consciousness and Social Change*, Columbus, University of Ohio Press, 1973; and *Possession*, San Francisco, 1976; *Trance Dance*, New York, 1968.

Vincent Crapanzano and Vivian Garrison (eds.), *Case Studies in Spirit Possession*, New York, 1977.

J. A. Elliot, *Chinese Spirit-Medium Cults in Singapore*, London, 1955.

Michel Leiris, *La possession et ses aspects théatraux chez le Ethiopiens de Gondar*, Paris, 1958.

I. M. Lewis, *Ecstatic Religion: An Anthropological Study of Spirit Possession and Shamanism*, Harmondsworth, 1971.

Traugott K. Oesterreich (trans. D. Ibberson), *Possession, Demoniacal and Other, among Primitive Races, in Antiquity, the Middle Ages, and Modern Times*, New York, 1930.

Sheila Walker, *Ceremonial Spirit Possession in Africa and Afro-America*, Leiden, 1972.

Witches Old and New

Julio Caro Baroja, *The World of Witches*, Chicago, 1964.

E. E. Evans-Pritchard, *Witchcraft, Oracles and Magic among the Azande*, Oxford, 1937.

Pennethorne Hughes, *Witchcraft*, Baltimore, 1965.

John Middleton, (ed), *Magic, Witchcraft and Curing*, Garden City, New York, 1967.

Barrie Reynolds, *Magic, Divination and Witchcraft among the Barotse of Northern Rhodesia*, London, 1963.

M. Stephen (ed.), *Sorcerer and Witch in Melanesia*, Melbourne, 1987; and *A'aisa's Gifts*, 1995.

Gillian Tindall, *A Handbook on Witches*, London, Panther Books, 1967.

Doreen Valiente, *Natural Magic*, London, Hale, 1975.

Vaudou and Santeria

Maya Deren, *Divine Horsemen: The Living Gods of Haiti*, New York, Thames and Hudson, 1953.

Migène Gonzalez-Wippler, *Santeria: African Magic in Latin America*, New York, Julian Press, 1975.

Melville J. Herscovits, *Life in a Haitian Valley*, New York, Doubleday, rpt. 1971.

Alfred Metraux (trans. Hugo Charteris), *Voodoo*, New York, Oxford, 1959; and "The Concept of Soul in Haitian Vodu," *Southwestern Journal of Anthropology*, 2, I, Spring 1946.

Luis Manual Nunez, Santeria: *A Practical Guide to Afro-Caribbean Magic*, Dallas, Spring Books, 1992.

Milo Riguad, (trans. Robert Cross), *Secrets of Voodoo*, San Francisco, City Lights, rpt. 1985.

Selden Rodman, *Where Art is Joy*, New York, Ruggles de Latour, 1988.

Seldon Rodman and Carol Cleaver, *Spirits of the Night: The Vaudun Gods of Haiti*, Dallas, Spring Books, 1992.

Dowsing

Christopher Bird, *The Divining Hand*, New York, E. P. Dutton, 1979.

Tom Graves, *Pendulum Dowsing*, Shaftesbury, Element Books.

Sig Lonegren, *The Pendulum Kit*, New York, Simon and Schuster 1990; London, Virgin, 1992; and *Spiritual Dowsing*, Glastonbury, Gothic Image, 1986.

Edward T. Ross and Richard D. Wright, *The Divining Mind*, Rochester, Vermont, Destiny Books, 1990.

Numerology

Rodford Barrat, *Numerology*, Shaftesbury, Element Books, 1994.

Ruth Drayer, *Numerology: The Language of Life*, El Paso, Texas, Skidmore-Roth, 1990.

Count Louis Hamon Chiero, *Chiero's Book of Numbers: The Complete Science of Numerology*, New York, Prentice Hall, 1988.

Harish Johari, *Numerology with Tantra, Ayurveda and Astrology: A Key to Human Behaviour*, Rochester, Vermont, Destiny Books, 1990.

Marie-Louise von Franz, *Number and Time*, Toronto, Inner City Books, 1985.

Geomancy

Nigel Pennick, *Secret Games of the Gods*, York Beach, Minnesota, Samuel Weiser, 1992; and *The Ancient Science of Geomancy*, London, 1979.

The magical interpretation, with rituals and astrological associations:

Aleister Crowley, *Magick in Theory and Practice*, Paris, 1929.

Francis Israel Regardie, *A Practical Guide to Geomantic Divination*, London, Aquarian Press, 1972.

Stephen Skinner, *Terrestrial Astrology: Divination by Geomancy*, London, Routledge and Kegan Paul, 1980.

See also:

Robert Ambelain, *La geomancie arabe et ses miroirs divinatoires*, Paris, 1984.

Robert Gascon, *Practique de la geomancie*, Paris, 1987.

On earth lights and electropsychic signs:

Paul Devereaux, *Earth Lights Revelation*, Blandford, 1989.

Ifa Divination and Yoruba Myths

Wande Abimbola, *Ifa Divination Poetry*, New York, Nok Publishers, 1977.

William Bascom, *Ifa Divination*, Bloomington, University of Indiana Press, 1969.

E. Bolaji Idowu, *Olodomare: God in Yoruba Belief*, London, Longman's, 1962.

Henry Drewall, John Pemberton III, and Roland Abiodun, *Yoruba: Nine Centuries of African Art and Thought*, New York, Center for African Art, 1989.

Judith Gleason, *A Recitation of Ifa, Oracle of the Yoruba*, New York, Grossman, 1973.

Bernard Maupoil, "La Geomancie a l'ancienne Côte des Esclaves," *Travaux et memoires de l'Insitut d'Ethnologie*, XLII, Paris, 1943.

Pierre Verger, Orisha: *Les Dieux Youruba en Afrique et au Nouveau Monde*, Paris, Editions Métailié, 1982.

Feng Shui or Chinese Geomancy

Stephen Feuchtwang, *An Anthropological Analysis of Chinese Geomancy*, Vientiane, Laos, Editions Vithagna, 1974.

Lillian Too, *The Complete Illustrated Guide to Feng Shui*, Shaftesbury, Element Books, 1995.

Derek Walters, *The Feng Shui Handbook*, London, Aquarian Press, 1991; and *Chinese Geomancy*, Shaftesbury, Element Books, 1991.

On Sikidy and Vintana:

Nigel Pennick, *Madagascar Divination*, Cambridge, Fenris Wolf, 1975.

Pierre Vérin and Narivelo Rajaonarimanana, "Divination in Madagascar", in *African Divination Systems: Ways of Knowing.*

Tarot

The Tarot has proved an effective way to turn a mythology into a divination system. Since 1976, there has been an enormous number of new decks, using Mayan, Egyptian, Hermetic, Norse, Tibetan, Japanese, Native American, Arthurian, Feminist, and classical Greek myths and symbols. These books may help you locate yourself in the new world of Tarot.

Gail Fairfield, *Choice Centered Tarot*, North Hollywood, 1985.

Cynthia Giles, *The Tarot: History, Mystery and Lore*, New York, Simon and Schuster, 1992.

Mary Greer, *Tarot for Yourself*, North Hollywood, 1984; UK: *Tarot Transformations*, London, Aquarian Press, 1987.

Stuart Kaplan, *Encyclopedia of Tarot* (3v), New York, US Games Systems, 1978-86.

A.T. Mann, *The Tarot*, Shaftesbury, Element Books.

Rachel Pollack, *78 Degrees of Wisdom* (parts I & II), London, Aquarian Press, 1980-83; and *The New Tarot*, London, Aquarian Press, 1985.

Cabala

Cherry Gilchrist, *Divination: The Search for Meaning*, London, Dryad Press, 1987.

Z'ev ben Shimon Haleri, *Kabbalah: Tradition of Hidden Knowledge*, London, Thames and Hudson, 1979.

Will Parfitt, *The New Living Qabalah*, Shaftesbury, Element Books, 1995.

Gerschom Scholem, *Major Trends in Jewish Mysticism*, New York, Schocken Books, 1971.

I Ching

Stephen Karcher and Rudolf Ritsema, *I Ching: The Classic Chinese Oracle of Change*, Shaftesbury, Element Books, 1994.

Stephen Karcher, *The Elements of the I Ching*, Shaftesbury, Element Books, 1995.

Willard Peterson, "Making Connections: Commentary on the Attached Verbalizations of the Book of Change," *Harvard Journal of Asiatic Studies*, 42/1, June 1992.

W. A. Sherrill and W. K. Chu, *An Anthology of I Ching*, London, Routledge and Kegan Paul, 1977.

Helmut Wilhelm, *Heaven, Earth and Man in the Book Of Changes*, Seattle, University of Washington Press, 1977.

Richard Wilhelm and Cary F. Baynes, *The I Ching or Book of Changes*, 3rd edition, Princeton, Princeton University Press, 1967.

Wu Jing-Nuan, *Yijing*, Washington DC, Taoist Study Series, 1991.

Runes

Two sets of rune stones with instructions on their history, mythology and use:

Ralph Blum, *The New Book of Runes*, London, Headline, 1990.

D. Jason Cooper, *A Comprehensive Introduction to the Art of Runecraft*, London, Aquarian Press, 1990.

More information on the runes and how they were used:

R. W. V. Elliot, *Runes: An Introduction*, Manchester, Manchester University Press, 1980.

Bernard King, *The Runes*, Shaftesbury, Element Books, 1993.

Nigel Pennick, *Practical Magic in the Northern Tradition*, London, Aquarian Press, 1985, and *The Secret Lore of Runes and Other Ancient Alphabets*, London, Rider, 1991.

E. O. G. Turville-Petry, *Myth and Religion in the North*, London, Weidenfeld & Nicolson, 1964.

The Ogham alphabet or "Celtic Runes" have also become popular as a divination system. Here are two modern divination decks based on the Celtic alphabet:

Nigel Jackson and Nigel Pennick, *The Celtic Oracle*, London, Aquarian Press, 1992.

Colin and Liz Murray, *The Celtic Tree Oracle*, London, Rider, 1988.

See also:

Courtney Davis, *The Celtic Tarot*, London, Aquarian Press, 1990.

Caitlin Matthews, *The Celtic Book of the Dead*, London, Aquarian Press, 1992; and *The Celtic Tradition*, Shaftesbury, Element Books, 1994.

Rolling the Dice

Lama Chime Rinpoche, "Tibet," in *Oracles and Divination*.

Robin Lane Fox, *Pagans and Christians*, New York, Alfred Knopf, 1987.

Jay L. Goldberg and Lobsang Dakpa, *MO: Tibetan Divination System*, Ithaca, New York, Snow Lion, 1990.

F. Heinevelter, *Würfel und Buchstabenorakel*, Stuttgart, 1913.

Austine Waddell, *Tibetan Buddhism*, New York, Dover Publications, rpt. 1972.

Derek Walters, *Your Future Revealed by Mah Jongg*, London, Aquarian Press, 1982.

Astrology

AN INTRODUCTION:

Lyn Birkbeck, *Do it Yourself Astrology: A User Friendly Guide*, Shaftesbury, Element Books, 1995.

Janice Huntley, *The Elements of Astrology*, Shaftesbury, Element Books, 1991.

MORE COMPLETE EXPOSITIONS:

Margaret E. Hone, *A Modern Textbook of Astrology*, Romford, Essex, L. N. Fowler, 1978.

Alan Leo, *Esoteric Astrology*, New York, Astrologer's Library, 1913, rpt. 1978.

Derek and Julia Parker, *The New Compleat Astrologer*, London, Mitchell Beazley, 1990.

Dane Rudyar, *Astrology for the Modern Psyche*, Davis, California, CRCS Publications, 1976.

ON SPECIFIC APPLICATIONS OF THE HOROSCOPE:

M. Baigent, N. Campion, C. Harvey, *Mundane Astrology*, London, Aquarian Press, 1991.

Olivia Barclay, *Horary Astrology Rediscovered*, Pennsylvania, Whitford Press, 1990.

Doris Chase Doane, *Profit by Electional Astrology*, Tempe, Arizona, American Federation of Astrologers, 1990.

ON THE HISTORY OF ASTROLOGY AND ITS CULTURE:

Alexandre Bouché-LeClercq, *L'Astrologie Grecque*, Paris, 1889.

Nicolas Campion, *An Introduction to the History of Astrology*, London, ISCWA, 1982.

Franz Cumont, *Astrology and Religion among the Greeks and Romans*, 1912, rpt. New York, 1960.

Eugenio Garin (trans. Carolyn Jackson and June Allen), *Astrology in the Renaissance: The Zodiac of Life*, London, Routledge and Kegan Paul, 1983.

William and Hans-Georg Gundel, *Astrologumena: Die astrologische Literatur in der Antike und ihre Geschichte*, Wiesbaden, 1966.

SIDEREAL OR INDIAN ASTROLOGY:

Valerie J. Roebuck, *An Introduction to Indian Astrology*, Shaftesbury, Element Books, 1992.

CHINESE ASTROLOGY:

L. de Saussure, *Les origines de l'astronomie Chinoise*, Paris, 1930.

Martin Palmer (ed. and trans), *T'ung Shu, the Ancient Chinese Almanac*, Kuala Lumpur, Vinpress, 1990.

Derek Walters, *Chinese Astrology*, Wellingborough, Aquarian Press, 1986.

ON THE CIRCLE OF ANIMALS:

Laurine Petit, *La nouvelle astrologie chinoise*, Paris, Crealivres, 1986.

Lori Reid, *Chinese Horoscopes for Lovers*, Shaftesbury, Element Books, 1995.

MESO-AMERICAN ASTROLOGY:

José Arguelles, *The Mayan Factor*, Santa Fe, New Mexico, Bear & Co, 1987.

Bruce Scofield, *Day Signs: Native American Astrology from Ancient Mexico*, Amherst, Massachusetts, One Reed Publications, 1991.

Barbara Tedlock, *Time and the Highland Maya*, Albuquerque, New Mexico, University of New Mexico Press, 1982.

Dreamworld

These collections of articles on dream and culture contain a wide range of imaginative, spiritual, historical, and psychological perspectives.

Carolyn T. Brown (ed.), *Pyscho-Sinology: The Universe of Dreams in Chinese Culture*, University Press of America, 1988.

Stanley Krippner (ed.), *Dreamtime and Dreamwork*, Los Angeles, Tarcher, 1990.

G. von Grunbaum and R. Callois (eds.), *The Dream and Human Societies*, Los Angeles, University of California Press, 1966.

Les songes et leur interpretation, Paris, Editions du Seuil, 1956.

R. L. Wood (ed.), *The World of Dreams*, New York, Random House, 1947.

DREAM TEXTS FROM THE ANTIQUE WORLD:

Aristides, *Sacred Histories* (dreams of Asklepios), (trans. C. Behr), Cambridge, Massachusetts, Harvard University Press, 1973.

Artemidorus (trans. Robert J. White), *The Interpretation of Dreams*, New York, Noyes Press, 1975.

E. and L. Edelstein, *Asklepius: A Collection and Interpretation of the Testimonies* (2v), Baltimore, Johns Hopkins University Press, 1945.

A. Oppenheim, The Interpretation of Dreams in the Ancient Near East, with a translation of an Assyrian Dreambook, *Transactions of the American Philosophical Society* 46/3, 1956.

W. Stahl (trans. and ed.), *Macrobius: Commentary on the Dream of Scipio*, New York, Columbia University Press, 1952.

A VARIETY OF APPROACHES TO DREAMING:

Edgar Cayce, *Dreams and Dreaming: The Edgar Cayce Readings*, Virgina Beach, 1976.

C. Comstock, "Internal Self Helpers or Centers," *Integration* 3:3-12, 1967.

Joel Covitz, *Visions of the Night: A Study of Jewish Dream Interpretation*, Boston, Shambhala, 1990.

James Cowan, *Mysteries of the Dreaming: Spiritual Life of Australian Aborigines*, Dorset, Prism Press, 1989.

Gayle Delaney, *Breakthrough Dreaming: How to Tap the Power of Your 24 Hour Mind*, New York, Bantam Books, 1991.

J. Fagan and S. Shepherd, *Gestalt Therapy Now*, Palo Alto, Science and Behavior Books, 1970.

Thomas French and Erika Fromm, *Dream Interpretation*, International Universities Press, 1985.

Jayne Gackenbach, *Sleep and Dreams, A Sourcebook*, Garland, 1987.

Patricia Garfield, *Creative Dreaming*, New York, Simon and Schuster; and *The Healing Power of Dreams*, 1991.

K. Das Gupta, *The Shadow World: A Study of Ancient and Modern Dream Theories*, Delhi, Atma Ram, 1971.

E. Gendlin, *Let Your Body Interpret Your Dreams*, Williamette, Illinois, Chiron, 1986.

Calvin Hall and Robert Van de Castle, *The Content Analysis of Dreams*, New York, Apple-Century-Croft, 1966.

James A. Hall, *Jungian Dream Interpretation*, Toronto, Inner City Books, 1983.

James Hillman, *The Dream and the Underworld*, New York, Harper and Row, 1979.

C. G. Jung, *The Meaning and Significance of Dreams* (I & II), Sigo Press, rpt. 1990.

Stephen LaBerge, *Lucid Dreaming*, New York, Ballantine Books, 1986.

Arnold Mindell, *Working with the Dreambody*, New York, Routledge and Kegan Paul, 1985.

Montague Ullman and Claire Limmer, *The Variety of Dream Experience: Expanding our Ways of Working with Dreams*, New York, Continuum, 1988.

Robert L. Van de Castle, *Our Dreaming Mind*, New York, Ballantine Books, 1994.

Marie-Louise von Franz, *Dreams and Death*, Boston, Shambhala, 1986.

Fred Allan Wolf, *The Dreaming Universe*, New York, Simon and Schuster, 1994.

Index

Acknowledgments

THE PUBLISHERS WISH TO THANK THE FOLLOWING FOR THE USE OF PICTURES:

Bridgeman Art Library: pp. 65, 208/209, 226; 124 (Bonhams); 42R (Christies); 13B, 17, 222 (British Library); 35M, 57B, 100L&T, 180T, 194B (British Museum); 49 (Galeria dell Accademia); 15B (Greek Museum, University of Newcastle upon Tyne); 2 (Gustav Moreau Museum, Venice); 223, 225 (Lambeth Palace); 193 (Musée Municipal Billancourt, Boulogne); 192L (Museum of the History of Science); 110L (National Archeological Museum, Athens); 188R (National Museum, Stockholm); 93 (The National Trust); 50T (Olympia Museum); 216 (Palais de Tokyo); 47R (Peabody Museum); 218 (Victoria & Albert Museum); 10L (Villa dei Pompei); 183L (Bridgeman Giraudon/Musée Guimet); 28L (Bridgeman Index/Archivo Capitular de Osma); 101R (Bridgeman/Link/Orde Eliason); 118T (Bridgeman/K&B Newsfoto, Florence).

The British Library: p. 170R.

C. M. Dixon: pp. 110/111.

Nevill Drury: p. 235L.

e.t.archive: pp. 21, 35R, 36M, 44/45, 46T, 52R, 60L, 63, 64, 68L, 70TR, 71TL, 86, 88R, 92R, 128M, 166R, 180B, 181T&B, 182, 194TR, 195, 200B, 212T, 228B.

Fine Art Photographic Library: pp. 23, 50B, 224.

Fortean Picture Library: p. 119L, 148.

By permission of Games System Inc., Stamford, CT 06902 USA: pp. 8L, 108L, 113BR, 148, 151, 152, 153, 156, 160.

Hammer Coll.: p. 125L.

Hulton Getty Collection: pp. 20T&B, 88L, 229T, 229B.

The Hutchison Library: pp. 16B, 47B, 98B; 90B (John Burston); 37R (Mick Czaky); 16T, 73, 84L, 144B (Sarah Errington); 74B (Carlos Freire); 12L (Bernard Gerard); 22B (Felix Greene); 74TL (Juliet Highet); 16 (Victoria Juleva); 96T (R. Ian Lloyd); 33T, 91R, 221R (Michael Macintyre); 52 (Lesley Nelson); 94B, 97T (Trevor Page); 38B (P. E. Parker); 55R (Christine Pemberton); 119B (Stephen Pern); 12T (J & A Reditt); 82/83 (Kerstin Rodgers); 52T, 57TR, 101L (John Ryle); 48B (Micha Scorer); 69R (André Singer); 78/79T, 236B (Liba Taylor); 79R (Val Wilkinson); 34, 35BL (Leslie Woodhead).

The Image Bank: pp. 177; 219 (Derek Berwin); 20M (Romilly Lockyer); 22TR (Alberto Incrocci); 145B (Zhen de Feng).

Images Colour Library: pp. 24/25, 36B, 41T, 43L, 47ML&T, 54, 55L, 58/59, 60T, 72, 75R, 80L&R, 85B, 89BL, 92L, 95, 98T, 99, 102L, 108B, 118L, 127T, 128T, 129, 130L, 131M, 132T&B, 133, 134, 144T, 146R, 147T, 149L&R, 166L, 172L, 173R, 190/191, 196, 204, 205T, 212B, 213, 224B, 234, 235T, 236T; 237 (Fay Pomerance).

Science Picture Library: p. 15T.

Stuart Littlejohn: pp. 30/31.

Danuta Meyer: p. 26T.

Laura Perls: p. 229

Shining Woman Tarot, Rachel Pollack: © HarperCollins*Publishers* 1992 p. 158.

Werner Forman Archive: pp. 68B, 100R; 46BR (British Library); 71BR (National Museum of Man, Ottowa); 70TL (C. Court Coll., Plains Indians Museum); 9R (P'yongyang Gallery, N. Korea); 162L (Statens Historika Museum).

SPECIAL THANKS GO TO:
Judith Cox, Carly Evans, Julia Holden, Janice Jones, Sally-Ann Russell, Stephen Sparshatt *for help with photography.*